Killer Web Design: NetObjects FUSION

Stella Gassaway

Hayden Books

ASSOCIATE PUBLISHER
JOHN PIERCE

PUBLISHING MANAGER
LAURIE PETRYCKI

MANAGING EDITOR
LISA WILSON

PRODUCT MARKETING MANAGER
KIM MORGOLIUS

ACQUISITIONS EDITOR
MICHELLE REED

DEVELOPMENT EDITOR
ROBYN HOLTZMAN

TECHNICAL EDITOR
VIC ZAUDERER

PUBLISHING COORDINATOR
KAREN WILLIAMS

COVER DESIGNER
SANDRA SCHROEDER

BOOK DESIGNER
STELLA GASSAWAY

MANUFACTURING COORDINATOR
BROOK FARLING

PRODUCTION TEAM SUPERVISORS
LAURIE CASEY
JOE MILLAY

PRODUCTION TEAM
STELLARVISIONS
DANIELA RADERSTORF

INDEXER
CHRIS BARRICK

Killer Web Design: NetObjects Fusion

Library of Congress Catalog Number: 96-78596
ISBN: 1-56830-340-8

Printed in the United States of America 1 2 3 4 5 6 7 8 9 0

Warning and Disclaimer

This book is sold as is, without warranty of any kind, either express or implied. While every precaution has been taken in the preparation of this book, the authors and Hayden Books assume no responsibility for errors or omissions. Neither is any liability assumed for damages resulting from the use of the information or instructions contained herein. It is further stated that the publisher and authors are not responsible for any damage or loss to your data or your equipment that results directly or indirectly from your use of this book.

Trademark Acknowledgments

All terms mentioned in this book that are known to be trademarks or services marks have been appropriately capitalized. Hayden Books cannot attest to the accuracy of this information. Use of a term in this book should not be regarded as affecting the validity of any trademark or service mark. **NetObjects Fusion** is a trademark of **NetObjects, Inc.**

Credits

Photo: Stephen Coan pp. 215 & 231; Gerry Mathews pp. 210, 223 and part openers
Illustration: Seth Jabour pp. 17, 40, 107, 108
p. 10 Designing Business cover ©Adobe Press, used by permission; p. 29 Information Architects cover ©Graphis Press, used by permission; p. 54 FontBook ©FontShop, used by permission; p. 213 Chestnut Hill Local, used by permission

Dedication

to Margaret Stewart Anderson

Acknowledgments

The folks at NetObjects were very helpful throughout the process of writing this book: Marc Escobosa, Laura Zung, and Brook Stein cheerfully answered our email, postings, and telephone calls. I especially thank Vic Zauderer for taking the time to review the entire manuscript for accuracy.

I would like to extend my deep appreciation to Clement Mok for sharing his design process in *Designing Business*, for his inspiring and ever expanding vision, and for writing the Foreword for this book.

The entire staff of STELLARViSIONs and bYte a tree were involved in this project and each made an invaluable contribution. Arthur Knapp is our JavaScript specialist, Seth Jabour provided those whimsical illustrations, and Gretchen Dykstra's editorial and proofreading skills were indispensable. My partner in bYte a tree productions, Gerry Mathews, is integral to all web design projects including the case studies described in this book.

Thank you to our clients and others who gave us permission to reproduce materials, clippings, and photographs in the case studies, especially Jeff Appeltans and Peter Fraterdeus.

Weekly telephone promptings from my Mom helped keep everything moving along. In the last minute rush to produce all of these pages, the entire staff and friends, especially Jayne Stokes, pitched in doing whatever was needed.

Hayden Books

The staff of Hayden Books is committed to bringing you the best computer books. What our readers think of Hayden is important to our ability to serve our customers. If you have any comments, no matter how great or how small, we'd appreciate your taking the time to send us a note.

You can reach Hayden Books at the following:
Hayden Books
201 West 103rd Street
Indianapolis, IN 46290
317-581-3833

Email addresses:
America Online: Hayden Bks
Internet: hayden@hayden.com
Visit the Hayden Books Web site at http://www.hayden.com

About the Author

Stella Gassaway is creative director of two "interwoven" companies. STELLARViSIONs is a graphic design firm she founded in 1987 (working on a MacPlus with a 20 megabyte external hard drive the size of a bread box). In 1994, she and her partners launched bYte a tree productions "applying creative intelligence to interactive, multi, and cybermedia."

In the New Media QuickTime web Challenge, bYte a tree won best of category, animation, for the gordian emoticon puzzle at www.dol.com and their soundbYtes page was a finalist in the audio category. The firm's work has been featured in publications on web and interface design, and Stella has been an invited presenter at conferences around the country.

Stella has often felt that she was in that overlap area in a Ven diagram, where design and technology meet. She seems to spend half her time trying to get designers to embrace technology and the other half trying to get technocrats to value design.

A longtime member of the AIGA, Stella was active in the first year of the Philadelphia Technology Special Interest Group [techSIG], where she and other "bleeding edge" designers pooled experience and arranged for guest speakers. She is now a member of the Chapter's Executive Board and principal architect of AIGAlink, a chapter hub and gallery space as well as the Philadelphia Chapter Web site. Also design director for designOnline's dezine café, www.desginOnline.com, she works toward her continuing goal to share experiences, knowledge, and the common language of design with designers of all disciplines.

contents at a glance

contents

part 2
{a tool} NetObjects FUSION

part 3
{the practice} case studies

foreword

If one were to ask if I had any interest in designing a piece of software 10 years ago, I would have laughed and seriously challenged the sanity of the requester. What does a high school math flunky know about computer science, let alone software engineering? It's 10 years later, the world has changed and so has my mind. I've started two software companies and my design consulting practice, Studio Archetype, is now engaged in designing numerous electronic-commerce efforts for Fortune 100 companies. If I were asked again about software design, I would not ask "why?" but rather "why not?"

It's not that I've turned my back on design and become a tech-weenie but rather, I've extended my definition of what design must accomplish. That extended definition of design is about embracing and integrating the digital medium—powerful force that is altering our interaction with daily life. Looking at the similarities. Looking at the differences. And trying to find access and connection points. Points, which require designers who can provide narratives and experiences with moral guidance and social purpose. The digital medium without context and intent is just data. The multiple disciplines required to provide such a framework define the new role design must take.

Design that will give meaning to our history, elucidate the present and give direction to our future. The challenge is enormous.

The journey to designing software was by no means planned. It came as the culmination of learning and working with new media. It came because of the acceptance and the need for design to play a broader role in shaping the electronic world around us. Design, as experiences impart to me, is a process. It's a process that facilitates and mediates between "the idea" and its "expression" irrespective of its media. The quality of that process is directly proportional to the quality of "the expression of the idea." In *Killer Web Design: NetObjects Fusion* the author and her team share their design process and demonstrate how our software can play a key role in that process.

THE PRODUCT IS ABOUT UNDERSTANDING THE TRAUMA OR THE CHALLENGE THE WEB SITE DEVELOPER ENCOUNTERS IN BUILDING A WEB SITE.

In any effort to develop software products, it's important to understand the needs of the customers—not just product features but also the social science behind it. A real advantage in this pursuit is having the 24 Hours in Cyberspace event and Studio Archetype to draw on for real-world experience. What sets NetObjects Fusion apart from all other Internet authoring software is its focus on the user-model. It's about making the possible or the impossible usable and relevant. The product is about understanding the trauma or the challenge the web site developer encounters in building a web site.

The nature of the challenge is that web sites continue to evolve in size, depth, and sophistication both graphically as well as functionally. It's too tedious, and it takes too much time and money to build a web site. Web site authoring tools are too limiting. Most are glorified word processing applications. They are either page-based or not open enough to support rapidly changing technology. To create breakthrough site-building products require a new model. Retrofitting old technologies or products that were built for a different paradigm or medium will not deliver radical gains in ease-of-use.

THE NATURE OF THE CHALLENGE IS THAT WEB SITES CONTINUE TO EVOLVE IN SIZE, DEPTH AND SOPHISTICATION BOTH GRAPHICALLY AS WELL AS FUNCTIONALLY.

The tool has to be scalable to support growing complex web sites. It has to provide explicit support for the information design that lets the author structure the information site-wide. It has to provide an intuitive graphical user interface that does away with complexity while providing access to sophisticated functionality. It has to support all major standards and platforms. It has to support the depth needed for advance users and usage. And most importantly, it has to automate and simplify the process of designing, authoring, publishing and updating a web site.

Ambitious goals required unconventional strategy and tactics. It required out-of-the-box thinking and the ability to focus. Many of the key features of the product came about just watching and interviewing web site builders.

RETROFITTING OLD TECHNOLOGIES OR PRODUCTS THAT WERE BUILT FOR A DIFFERENT PARADIGM OR MEDIUM WILL NOT DELIVER RADICAL GAINS IN EASE-OF-USE.

The notion of an application that would take into account site structure evolved out of the mapping practice Studio Archetype developed to communicate the breadth and the depth of a complete site to their clients. The idea of site view came from the belief that the user should be able to look at the whole site, just like a presentation software package can look at the whole presentation, as opposed to doing it in MacDraw page-by-page.

Pixel-level control and WYSIWYG requirements were the basis for the page-layout capabilities of NetObjects Fusion. Editing web pages with enhanced word processing-like applications was at best a dysfunctional model for serious web site building. It needed to be as sophisticated as the layout functionality of PageMaker, QuarkXPress, or Macromedia Director.

Another area of need NetObjects focused on was dealing with the "graphically-challenged" and "technically-challenged" users. Most web site developers do not have either a graphic design or engineering degree. By providing a library of professionally designed and programmed web sites eliminates the intimidation threshold inherent with any web building effort.

The bar has been set. Have at it.

Clement Mok

Chief Creative Officer, NetObjects, Inc.

Clement Mok

STUDIO ARCHETYPE

Identity and Information Architects

600 Townsend Street,

San Francisco, CA 94103

55 Broad Street New York, NY 10004

clement@studioarchetype.com

preface

Designers are constantly objecting to the amount of time they spend in front of a computer. They want to design. *It seems for many that the same pleasure isn't derived from digital tools as there has been for analog tools. Designers have a relationship with paper and print which, for convenient reasons, they seem to have forgotten was always a love-hate relationship.*

IT TAKES TWO TO SPEAK THE TRUTH–ONE TO SPEAK AND ANOTHER TO HEAR.

–HENRY DAVID THOREAU

This relationship between designers and their tools is an important one. We redesigned our analog tools as we worked with them. Sharpening our pencil to the point of a nail. Tossing away a dull blade for a sharp new one. So why is it that we have been absent in the creation and sharpening of these new digital tools? Is the responsibility somehow less in these digital times? I think not. This digital age, as Clement Mok says, requires the expansion of what design must accomplish. The active participation in shaping the process, practice and tools of design. We must look at inventing, not recycling ideas.

Long before I first signed up as a member of the NetObjects Fusion Seed development program I had been awed by the 24 Hours in Cyberspace Project. I was amazed at the preparation, organization, and implementation that made it a reality. How had they managed to make it happen? It took the cooperation of designers and engineers to create a new technology. That new technology has been molded into a tool that is a designer's tool, NetObjects Fusion. It required a combination of technology how technology works and understanding the way a designer works. *How could that be?* Simple. A designer decided to participate in making a tool with which he could more efficiently, more intuitively design. That designer was Clement Mok. He has also generously shared his DADI process with designers and clients. It's a system that helps both the designer and client understand their responsibilities in the process of design.

CREATE A VIEW OF NEW THINGS IN A COMFORTABLE WAY AND OLD THINGS IN A NEW LIGHT

We have taken the DADI process and the tool NetObjects Fusion into our studio. We have participated in the evolution of both the system and the tool to fit our projects and our needs. This is the process of design; to look at what is available and to provide access to it, to make it understandable so that someone else will be enlightened or inspired by the experience.

As a result of our involvement in experimenting and being a participant in helping design digital tools for the future, I have written this book. From now on however, the voice for the book is "we" because everything out of my studio is a collaboration among the team members. In this book we're going to talk about some dicey stuff like designer/client responsibility, the partnership of technology and design, and the incredibly close proximity of order to chaos. I hope it will inspire you to participate in sharpening your tools, expanding your role as a designer, and embracing the chaos the Web offers.

It's an exciting time to be a designer.

Stella Gassaway

sm gassaway

STELLARViSIONs | bYte a tree

4200 Mitchell Street, Second Floor

Philadelphia, PA 19128

stella@designpractice.com

part 1

{in} theory

design issues

In this first part of the book we talk in general about the design process, and more specifically, Web site design. We begin in Chapter 1 with an overview DADI: definition, architecture, design, implementation—a system developed by Clement Mok. This process can be applied to any design challenge, but is especially useful in authoring interactive media, applications or Web sites. Because of Mok's involvement with the development of NetObjects Fusion software, there are ways in which the application lends itself particularly well to these four stages. We explore this further in Part 2, in the discussion of how NetObjects Fusion can be helpful to the design process. Then, in Part 3, you see how the DADI system is applied to actual practice through case studies.

Chapter 2 elaborates more extensively on the architecture stage of DADI and sets out some principles for approaching Web site structure. Chapter 3 looks at the specific challenges and considerations of web page design, and how it is both like and unlike designing for other media. An understanding of the process, and the ideals to which we aspire, is an essential precursor to a discussion of how NetObjects Fusion can be a useful servant. The guidelines set here for both process and result are the standard against which the software and the case study sites are measured.

1

The DADI Process:

Definition → Architecture → Design → Implementation

Figure 1.1
Studio Archetype's logo: a hybrid drafting tool and sextant create the letter "A".

The DADI process is the brainchild of Clement Mok, founder of Studio Archetype (Figure 1.1), former Apple Computer creative director and now Chief Creative Officer at NetObjects, Inc. In his book *Designing Business, Multiple Media Multiple Disciplines*, Adobe Press. Mok detailed the DADI approach (definition, architecture, design and implementation) with regard to identity design, information design and the design of interactive media. He also emphasized the importance of collaboration with other professionals, especially where technology is concerned.

IN THIS BOOK THE TERM WEB SITE REFERS TO PAGES THAT ARE VIEWED ON COMPUTER SCREENS USING BROWSERS. THIS INCLUDES PUBLIC, MEMBER-ONLY, AND INTRANET WEB SITES.

In this chapter we review Mok's DADI system, as we understand it, and how it can be applied to a web project. We begin with this theory because it will be referred to throughout the book, especially in the case studies. Following the stages of DADI can help to avoid many pitfalls in a project. There is also the challenge of working closely with a multi-disciplinary team and defining team roles, including that of the client. (Remember in-house projects also have a client—usually the boss.) First, however, we look more closely at a word that is used quite loosely, especially with regard to Web sites, and that is "design".

What is Design?

Consider the contradiction inherent in the statement:

The design process consists of definition, architecture, design, and implementation.

Is design the entire process or just stage three? Are designers only involved in stage three, and should they leave the other stages to others? What about this implementation stuff, isn't that production, not design? If the professionals are not consistent in how they use the terms, no wonder the buying public is confused.

The confusion stems partly from that fact that the word "design" has become associated with graphic design unless otherwise specified (that is fashion design, software design, interior design). Those that do not understand graphic design confuse it with decoration and undervalue its contribution. Even those with a serious respect for the field of design usually think of two-dimensional (print-like) solutions, arrangements of type, graphics, colors, and white space to communicate a message.

Therefore clients often think of hiring a technical firm to "build" the site, and a designer (read graphic designer) to design the pages of the site. There are several problems with this. First, web page design has more in common with designing an interactive interface than a magazine page. Second, web pages are not isolated entities but part of an organic whole, a site. Given the common undervaluing of design, however, it is tempting to bask in the fact that expertise in presenting visuals and designing a user-interface is actually appreciated, and not insist on a wider role.

WE FIRST MET CLEMENT MOK IN 1988 AT A DESIGN CONFERENCE ON THE SOUTH RIM OF THE GRAND CANYON, WHERE HE WAS BRIMMING OVER WITH EXCITEMENT ABOUT THE BRAND NEW HYPERCARD AND THE REVOLUTIONARY CONCEPT OF HYPERTEXT.

What DADI points out is that the entire process requires design, starting at a much earlier point than designers are usually involved. There is not general agreement as to what discipline is qualified to head up the progress from definition to architecture, design and finally, implementation. (Clement Mok has been called an information architect, a new breed of designer.) What is clear is that there must be a team that follows the process from start to finish. DADI is design in the widest sense, a process of making decisions, solving problems, and testing solutions. Whatever the background of the team leader, if he or she has a clear grasp of the DADI system and involves specialized colleagues throughout the *entire* process, the results can be amazing. To avoid confusion on the part of clients, however, we usually refer to the third stage as *design of look and feel* rather than *design*.

Throughout this book the term "designer" is generally used to refer to the person making decisions about how the site should be experienced by visitors. The *client* is the company that is putting the site on the web (represented by one or more individuals), whose goals the site must serve. Most of the discussion refers to a design firm and separate client, because that is the situation of this author, but the principles apply equally to in-house teams working with the company management.

The Team

In the old days print designers worked closely with an array of allied professionals upon whom they were dependent to have their work succeed: typesetters, mechanical artists, scanner operators, and the like. Desktop technology has isolated many graphic designers and put the burden of most of the process, through production, squarely on their shoulders. With interactive media you cannot operate in this isolation, you must engage with colleagues who each bring something to the process (Figure 1.2). This may include programmers, content developers, database professionals, multimedia artists, and so forth. (This is written from a designer's point of view. If you fill a different role, take note and include on your team a designer with experience in structural, navigational, and interface design as well as visual presentation.) Most importantly, the team works with the client, who plays a crucial (and pivotal) role.

PHOTO COURTESY A.R. EDDY

Figure 1.2
A team must be versatile, with many interests and expertise. The members may come from a different state of mind and have challenging points of view. However, together they work toward a common goal. Uniforms not required.

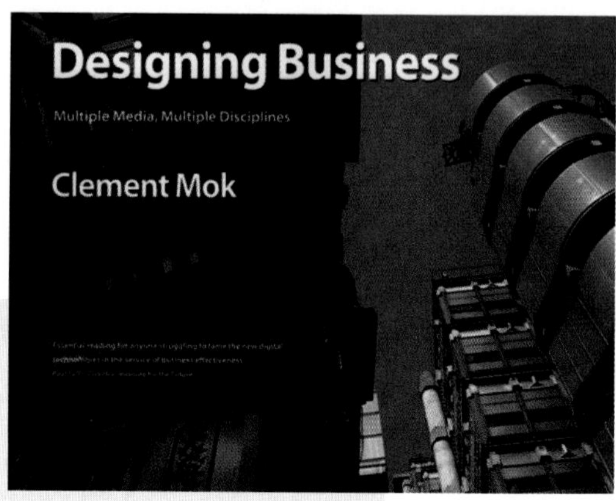

Figure 1.3
Designing Business *by Clement Mok shares the approach of one designer, or information architect, as he now calls himself.*

Roles Gone Astray

Clients who want web sites are bewildered as to who they should hire if Clement Mok is busy (Figure 1.3), and what they buy when they pay for *design* (after all, any college student can put up HTML pages). The following scenarios are not condemnations of any one of these roles or fields, but examples of how some sites have gone astray due to the lack of a full team or to inappropriately assigned roles:

Astray 1:
An Internet Service Provider sets up the site, a digital artist is hired to pick the colors and draw some icons. The links all *work* but visitors complain that they get easily lost.

Astray 2:
A print designer lays out each page like a magazine and the HTML production staff in-house says *it can't be done*. The designer gives up in despair.

Astray 3:
A multimedia artist creates a cool animated entrance page and interactive menus for the core page, but the third-level pages have dense text that extends across the full screen width.

Astray 4:
A company spends thousands of dollars to connect their database to the web, but somehow the most relevant information is difficult to access.

The Client's Role

A conversation at cross-purposes that occurs every day:

CLIENT: SO **WHEN** CAN I HAVE MY WEB SITE?

designer: What do you want to accomplish through this site?

CLIENT: SO HOW MUCH WILL IT **COST**?

designer: What exactly is the extent of the content that needs to be online?

CLIENT: WHAT WILL THE ICONS **LOOK LIKE**?

designer: What audience are you targeting?

CLIENT: DO I HAVE TO GET SOMEONE ELSE WHO WILL REALLY **GIVE ME ANSWERS**?

designer: (sigh) You can have it in two months, for $25,000, and the icons will be red and black with a fuzzy drop shadow.

Here the client has abdicated their crucial role and has eventually beaten down the designer. After all, you have children to send to college, you can't fight the battle forever. We have found that it is essential to make client responsibilities clear from the very beginning, spelled out in writing in the proposal. These are referred to later in the description of each step of DADI, and consist mainly of providing information about the company and their business, engaging fully in the definition phase of the project, and signing off on agreed-upon solutions. The most essential step the client must take, however, is understanding and subscribing to the DADI process and not insisting on putting the cart before the horse. Not insisting on the classic:

"ready, FIRE! ...aim..."

The Design Team

In our office, the partners meet to decide which partner will take the lead on a project. The considerations include how many projects that partner is already managing, whether they have a relationship with the client, or who should develop the relationship with a potential client. The lead partner will create a proposal for consultation with the prospective client. After the client accepts this proposal, the project leader is determined (usually the same partner), and the leader forms a team.

We are a small studio, so it's very likely that everyone will be involved in each project, but not necessarily in every phase or to the same extent. However, all team members must be kept up to date on the project and involved in key meetings even if they have no hands-on role in the current phase. Implementation may be the last phase, but the programmer sits in on early brainstorming sessions to respond to the frequent "can that be done?" queries. Sometimes research is needed before the answer can be given, so the early alert is essential.

The role each member will play may not be distinct; often one team member will wear several hats—but always the team jersey. Creating a team helps define responsibilities and roles in ongoing projects. A team also allows the client to have contact with a staff member who is aware of project status when the project leader may not be available.

The key functional roles on the team outlined by Mok are: strategy, information design, creative design, producer, and project manager. Each has specific roles and duties. At each phase, a particular function will drive the process. So the project leader is really a coordinator, allowing each function to take the lead when appropriate. Each leader focuses on the goals specific to a particular phase of the process. The following list is adapted from Mok's book *Designing Business*:

- Strategy (leads during definition)
- Information design (leads during architecture)
- Visual and interface design (leads during look & feel design)
- Producer (leads during implementation)
- Project manager (coordinates throughout, communicates with client or lead partner)

The DADI System

For a more comprehensive explanation of DADI, we recommend Clement Mok's book *Designing Business*. There is also a good deal of information at his studio's web site (Figure 1.4). Here we will present what we have found to be the most useful elements of the system, briefly reviewing the four stages, especially the first (definition) and the last (implementation). Issues specific to web site design that arise in stages two

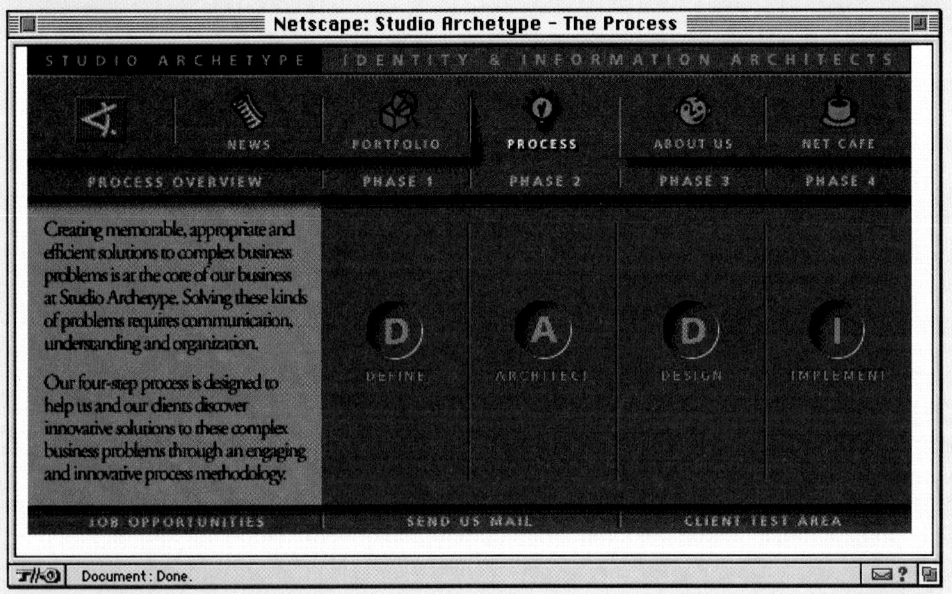

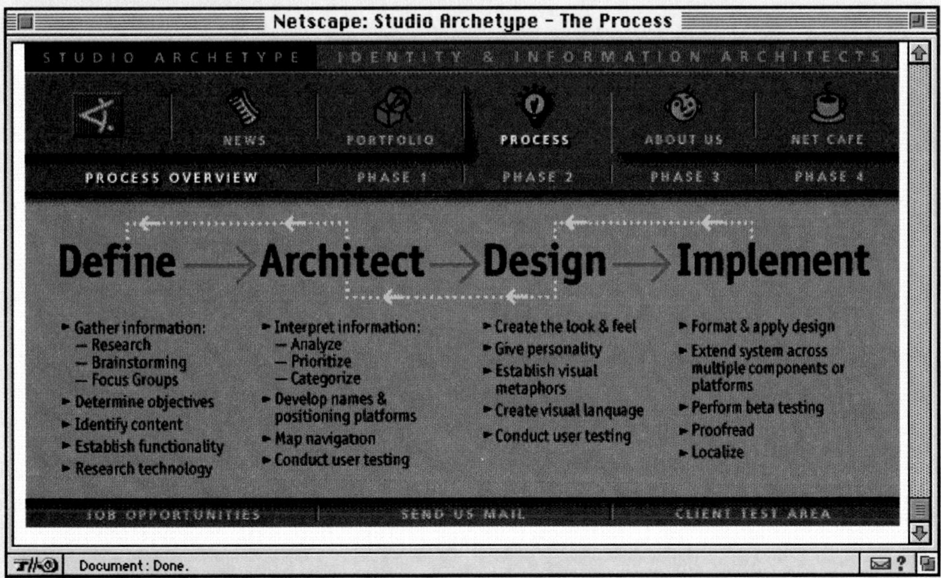

Figure 1.4

The site for Studio Archetype has a good deal of information about the DADI process. As this system is constantly evolving, there are some differences between the terms used at the site and those originally presented in the book. The pages shown are available at http://www.studioarchetype.com.

IF THE BUDGET IS PROPOSED AT THE END OF THE DEFINITION STAGE, DOES THAT MEAN THAT ALL OF THE WORK SO FAR HAS BEEN FREE? NO! DO NOT GIVE AWAY YOUR EXPERTISE. PROVIDE A DETAILED EXPLANATION OF YOUR PROCESS, SOME EXAMPLES OF YOUR WORK AND (IF THEY INSIST) A BALLPARK ESTIMATE OF PRICE AND TIMELINE. AGREE ON A CONSULTATION FEE THAT WILL TAKE YOU THROUGH THE DEFINITION PHASE, DEPENDING ON HOW MUCH OF THE RESEARCH YOU MUST DO AND HOW MUCH THEY CAN PROVIDE.

(architecture) and three (look and feel design) are explored in more detail in Chapters 2 and 3 respectively. We also refer to this system and stages throughout the case studies.

Definition →

Team Leader: Strategy

When? Where? What? How? Once the team has been assembled members will begin to collect all the bits and pieces relating to the project and analyze them. The team will identify the objectives and consider practical parameters such as budget and time frame. The scope of the project begins to make itself known. In these meetings the real investigation process takes place. A rigorous but friendly questioning of the client can often yield surprising and enlightening results. Approach this phase with a questioning attitude and from several different points of view.

The definition phase can take a couple of meetings or it can take months. Here is what you need to do during this phase:

1. Determine the objectives.
2. Determine the competition.
3. Identify the content.
4. Identify desirable features.
5. Identify the customer (audience).
6. Explore technological issues.
7. Determine the timeline.
8. Determine the budget.

The result of this process, as we apply it, is a comprehensive plan for the project that includes a timeline for each of the upcoming phases, and a budget. It does not include any sketches of site structure, sketches of page layout, or any graphics for the site. Do not proceed to the next phase without a sign-off on a plan that includes: goals, audience, content, schedule, budget—and specific statements of who is responsible for what.

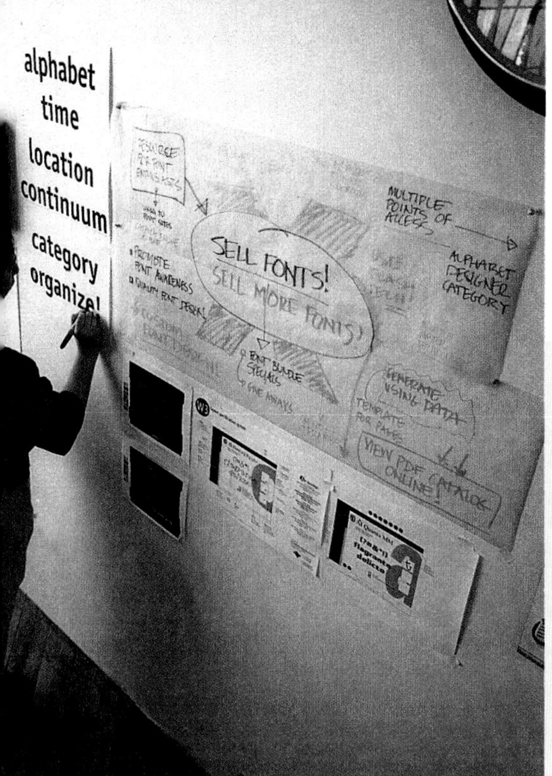

PHOTO GERRY MATHEWS

Figure 1.5

Our meeting room walls are covered with lists, goals, and proposed screen designs for sites that are under development. These charts and visual devices aid the team members.

Clarifying Goals

The client needs to be engaged in the process of establishing and prioritizing objectives for the site. Do not proceed based on a verbal discussion of goals. Return to the client with a written statement of goals that he or she can have approved by higher management, if necessary. Write these out large and tape them up in the project meeting room (Figure 1.5). Everything you do from here on must relate back to these objectives.

Be careful to distinguish between desired content or features and goals. For example, perhaps the client says they want a form online for customer feedback. This is NOT a goal. The goal may be increased customer satisfaction with the company. The hope is that the feedback form will help the customers feel (psychologically) important, and the company response to feedback may make an actual improvement in the product or service.

Another trap is *we want the coolest site on the Web.* Is that a legitimate goal? Obviously anything that spreads the word about a site will increase traffic and the word about truly *cool* sites travels fast. But this is really a strategy, not an underlying objective. The objective might be to increase the visibility of the company and recognition of the company name.

Internal versus External Agendas

Be careful not to get caught in the internal politics of a company. The individual you are dealing with may have several agendas: to please her boss, outshine another department, show off technological knowledge, and so on. Often the individual most excited by the web is delegated to look into getting a web site. This person might be determined to have a spinning logo (or a logo on fire!) when that may or may not be relevant to the overall strategy for the company. Here a gentle educational approach is

THE MOST COMMON INTERNAL AGENDA IS REFLECTED IN THE UBIQUITOUS ABOUT OUR COMPANY PAGES OF CORPORATE SITES. THE EGOS OF THE VARIOUS DEPARTMENTS DEMAND THAT THEY GET EQUAL SPACE ON THE WEB WHEN, OFTEN, THIS INFORMATION IS OF NO INTEREST TO THE TARGET EXTERNAL AUDIENCE.

best, basing your statements on what has been found to succeed for other companies in your experience. If you follow the lead of a client in the wrong direction, the site will not be successful in the end. Also, redirect the focus from what the boss wants to what the visitor will want. Be an advocate for the end-user and keep the focus there. "It's the user, stupid!".

Is a Web Site the Answer?

Don't be afraid to evaluate whether or not a web site (or intranet) is the best medium to reach the client objectives. Remember the strengths of the web:

- It breaks down geographical barriers.
- It allows for information to be distributed on demand.
- It allows frequent updating (if resources are allocated).
- It allows the inclusion of multimedia elements (sounds, motion, interactivity).
- It can be a two-way medium inviting visitor participation.

Beware of those who just want to join the crowd.

Identify the Content and Desirable Features

Get your client to talk freely about all the possible content that might go on the web. Let them fantasize about features (wouldn't it be great if...). Don't promise anything, but don't dampen their enthusiasm with technological barriers, yet—just keep them talking. They might even want to solicit suggestions from staff. Start with an unedited list. Collect any and all resource material about your client and their business including printed matter and products (Figure 1.6).

Take the list and material to your in-house team and add to it in brainstorming sessions. Look into the viability of some of the desired features (and the price tag attached). Ideally, let at least a week go by and then have a second team meeting to pare down the list. Now you are ready to

ONE OF THE EARLY CORPORATE WEB PIONEERS WAS SATURN CARS. IN OCTOBER OF 1995 WE HEARD A PRESENTATION BY DORIS MITSCH, THE DESIGNER OF THE ORIGINAL SITE. HER STORY TOLD OF HOW SHE WAS LITERALLY FLOODED WITH EMAIL ABOUT WHAT COLOR THE SEATS COULD BE IN A PARTICULAR MODEL AND HOW THE CARS COULD BE IMPROVED. SHE HAD MADE HER STUDIOS EMAIL ADDRESS AVAILABLE AT THE SITE. PLAN AHEAD. VISITORS WANT THEIR EMAIL ANSWERED, SO BE SURE TO HAVE A SYSTEM TO SEND MAIL TO THE APPROPRIATE PERSON.

meet with the client and reduce the list and prioritize the content according to the agreed upon objectives. Be sure that if they are talking about features that require constant updating they are willing to allocate resources to accomplish this. Consider any technological issues involved in features such as linking to a database or custom response to visitors.

Figure 1.6

The assets a client brings to the table may be overwhelming. Chapter 10 is a case study of a site for TimeCycle Couriers—boy do they have a lot of stuff!

Identify the Audience(s), their Technology, and Agendas

Often there are multiple audiences for a site. Some examples include:

- Existing and potential customers
- Existing and potential investors
- Existing and potential employees.

Some audiences may be more important than others, and some may be more motivated than others. Potential employees, for example, will generally explore a site fairly thoroughly. Unless recruitment is a pressing problem for the client, this audience does not have to be catered to in the way others do.

Review the content list and be sure that everything you are putting at the site is of interest to at least one of these groups. Also, be sure there isn't content omitted that would be useful to someone. Conversely the competition will surely be visiting the site, so be sure there isn't anything there that they shouldn't see.

Will the visitors be coming to the site from work, on a high-speed connection and a powerful CPU? Or will they be consumers dialing up from home who might have older computers and older browsers? Review the feature list and be sure you are not shutting out important audiences with technological barriers.

DON'T LOOK AT WORDS AND DOCUMENTATION AS YOUR ENEMY. DESIGNERS CAN UNDERESTIMATE THE VALUE OF THE DOCUMENTATION OF MEETINGS AND SIGNED CHARTS AND PROOFS. THESE PIECES OF PAPER ARE MORE THAN A PROTECTION IF SOMETHING GOES WRONG; OFTEN DOCUMENTATION CAN PREVENT A SERIOUS MISUNDERSTANDING.

IF THERE ARE DIFFERENCES BETWEEN WHAT IS BEING DELIVERED AND THE EXPECTATIONS OF EITHER THE CLIENT OR THE DESIGNER THE CAUSE MUST BE IDENTIFIED BEFORE THE PROCESS MOVES TO THE DESIGN PHASE. THIS MAY REQUIRE A REEVALUATION OF THE DEFINITION PHASE.

Architecture→

Team leader: Information design

What matters and where does it go? Information design is implemented at this phase. Here the team decides if all the information gathered at the definition stage is relevant. What has the highest priority? Refer back to the objectives. How difficult will building the structure be? The designer determines where the information will fit into the structure and which medium to use. The steps in this phase include:

1. Identify key messages that emerged from the definition phase.
2. Define the information types and how they will be manifested.
3. Define logical relationships.
4. Define links between information types.
5. Brainstorm and conceptualize.
6. Test the navigation using prototypes.
7. Identify specialized resources required to complete the project.

We address the issues of site architecture: organizational structure, navigational structure, prototypes and testing, in Chapter 2, "Constructing Site Frameworks". Prototypes are used to analyze, prioritize, categorize, and interpret the information that was gathered at the definition phase. Prototypes help both the designer and client to be aware of difficulties. It is through this process that the priorities and their implementation become more dimensional.

This is the phase that provides the framework on which the project's look and feel will be built. The designer's work should be examined against the client's expectations at this point. Do not underestimate the importance of this step. Both parties involved in the process MUST understand each other's expectations. The simple nodding of heads is a danger sign. Question your client and document your findings because misunderstanding can lead to disaster. Do not proceed to the design phase without sign-off on an approved structural (or logical) prototype.

SIGN-OFF DOES NOT MEAN THAT REVISIONS CANNOT TAKE PLACE AT A LATER POINT. IT DOES MEAN, HOWEVER, THAT IF THESE REVISIONS REQUIRE A CHANGE IN BUDGET OR SCHEDULE THE RESPONSIBILITY IS FIRMLY ON THE CLIENT'S SHOULDERS. OFTEN A CLIENT WILL NOD AND SMILE BUT, WHEN ASKED TO SIGN, SUDDENLY FINDS PROBLEMS WITH THE STRUCTURE WHICH OTHERWISE WOULD HAVE BEEN RAISED AT LATER STAGE.

Design of Look and Feel→

Team leader: Visual and interface design

This is where the project takes on form. The audio and visual elements that elevate the parts developed in the previous phases are developed. This is where the creativity that gives the project its personality begins to bring the project from a two-dimensional plan to a four-dimensional experience. The visual metaphors that support and enhance the architecture are devised and tested.

This phase maximizes the results of creative time by following the information structures defined in the architecture phase. Properly implemented, the definition and architecture phases create a solid foundation on which to build a functional and memorable look and feel. We have learned the hard way that prematurely designed pages may be torn to shreds if it is discovered that they don't work with the structure.

Again, at this stage the costs should be estimated and timeline should be evaluated. The need for special technologies and development costs should be estimated. The following list is based on our own process and differs considerably from the tasks listed by Clement Mok at his site:

1. Develop a custom color palette for the site.
2. Choose fonts for use in GIFs.
3. Determine screen size, especially page width.
4. Create illustrations, photography, audio, or video assets.
5. Choose the metaphor, if any, and design the visual interface.
6. Determine the names of the major sections and features.
7. Create navigational graphics and any site-specific icon systems (help, sitemap, index, and so on).
8. Create comps (not live HTML) showing the layout of key pages.
9. Begin content development (if part of your brief) especially for key pages.
10. Proceed with research and development of specialized technology (scripts, database preparation, and so on).

The issues of web page design (or screen design) are addressed in detail in Chapter 3. At this stage the comps are presented as hard copy (or static screen images), not live HTML. We put most of these together in Adobe Illustrator and know other firms that use primarily Photoshop or QuarkXPress for comp pages. Use actual copy wherever possible.

Before proceeding to implementation, approval of the color palette, section names, navigational interface (metaphor), and layout of key pages must be secured.

Words Have Feelings, Too!

In designing the look and feel of a site do not overlook the style of the copy, and the choice of titles for sections of the site. Some sites have playful copy and section titles, others are more straightforward. If a visual metaphor is being used the words should reinforce this (Figure 1.7). Be sure that playful, or intellectual, does not equal obscure and confusing. Put the names in your prototype from the architecture phase and test them!

One simple and practical reason to get the section titles approved early in this stage is that after you have created images with anti-aliased text, it is really not fun to change that text. Of course, NetObjects Fusion makes this much easier if you allow the application to generate the image with the text. Consider a longer version of a section name for the heading of a page, and a shorter version for navigation bars. No one wants to put *Recent Technological Advances in the Industry* on a button!

Key Pages

The pages for which layouts will be approved at this stage should be listed in the plan that you prepared in the definition stage. Use actual copy for these comps wherever possible. We generally include:

- An entrance (or splash) page
- The core page
- The opening page of each major section
- A What's New page (if appropriate)
- A sample page of each significant type of content page (articles, catalog pages, employee profile)
- The visual interface of significant functions at the site (submission forms, site map, search page)

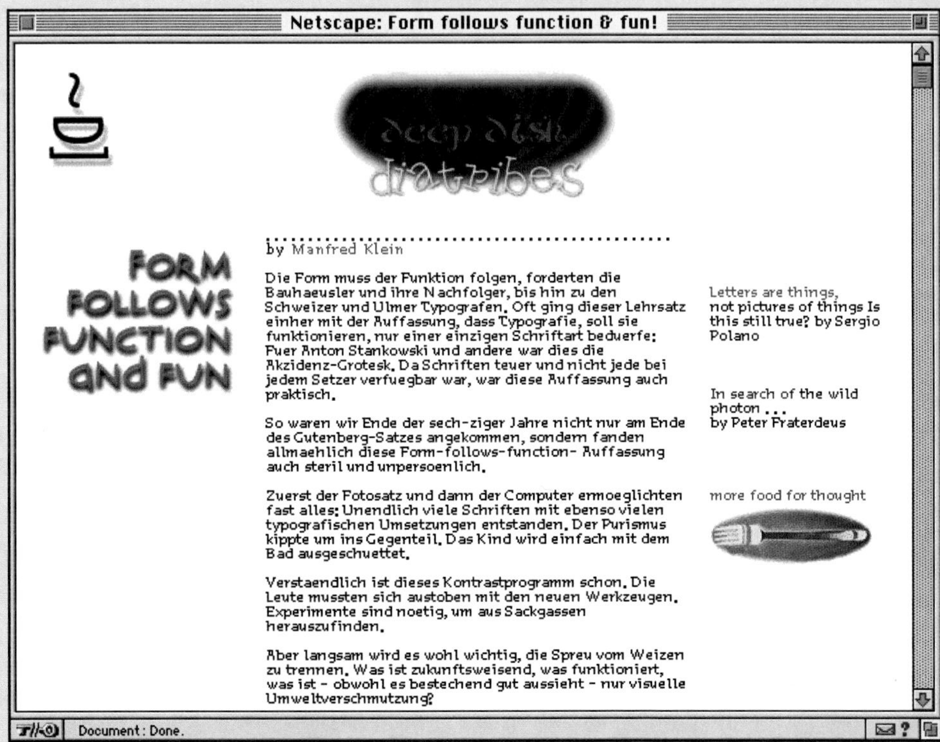

Figure 1.7

The section titles for the dezine café:—conversation, inspiration, and food for thought—which evoke the designer's ideal coffeehouse. The original text for one of the subsections Deep Dish Diatribes *(in food for thought) was* Meat and Potatoes. *We made a complex graphic with a great drop shadow before checking with our vegetarian client, who objected strongly!*

Implementation→

Team leader: Producer

In this phase, the project becomes *real* as the project team implements the ideas, activities, and assets developed in the first three phases. Testing with actual HTML pages takes place. Does the look and feel succeed? Is the right impression created? Do visitors become disoriented? This is not really production, the design process continues during this phase.

The key pages are implemented following the approved layouts, using approved text. Several content pages for each type are implemented, again using actual material. Sounds, animation, and interactivity are implemented. The prototype at this point is not a full beta site (all content is not yet in HTML) but systems to implement the full site are developed.

If NetObjects Fusion is used, this is where the components of a SiteStyle that was designed specifically for the client might be turned over to in-house staff to produce the full site in-house.

This phase includes the following steps:

- Implement the design including multimedia or database components.
- Perform beta testing across multiple platforms and browsers.
- Proofread all copy.
- Provide HTML templates.
- Provide live web pages for key pages (and multiples of content pages).

If desired, this phase can be followed by a fifth stage of production, bringing all material online and assuring quality control, and the sixth of ongoing site maintenance (and quality control). Site maintenance should be quite distinct from site enhancement, revision, or redesign. Maintenance is simply updating content. Be sure that your proposal specifies separate pricing for the addition of new features or sections of the site, or for revisions to the design.

2

Constructing Site Frameworks

WHEN I AM WORKING ON A PROBLEM, I NEVER THINK ABOUT BEAUTY, I THINK ONLY OF HOW TO SOLVE THE PROBLEM. BUT WHEN I HAVE FINISHED, IF THE SOLUTION IS NOT BEAUTIFUL, I KNOW IT IS WRONG.

R BUCKMINSTER FULLER.

In this chapter we discuss the methods for organizing and creating navigational structures for a site. We look at organizational models and how to conduct testing using a logical prototype. We talk about how to incorporate the information that was gathered in the definition phase into a structure that works (Figure 2.1). Finally, we'll warn you about some common pitfalls.

There is a complex, causal relationship between the goals, content, organizational structure, and the navigational structure (or paths) of the site. Note the distinction between *organizational* structure and *navigational* structure, they are distinct concepts (Figure 2.2). The organizational structure of the material comes out of the nature of the information itself. The navigational structure or access is designed to meet the goals, for example, enable this audience to reach this information.

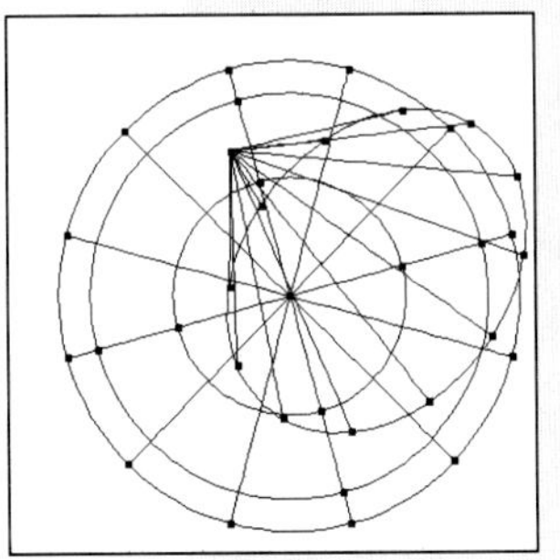

Figure 2.1
Don't be confined to thinking of structure as a hierarchical chart.

1. The goals determine the content.
2. The content determines the organizational structure.
3. The structure defines the *location* of the content for organizational purposes.
4. The goals determine the path to the content—the navigational structure.

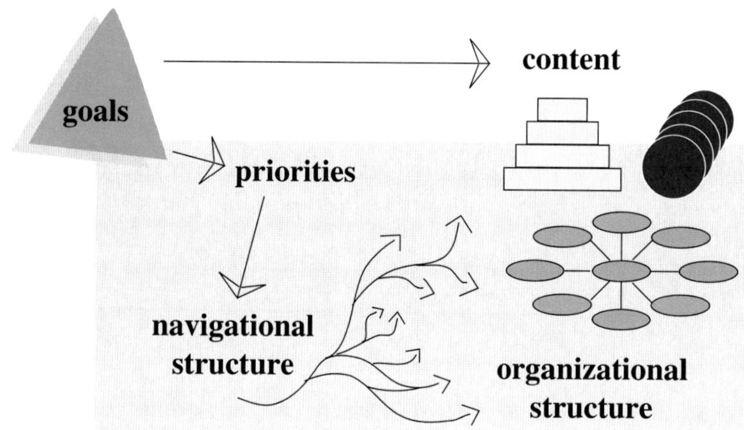

Figure 2.2
Here you see how the goals of a site determine the content and also the priority of that content, how accessible it must be. This is distinct from the organizational structure, which simply arranges the information logically.

With designing for a new medium comes the ability to directly measure our success. Now designers must actually measure the results of their work based on visitor response, which is tracked by the server. Aesthetics, grids, and other applied graphic arts are not enough in this new environment. The needs at sites are being reevaluated every week when the log reports come in. You want to know if your design is working? Your client will want to know too.

We have protested against those who undervalue a designer's role in the site design process and try to restrict us to making icons or banners. Now we will counter by addressing some misconceptions that are being perpetuated specifically by some designers.

It's not Print, It's GUI

Designers have formed opinions about the organization and design of sites based on a print model; however, these assumptions are not always true. Designers, some pretty famous ones too, are saying that the days of the techno cyberculture are over and we, as the smart designers, are here to fix the mess. It's as if they are saying "Yep, us civilized folks are going to beat the heathens into submission."

Amazing isn't it? See an opportunity and crush it with old ideas. Not us, we're not joining that club and we hope you won't either. One of the most exciting things about the Internet and intranets is the opportunity to create something that is totally new. Who wants to look at a hundred sites that look like *Time Magazine* moved to the web, or visit two-dimensional spaces in a medium that offers so much more?

It is time for us all to wake up and realize that a web site is about creating an environment, an experience, a world. All the content in the world is useless if the visitor can't get access to the content. So what do you do? You either hire an interface specialist as a consultant or make one part of your team. And you test, test, test.

So, start reading those books and journals on creating human interfaces. You can find reading suggestions at our companion web site www.designpractice.com. This isn't print—let's not dull the medium. Let's use the opportunity to find out more about ourselves as designers, the new medium we are working within, and how people will use it.

The visual interface is the surface representation of the underlying navigational structure. We talk more about the visual aspects of the interface in Chapter 3, but the place to begin is with the structure of the site.

THE TEN COMMANDMENTS OF SITE STRUCTURE

1. **Organizational structure does not equal navigational structure.**
2. **Don't force content into categories.**
3. **Every page must have content.**
4. **Provide the simplest path of accessibility.**
5. **Don't throw obstacles into the visitors' path.**
6. **Build back doors and escape hatches.**
7. **Prepare for multiple audiences.**
8. **Be flexible.**
9. **Allow for growth.**
10. **Be prepared for change.**

Organizational versus Navigational Structure

Organizational structures are usually represented by charts that look like company organizational charts, called organizational *trees*. These are sometimes called *flow charts* but they are not flow charts. Figure 2.3 shows a true flow chart, where the progress over time, from point A to point B, goes through many possible routes. Our beloved site trees are static—there is absolutely nothing flowing about them. They are helpful, however, in grouping related information in categories and sub-categories (Figure 2.4).

The chart shown in Figure 2.4, however, should not represent a navigational structure. That is, unless you restrict your visitor to three choices: up, down, or over. We have actually seen this on the web, and it is very painful. The path that a visitor will need to take does not always conform to pages that are adjacent on the organizational chart.

Navigation happens over time. See how complex the flow chart is for interNIC where the origin and destination are set. On a web site there are myriad destinations. We try to portray it on these charts by drawing lots of lines, and arrows, often in different colors. This is a good place to start, but eventually you must actually experience the journey of the visitor to evaluate the navigational structure.

Organizational Structures

When building a structure (like a building) you should begin from the bottom up. Look at the content. What things belong together in a way that will make sense to the visitor? How would they want to access the content? Look at the products, the articles, and the real content of the site. Remember the rule we set out at the beginning: The content determines the organizational structure. Don't start with the core page, decide you want four options from there and force the content into four artificial categories.

Your list of goals may contain several phases of a project. Define a timeline based on requirements of the client and divide the phases based

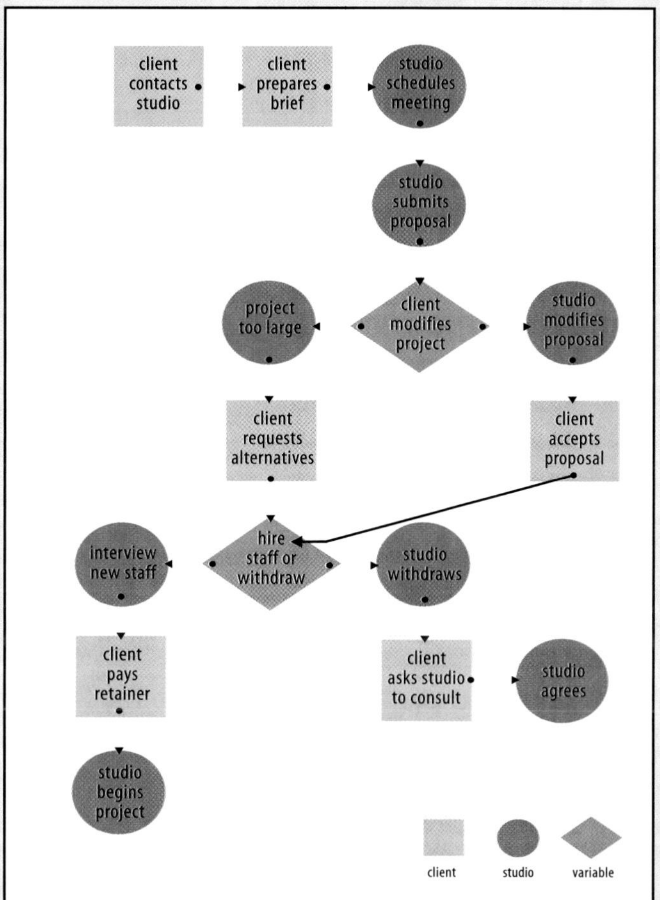

Figure 2.3

A sample flow chart. Flow charts show actions and points of decision making over time.

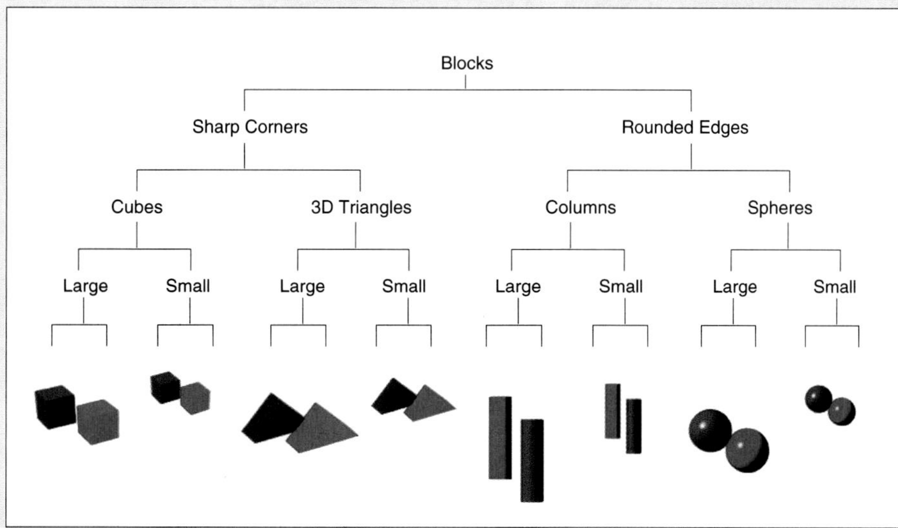

Figure 2.4

This is a typical structural chart, showing an hierarchical layering into 5 levels from top to bottom. It organizes what might have been a jumble of colored blocks. Only one level (the bottom) contains any blocks!

on time and priority. When a web project begins, certain parts of the site may contain more information than others, thus creating a lop-sided organizational tree. This is a natural condition that comes about from the focus of individuals supplying the information.

When you are considering how someone might access information, two main distinctions are the impulsive browsing visitor who might not know what they want (that you want to lead in), and the visitor seeking something specific who expects to find it in a logical place. You build the organizational structure like a reference work with material categorized in one system, the primary (or default) organization. You then overlay an alternate navigational structure that allows for browsing, adventure, exploration, serendipity, or impulsive linking following relationships other than the primary organizing parameters.

Information Types: Organizing the Content

In the classic book by Richard Saul Wurman, *Information Anxiety,* we find that information can be organized in five ways: **category**, **alphabet**, **time**, **location**, and **continuum** (Figure 2.5). This book is an incredibly useful reference, as is his more recent book, *Information Architects*. In our staff project room we have the categories for organizing information displayed prominently on the wall when we begin the process of creating an architecture for a web site (Figure 2.6). These are the categories we use to help define the organization; but not necessarily for the whole site. Again, you may use one method of organization for the foundation of the site and yet have several different methods of access. This is illustrated in the case study of the fontsOnline site, Chapter 10.

INFORMATION ANXIETY IS CURRENTLY OUT OF PRINT. CAN YOU BELIEVE IT? WE RECOMMEND THIS BOOK HIGHLY. SO START LOOKING FOR COPIES AT USED BOOK STORES.

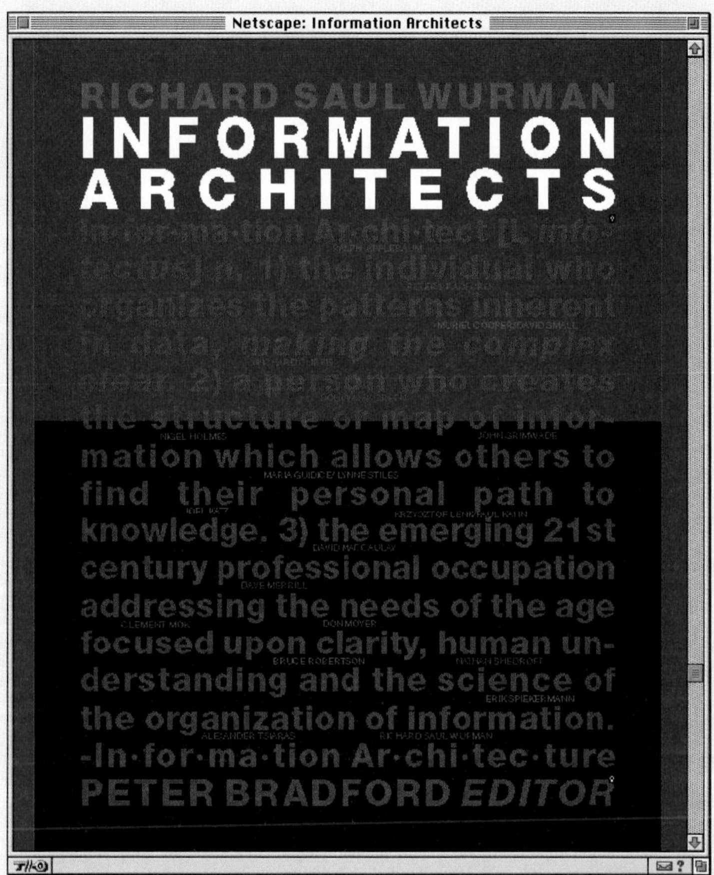

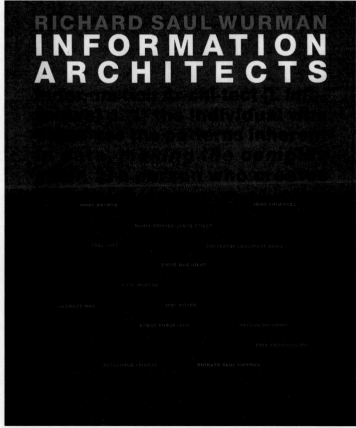

Figure 2.5
If you surf over to the site http://www.ted.com *You'll find information about Richard Saul Wurman, the TED conferences and his book* Information Architects *including this representation of the cover (below), but on the Web the names are links to more information about the individual architects. Read the copy, it's to the point!*

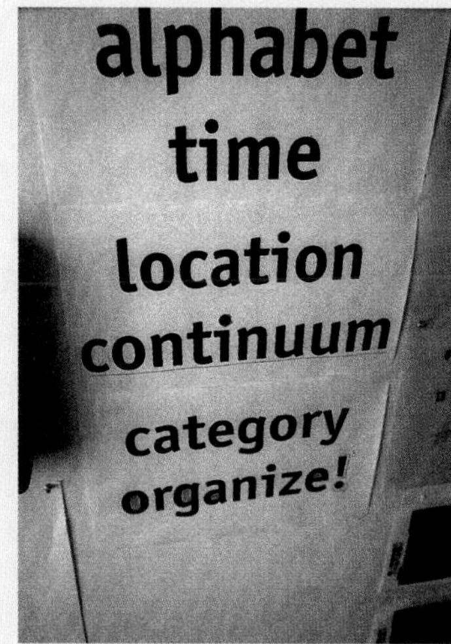

Figure 2.6
Keep reminders about key principles prominently displayed around your workspace.

Let's take a look at these organizational possibilities.

Category. These are groups that have similar importance. If you were to go to let's say www.toyota.com you would find the automobiles organized by categories such as different models, and then models with four-wheel drive, and so on. There is no set order, or set priority between one category and the next. At our Elements of Einstein site, material is organized into whimsical categories that are set up like the table of the elements (see Figure 2.7).

Alphabet. A great way to organize large bodies of information. This is more than a category because the material must be ordered in a particular (if arbitrary) manner. And everyone carries the key to the system around in their heads (at least in the Western world). The little song plays in our head: ABCD, EFG, HIJK, L-M-N-O-P... You can always find something this way, but only if you know the name of what you are looking for. Figure 2.8 shows how we put an alphabetical index at the Elements of Einstein site that was mentioned above, to serve the more directed visitor.

Time. Arrangement by what happened when, or when things will happen in the future. Examples include calendars, histories, and schedules. Figure 2.9 shows an imaginative graphic where information is arranged by time.

Location. Where proximity is used to relate one thing to another. Maps are the most common example of this, showing cities, parks, rivers, roads, and so on. Other examples are diagrams of the human body, or floor plans of a building. You can see visually what things are distant and what things are in close proximity.

Continuum. Here you assign value or weight to the information such as greatest importance to least importance, highest rated to lowest rated, most popular to least popular, smallest to largest, lightest to darkest, and so on. Usually these are associated with some kind of numerical measurement, but not necessarily—for example, most detailed to most general. Some continuums have many members at one level, such as a site that gives product ratings from 1 to 5. You might think there is a "5-star" category, but these categories have an order (based on increasing numbers of stars) so the overall structure is by continuum.

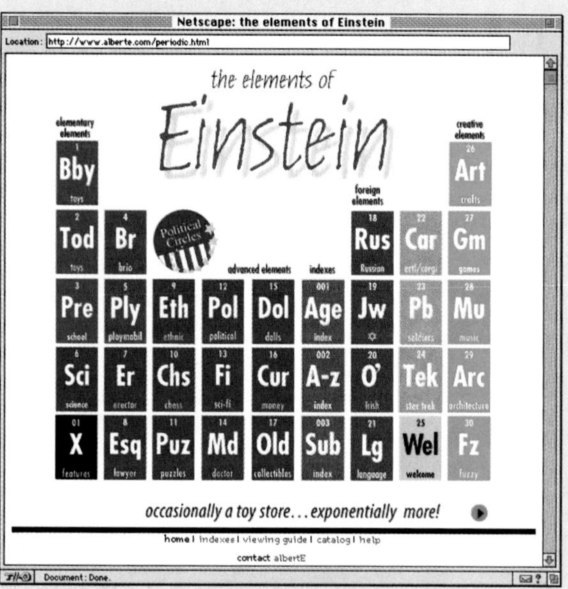

Figure 2.7

The home page of the Elements of Einstein, www.alberte.com/,periodic.html shows a mock table of the elements where you choose a category of products to see based on these playful categories.

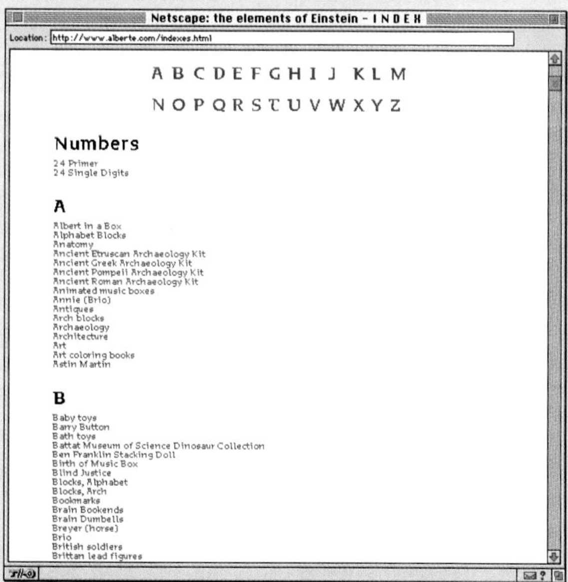

Figure 2.8

If you chose the A-Z element from the screen shown in Figure 2.7, you get an alphabetical index of the products.

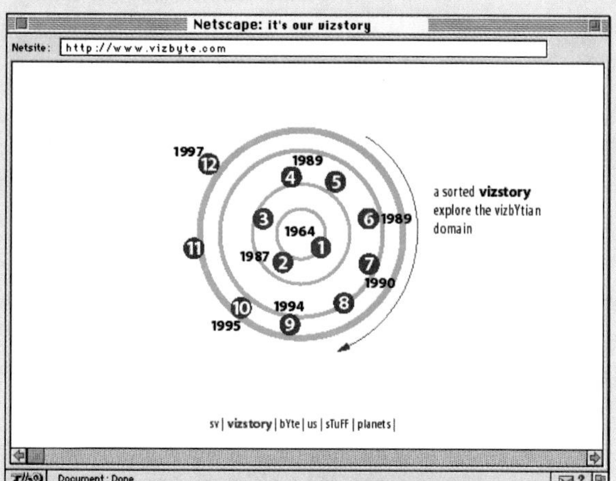

Figure 2.9

Here's a menu to our timeline at www.vizbyte.com. Click somewhere on the target and find out what we're up to in our vizstory.

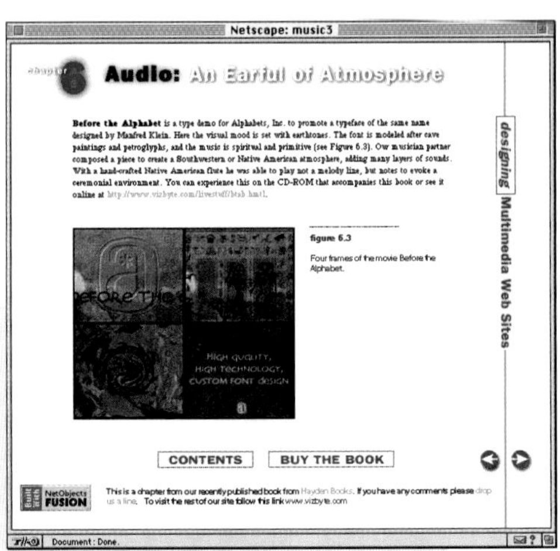

Figure 2.10
This is a page of the Audio chapter of Designing Multimedia Web Sites *(by Stella Gassaway, Gary Davis, and Catherine Gregory, Hayden Books). Here you can go forward, back, or to the contents.*

Logical Relationships, Mok's Models

Clement Mok presents seven organizational models—ways that data relates to each other.

Hierarchical. This is how the typical organizational tree is set up, the structure has overall categories, sub categories, and sub-sub categories. A corporate organizational chart leaps to mind.

Linear. A story that proceeds from one paragraph to the next. This is a challenge on the web because it is misrepresented by tree-like structures that do not allow continuous horizontal movement. Figure 2.10 shows a page from a book online, where the linear page organization of a printed book is mimicked on the web.

Web. This consists of inter-related information with no upper or lower levels, and no related groups. This kind of information becomes distorted when put in the tree, because it takes on an appearance of order that it does not really have.

Parallel. Here you present information that shares a commonality, like a timeline where you see what was happening in politics, or the arts and science for any given year.

Matrix. Where there is more than one organizing system, you need to see two axes. An example of one axis is a price list with one price for each item. A matrix is where you get a discount for ordering in quantity, so you must look at the product and the quantity to determine the price. This is simple enough to present within a page (as a table) but is more difficult when the pages themselves must be organized by more than one axis.

Overlay. This will become more applicable to the web with layers in Netscape Communicator. You can choose to see a map showing climate zones, or remove these and add political boundaries, and so on.

Spacial Zoom. The common practice of showing a small picture and allowing the viewer to click to see a larger picture, or a detail. Think of the classic film by Charles and Ray Eames, the *Powers of Ten* where the entire movie is a zoom that goes from microscopic to intergalactic.

Define Links Between Information Types

This is a difficult concept, but well worth grappling with. Consider the TimeCycle Couriers site that we discuss in Chapter 11. The information about levels of urgency (for example, Rush or Super Rush) is not enough for the customer to ascertain what they want to know: the price and speed of the delivery. These desired pieces of data are based on another *type* of information: the relative location of the origin and destination of the delivery. Therefore it is not enough to simply present the geographical information and the various levels of urgency available; there must be a way to link the two. You can see how we managed in Chapter 11.

The information and assets that comprise the content of the site will make the structure apparent. I know this sounds Zen-like, but if you create artificial methods for organizing information, the visitors to the site will not be able to find out what they want to know. We must provide a path through the content, which we call the navigational structure.

Navigational Structure: Decisions, Decisions...

In the definition phase we created a list of the site goals, and key target audiences. These help to prioritize the content and determine how it should be made accessible. The content may be organized in a logical way, but the visitor may want to skip the intervening layers of organizational structure directly to the item of interest.

Suppose you have a catalog of products that is organized by type of product, and the soap dish page is at the sixth level of the site, under housewares. This month you are having a special sale on soap dishes and so you put an announcement of the sale on your core page (with a link). The soap dish page doesn't have to move out of housewares to the first level simply because there is direct navigational access from the core page. Although according to the organizational structure the visitor has traversed several levels, the navigational path was one click. They then find themselves among other housewares (not on sale) that might also be of interest! The navigational structure does not reflect the organizational tree.

The previous example is quite obvious and simplistic but the same principle applies in more complex situations. Many sites actually move the location of a page when it moves from an active article to an archived back issue. There is no reason why all articles can't be assigned a permanent URL based on a fixed structure (such as content) and then the current issue would simply be accessed through the table of contents page for that issue (especially if frames allow you constant access to the table of contents). This way those that bookmark the page can always find it later. Find an organizational structure that does not require pages to move and then adapt the navigational structure as needed to point visitors toward the most important information.

THIS IS NOT A PARALLEL TO SHALLOW AND WIDE SITE STRUCTURES, BECAUSE THE VISITOR WILL GENERALLY WANT TO VISIT MORE THAN ONE PAGE. YOU DON'T OFTEN WEAR MORE THAN ONE (WELL, MAYBE TWO) SHIRTS. THE ONLY SITES THAT FIT THIS MODEL ARE SITES WHERE YOU ARE JUST LOOKING FOR ONE PAGE, SUCH AS A LISTING OF A PARTICULAR BOOK.

When you arrive at a web site, decision is the word of the moment. Is this what I thought it would be? Should I investigate? Where do I enter? Do I need to register? Why do I need plug-ins?

To define the process of making navigational choices we create decision trees. The navigational architecture of a site is made up of numerous decision trees. The content within a particular channel will define the tree structure. A site can contain numerous tree structures. At each level the visitor makes at least one decision: whether to continue. Decision trees are the geometry that makes up the site architecture. Don't try to draw all possible routes (as the true theorists would)—think of likely paths a real visitor might take.

Types of Decision Tree Structures

Shallow and Wide. In a shallow decision tree the agony is over pretty quickly. You have a wide range of choices (like facing your closet in the morning) but once the decision is made you are finished and can go on with your day. In life, when faced with too wide a range of choices, some people deliberately make the process deeper (adding more decisions) by narrowing it down. You can wear a long-sleeved shirt, a dark shirt, a black shirt, and so on until you arrive at one chosen shirt.

Narrow and Deep. In this structure few choices are available at any particular level, however, many levels must be accessed. Note that narrow is a relative term, a mere four choices at every level quickly becomes wide visually, but as decision trees go it is still narrow. Figure 2.11 is an example of a narrow and deep decision tree.

Wide and deep. A wide and deep decision tree has multiple decisions at each level. This structure allows a visitor to skim the surface laterally, diagonally, or drill straight down. Most large web sites fit into this category. If you truly represent all the choices a visitor has at each page (return home, leave site, go up one page, go to a related page, go down one page, and so on) you could never draw all the choices.

HERE'S A LOOK AT THE TREE THAT DESCRIBES A TRIP TO THE OFFICE IN THE MORNING.

wake up (no choice)

shower / not

choose something to wear

long sleeves / **short sleeves**

go to the garage

I drive / **Margaret drives**

park the truck

in lot / **on street**

enter the building

front door / **side door**

have coffee

milk / black

check email

mail / **not**

now what?

work / **pretend to work**

Figure 2.11
A narrow and deep decision tree.

Visitors with Widely Differing Needs and Agendas

As designers, we assist in defining the site audience and consider the site from the visitor's point of view. In our meetings, members of the team approach the information from a particular visitor's point of view. Consider the path each might take through the site, the choices they would probably make given their interests and mind set. Do they reach the information of interest to them? Do you lose them along the way? (Do you care?)

This becomes very difficult using paper and pencil. You can only draw lines with so many colors of ink on a static chart. You need a way to test the structure and assumptions dynamically. This is discussed in the next section, "The Logical Prototype."

The Logical Prototype

It is vital to get feedback on the architecture and navigation of a site long before the visual look and feel have been designed, as we discussed in Chapter 1. The **logical prototype** is a way that we have found to keep the focus on the architecture. This device allows us to check access to content and the effectiveness of navigational features. We use this for our internal testing as well as for client testing.

NetObjects Fusion has made it possible to make these prototypes quickly. Each page is a screen containing a description of the content that will be on the page, and navigational choices. A banner at the top tells the tester what page they have reached. The text description has to be enough to let the tester know that they have reached their destination, something like "a list of household products and prices appears here." The navigational choices may have relative emphasis (text links at the bottom, simple buttons at the left, some special links in the body of the page).

The lack of any graphics or real copy keeps the client (and the designers) from being distracted by the look and feel. Remember, avoid answering questions about what the icons will look like until you can get the client to sign off on the logical prototype. This is key, because clients get distracted by not liking that color, that image, or asking "Why doesn't that align?"

THE LOGICAL PROTOTYPE

NO ICONS, NO BLINKING, NO HIGHLIGHTS, NO SOUND. NO DISTRACTING EMOTION OR STIMULATION, JUST THE STRUCTURE.

The logical prototype also enables the design team to work with the engineers and programmers earlier in the process. In this way technological solutions can be discussed and evolve with the site design process. This can be seen in many of the case studies, especially the fontsOnline site, which is discussed in Chapter 10.

Designer and Client Testing

Don't ever let a client convince you that their site can go live without testing, and we don't just mean testing to see if the links work or the GIFs are corrupted. Sites must have numerous levels of testing, beginning with the logical prototype, through the look and feel, to the implemented alpha and beta level sites.

build it

test it

learn some stuff

build it again

test it some more

The first level of testing of the logical prototype is done by the design team. The team looks for any deficiencies in the content structure as well as any navigational problems. When the team is confident that it has created a successful logical prototype it will be presented to the client for testing. This is usually done by serving the pages in a client test area on the web.

Each tester will go through the site first as themselves, recording their human, personal reactions. Then they will assume the attitude of a member of a key audience that has been profiled by the team. For example, they might pretend to be an impatient customer seeking information about why a software product isn't functioning properly. Then they might take on the role of a potential investor deciding whether to buy stock in this particular software company.

For each role the same questions are asked including:

Are the key messages communicated?

Is the content accessible?

Were you frustrated or bored?

VISITOR TYPES

THE EXPERIENCED, DIRECTED NETIZEN SEEKING SPECIFIC INFORMATION

THE CONFUSED NOVICE SEEKING GUIDANCE

THE EASILY-BORED SURFER, SEEKING ENTERTAINMENT

THE IMPULSE BUYER, SEEKING TEMPTATION

THE COLLEAGUE WHO KNOWS THE CONTENT BUT IS INEXPERIENCED ON THE WEB, SEEKING RESOURCES

Tally Feedback and Results

Before making the logical prototype available for testing it is helpful to create feedback forms and give them to the testers to record their responses. This is true for testers in the studio, or the client. A logical prototype is useless without real feedback. Forms help to remind participants that the testing is for real, and to take it seriously. It also makes it possible to have quite a number of people test the logical prototype and give feedback. Interviewing them later is a good idea too—some people aren't good at filling out forms.

One simple form could be print outs of small screen shots from the pages so that the testers mark areas of confusion, frustration or missing content. The testing forms should be labeled with the scenario that is being tested (the visitor type). Clients may (and should) deviate from this testing, seeking out the goals of primary interest from their own personal point of view. You can be sure that if a member of the client team advocated for something to be included, they will be looking for how easily that feature is accessed.

Site Nightmares

With all of the complexity of content organization, navigational structure, and multiple audiences there are many pitfalls that await the developer of a web site. Here we describe three common structural problems that you see on the web all too frequently. The most common nightmare is a site that is built page by page, grows to hundreds of individual pages, and then has to be maintained and updated manually!

Menus, Menus, and Nothing to Eat

What is the distance between your site and the information the visitor wants to access? One click? Two, three? The worst thing you can do is drag the visitor through menu after menu without a morsel of information for consumption. Remember the blocks in Figure 2.4 at the beginning of this chapter? If a site followed this structure literally, the content (the colored blocks) would not appear until you had made four choices. Not only would you not see the content you were searching for, you would not see any content at all! This is one of the most difficult challenges facing a web designer— content and navigational choices must be integrated throughout a site.

A PARALLEL IS OFTEN MADE BETWEEN A HIERARCHICAL STRUCTURE AND THE FILING SYSTEMS IN THE WINDOWS OR MAC OS. THIS IS AN EXCELLENT PARALLEL: THE FOLDERS ON THE FILE DIRECTORY SYSTEM ARE NOT FILES THEMSELVES, THEY ARE MERELY CONTAINERS.

The visitor to your site isn't interested in your structural design. The shortest distance between two points is what they are looking for. Give them something to sink their teeth into or they'll go somewhere else. In Chapter 4 you will learn a trick to be able to keep a page in NetObjects Site view for organizational purposes, but avoid making visitors actually pass through it.

When we first built web sites, designers followed a print model and included introduction pages for each section that served the function of a table of contents. A different model is emerging now (as we will discuss in Chapter 3). The best way to find out what models are working is to go to sites and deconstruct them. Discover what has been successful in creating an interface. Don't take anything about the interface for granted.

Growth That Is Out of Control

More often than not, the original scope of the project will grow as conversations with the client bring to the surface all of the desirable features of a site. This continually expanded scope requires that the design of the structure accommodate growth both planned and unplanned. A plan for implementation with phases or stages must be created.

A site structure must be scaleable and lend itself to convenient updating and maintenance. A web presence can turn into a real life version of the sci-fi (or horror)movie *The Blob* if you don't watch out. It's almost a living thing that will expand to fill the space its given and ask for more. It must accommodate the addition of information. It is the design team's job to prepare for appropriate expansion at defined intervals.

If the design of the site and its goals are met, it is likely that the visitors to the site will make more of their needs known. When a visitor becomes a frequent visitor at your site, it means you have been successful. There is interest enough to make a commitment to returning to the site. As the feedback begins to come in on a launched site, the design and content teams must be ready to accommodate requests from those that use the site and will help define the sites direction of growth.

ONE OF THE COMPANIES WE WORKED WITH WAS ABSOLUTELY UNPREPARED FOR THE POSITIVE RESPONSE THEIR INITIAL WEB PRESENCE ACHIEVED. THE VISITORS TO THEIR SITE, THEIR CLIENTS, BEGAN TO REQUEST THAT MORE INFORMATION BE MADE AVAILABLE. IN A RUSH TO RESPOND THEY HAD CREATED HTML AND ADDED TO THE SITE IN A PATCHWORK MANNER. THIS CREATED MANY DEAD ENDS IN NAVIGATION, AND CONFUSION ABOUT WHERE YOU ARE WITHIN THE SITE.

The Nightmare of Democracy

The same kind of problems arise when autonomy is given to different parts of an organization to design "their section" of a web site. This may prevent the bruising of egos, but an overall master plan is still required. Otherwise, the absence of basic standards will become obvious when it's too late.

Simple guidelines, combined with a visual system that will prevent confusion and repetition of effort may be the only necessary mandate from an oversight committee for a large organizational site. The key is communication and cooperation between parties, and if that is missing some serious problems can occur.

What if you have a large non-profit organization with satellite "chapters" run by volunteers? The volunteers are putting up their own sites in their own time, and aren't interested in restrictions from a central authority. However, the central office could create a simple system that would help guide the chapters and still give them complete autonomy over site design, structure, and content.

The main office of the organization would conduct a dialog with its affiliates. The dialog would answer these questions. What would be the general content at a chapter site? How would the chapter link to the central site? How would the central site link to the chapter? To prevent duplication of effort, and keep content current and accurate, the chapter would link to the central site for various "organization-level" information. The central office would be responsible for providing the most current and accurate data. The chapter site would emphasize the local outlook and serve the chapter membership, while providing access to the central site.

3

Web Page Design:

Finding a New Paradigm

In this chapter we see a great deal of the struggles of this new medium, the web, to come into its own. There are many how-to books on the market that will instruct you in the correct way to design a web page. These books attempt to teach principles in a few pages that take design students and designers years to master. Positioning of graphics and text, use of color and white space, or how to use multimedia; these are only a few of the difficult issues that the web designer must face. Design cannot be packaged in lists of rules, recipes or formulas.

THE CONFLICT BETWEEN DESIGN AND TECHNOLOGY, LIKE THE CONFLICT BETWEEN FORM AND CONTENT, IS NOT AN EITHER/OR PROBLEM, IT IS ONE OF SYNTHESIS.

PAUL RAND, **FROM LASCAUX TO BROOKLYN**

THE DESIGN OF LOOK AND FEEL DOES NOT NECESSARILY REQUIRE THE ABILITY TO CREATE GRAPHICS. NETOBJECTS FUSION COMES WITH MANY PROFESSIONALLY RENDERED GRAPHICS THAT CAN BE USED EFFECTIVELY IN A SITE. GRAPHICS ALONE, HOWEVER, DO NOT. PROVIDE A SITE OR PAGE DESIGN.

Therefore, this chapter is not a step-by-step discussion or instruction about how to create effective page layouts. We prefer to teach by inspiration, and by stimulating thinking about the underlying issues involved. Study the pages shown in this chapter and throughout the book that strike you as the most effective. If you are building a site and do not have a designer on your team, you should at the very least seek some design consultation or request an analysis of your site or prototype pages.

The central issue that underlies most design for the web, is the uncertainty about what model to draw upon. Is the web in the tradition of a broadcast medium, or is it more like the print medium brought to the screen? Following either model blindly leads to some pitfalls but both traditions have a great deal to contribute to the new Web environment.

Right now they are the models that designers, and more importantly visitors, have to go by. The *U.S. News* site (Figure 3.1) is an excellent example of a site that uses the printed page metaphor. Figure 3.2 shows an excellent example of an exhibition, the Holocaust Museum, that presents its material like a series of screens in a multimedia piece. There is a clear dividing line between those that cleave to one model, and those that look to another, and the dividing line is based on the content of the site. Eventually the web will find its own model, but during this exploratory period there is some benefit to be gained from the tension between the two mindsets.

COLOR, WHICH TOOK YEARS TO BECOME PREDICTABLE FROM A DESIGNER'S SCREEN TO PRINT, AGAIN IS A DEVIL. NOW COLOR IS BEING VIEWED ON MONITORS THAT HAVE NEVER BEEN CALIBRATED, AND THAT WEREN'T INTENDED TO DISPLAY COLOR ACCURATELY. WE CONFRONT BIT DEPTH, CROSS-PLATFORM COLOR PALETTES, AND BROWSER PALETTES.

The technical challenges in designing for the web change everyday. The intellectual methods of design, however, remain the same. We meet with our clients, ask them questions, they answer the questions, and we ask them more questions. The design challenge is still to gather the information, determine the goals, define the approach, and execute the plan. As designers and developers, we jump at the new possibilities of publishing that include such things as video and audio, but a whole new set of limitations and constraints create new design challenges. Designing for a luminous vehicle (the screen) demands creative solutions to create readable type both as image and HTML text.

Let's not be overwhelmed by these new technologies. Rather let's look at the advantages that our previous experience with print can bring to approaching viable solutions and models within the new media. Using this experience will also allow us to draw a parallel that will help our clients approach their web site with an understanding of the process. In this way we can look at creating a site that will be a tool and communication vehicle like other vehicles before it.

New Setting, Old Metaphors

Creating interface standards on the web is still young. A visitor can arrive at any number of sites and find a completely different entrance, or an entirely different way to access the assets contained within the site which

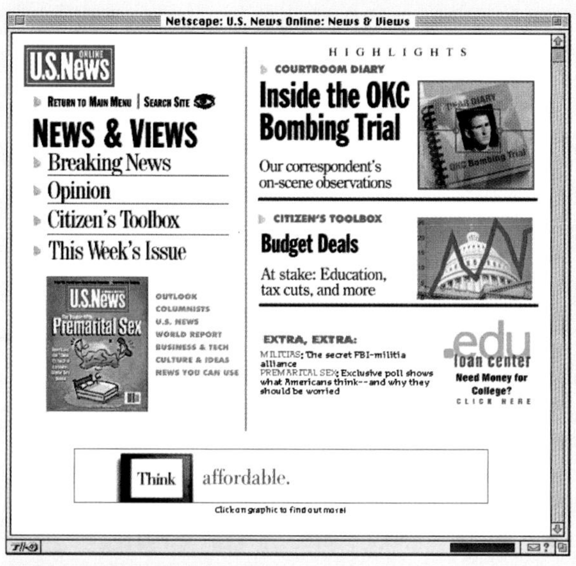

www.usnmm.org

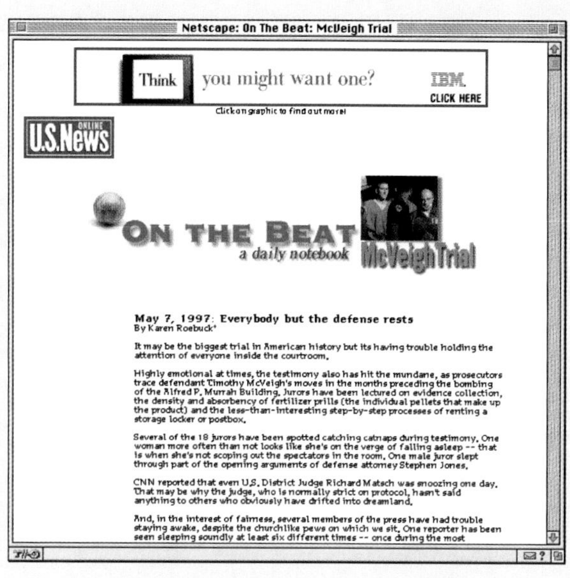

Figure 3.1

The U.S. News Online site moves the printed page directly to the web page. They gain mileage by bringing their print look and feel to the web. Their image is strong and consistent even when delivery isn't in print media.

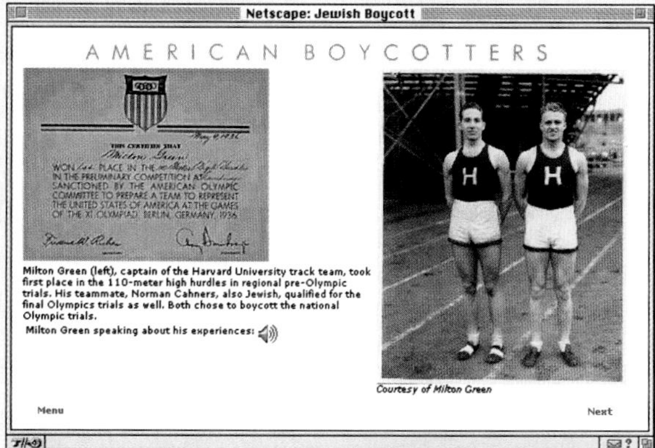

www.smithsonian.org

Figure 3.2

At the web site for The United States Holocaust Museum, there are numerous online exhibits. Here are two screens about the Olympics in Berlin, how Hitler used it for propaganda, and the U.S. response calling for a boycott. This exhibit is presented as a series of screens with forward arrows and a main menu.

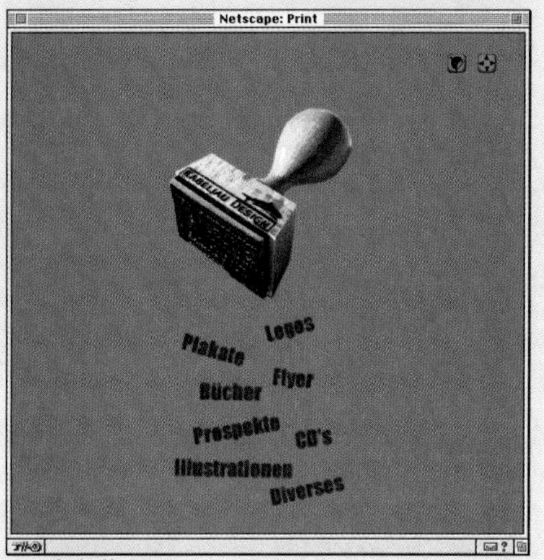

www.kabeljau.com

Figure 3.3

Even with the use of the same devices, maps and lists, we can see the diversity of web design.

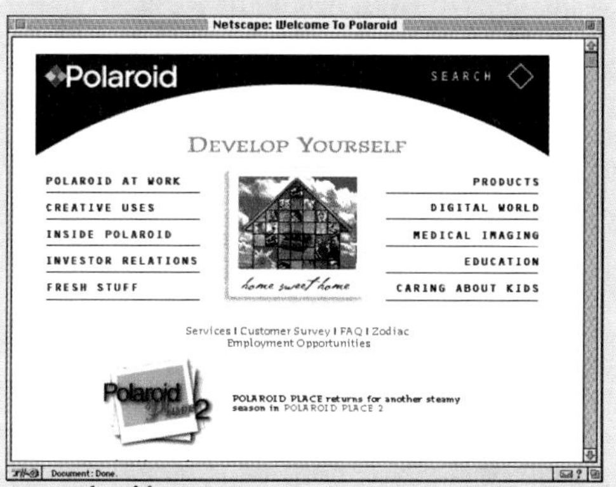

www.polaroid.com

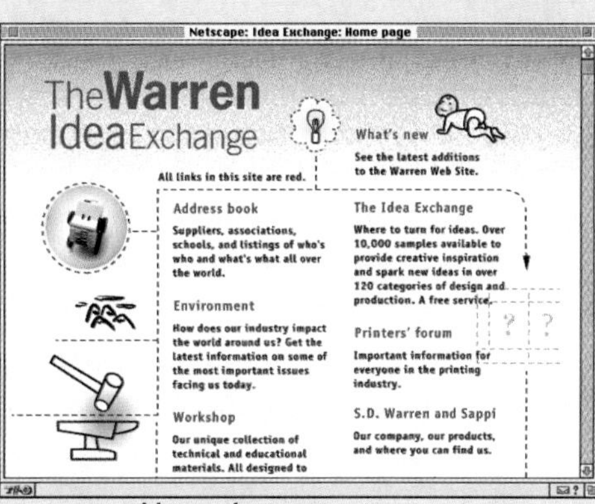

www.warren-idea-exchange.com

www.bradjohnson.com

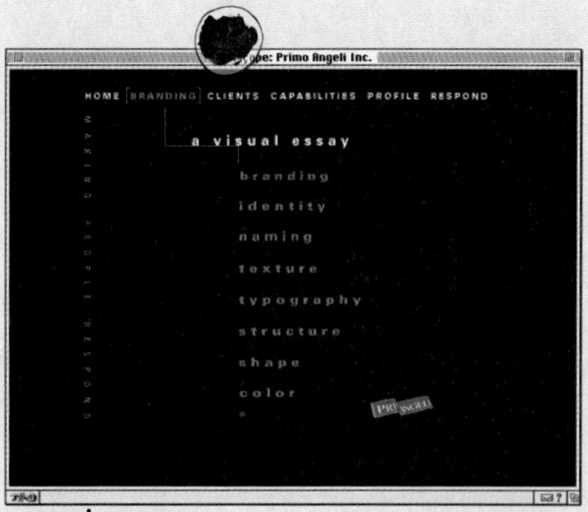

www.primo.com

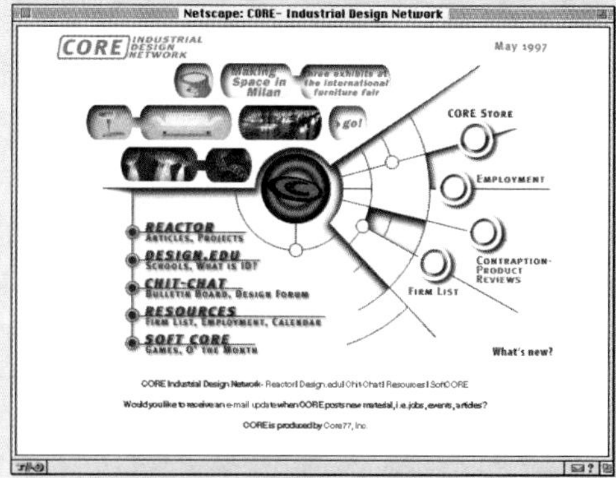

www.core77.com

Figure 3.4

If you would like to get a full grasp of the levels of designation and relationships in the design of books buy a copy of The Chicago Manual of Style, University of Chicago Press.

make up the content. As we experiment with interface and navigation, we use metaphors that allow the visitor to draw on past experience to navigate a site. Figure 3.3 shows a wide variety of examples of interfaces.

How is Something Old (Books) Like Something New (the Web)?

One wonders how a book—a tactile, paper, static, and linear end product—could have any relevance to designing for the web. A book is created within a linear structure model, yet is accessed from different points along that line. A book contains cross references, footnotes, glossaries, indexes, and images to which the reader expects nonlinear access (Figures 3.4 and 3.5). The book has a navigational structure that the reader expects and understands. It is a tried and true interface which we have grown to know and trust.

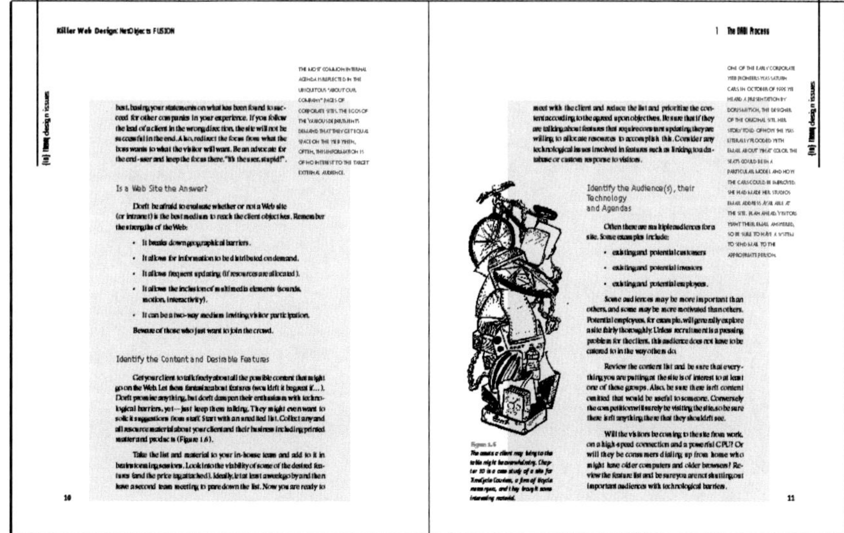

Killer Web Design: NetObjects FUSION

{in} theory design issues

THE MOST COMMON INTERNAL AGENDA IS REFLECTED IN THE UBIQUITOUS "ABOUT OUR COMPANY" PAGES OF CORPORATE SITES. THE EGOS OF THE VARIOUS DEPARTMENTS DEMAND THAT THEY GET EQUAL SPACE ON THE WEB PAGE. OFTEN, THIS INFORMATION IS OF NO INTEREST TO THE TARGET EXTERNAL AUDIENCE.

best, basing your statements on what has been found to succeed for other companies in your experience. If you follow the lead of a client in the wrong direction, the site will not be successful in the end. Also, redirect the focus from what the boss wants to what the visitor will want. Be an advocate for the end-user and keep the focus there. "It's the user, stupid!".

Is a Web Site the Answer?

Don't be afraid to evaluate whether or not a Web site (or intranet) is the best medium to reach the client objectives. Remember the strengths of the Web:

- It breaks down geographical barriers.
- It allows for information to be distributed on demand.
- It allows frequent updating (if resources are allocated).
- It allows the inclusion of multimedia elements (sounds, motion, interactivity).
- It can be a two-way medium inviting visitor participation.

Beware of those who just want to join the crowd.

Identify the Content and Desirable Features

Get your client to talk freely about all the possible content that might go on the Web. Let them fantasize about features (wouldn't it be great if...). Don't promise anything, but don't dampen their enthusiasm with technological barriers, yet—just keep them talking. They might even want to solicit suggestions from staff. Start with an unedited list. Collect any and all resource material about your client and their business including printed matter and products (Figure 1.6).

Take the list and material to your in-house team and add to it in brainstorming sessions. Look into the viability of some of the desired features (and the price tag attached). Ideally, let at least a week go by and then have a second team meeting to pare down the list. Now you are ready to

10

1 The DADI Process

{in} theory design issues

ONE OF THE EARLY CORPORATE WEB PIONEERS WAS SATURN CARS. IN OCTOBER OF 1995 WE HEARD A PRESENTATION BY DORIS MITSCH, THE DESIGNER OF THE ORIGINAL SITE. HER STORY TOLD OF HOW SHE WAS LITERALLY FLOODED WITH EMAIL ABOUT WHAT COLOR THE SEATS COULD BE IN A PARTICULAR MODEL AND HOW THE CARS COULD BE IMPROVED. SHE HAD MADE HER STUDIOS EMAIL ADDRESS AVAILABLE AT THE SITE. PLAN AHEAD. VISITORS WANT THEIR EMAIL ANSWERED, SO BE SURE TO HAVE A SYSTEM TO SEND MAIL TO THE APPROPRIATE PERSON.

meet with the client and reduce the list and prioritize the content according to the agreed upon objectives. Be sure that if they are talking about features that require constant updating, they are willing to allocate resources to accomplish this. Consider any technological issues involved in features such as linking to a database or custom response to visitors.

Identify the Audience(s), their Technology and Agendas

Often there are multiple audiences for a site. Some examples include:

- existing and potential customers
- existing and potential investors
- existing and potential employees.

Some audiences may be more important than others, and some may be more motivated than others. Potential employees, for example, will generally explore a site fairly thoroughly. Unless recruitment is a pressing problem for the client, this audience does not have to be catered to in the way others do.

Review the content list and be sure that everything you are putting at the site is of interest to at least one of these groups. Also, be sure there isn't content omitted that would be useful to someone. Conversely the competition will surely be visiting the site, so be sure there isn't anything there that they shouldn't see.

Will the visitors be coming to the site from work, on a high-speed connection and a powerful CPU? Or will they be consumers dialing up from home who might have older computers and older browsers? Review the feature list and be sure you are not shutting out important audiences with technological barriers.

11

Figure 3.5

*The interface we know as a book. Even though you shouldn't judge a book by its **cover,** it is the first thing we see. It tells us the title and author. The back cover and flaps usually tell us about the author and about the content of the book. The **parts, sections, chapters** and **running heads** help to define our location within the book. We use **table of contents** to experience the book out of its linear progression. **Folios** (page numbers) let us know where we are in the book as a whole—they are the progress bar in our reading. If we can't find a particular subject we head to the **index** and look for the page references. If we don't know a word we go to the **glossary.** If we want to know who and what influenced the author's writings we go to the **bibliography** and **references.** The structure of a book is overlooked due to its ease of use and our understanding of it.*

AS READERS WE DON'T EVEN THINK ABOUT NAVIGATING A BOOK. THE PHYSICAL, SEMANTIC, AND CULTURAL CONSTRAINTS HAVE BEEN DETERMINED AND HAVE BEEN IN PLACE FOR CENTURIES. THE RECOGNITION OF LETTERS BELONGING TO DIFFERENT LANGUAGES LETS US KNOW WHETHER TO READ LEFT TO RIGHT, RIGHT TO LEFT, OR TOP TO BOTTOM. NAVIGATING A BOOK IS EASY BECAUSE WE UNDERSTAND THE STRUCTURE AND THE INTERFACE.

Actually, a web site has much in common with a book. It usually contains a considerable amount of text and information, and it is created within a linear or hierarchical structure that is accessed from numerous points of the structure. It contains many *assets:* pieces of data, images, graphs, lists, indexes, footnotes, and references. These assets may be expressed as text, animated images, video, music, or sound. It will probably contain many aids to the visitor such as search, help, and glossary that are parallel to similar aids in a printed book.

There is also an amazing resemblance in the design and production of books with the design and production of web sites. Web sites are not 8 to 10 pages or screens that require individual crafting such as a brochure or small communications piece. Most of our site projects start at 100 pages. We don't see any reason why a designer or production staff needs to be creating HTML for 100 pages. We especially don't think we should be designing 100 pages individually.

THE IDEA OF CREATING TEMPLATES AND STYLES THAT CONTAIN THE ATTRIBUTES OF ANY GIVEN ELEMENT AND ITS RELATIONSHIP TO OTHERS WILL BECOME OF MORE INTEREST TO WEB DESIGNERS AND DEVELOPERS WITH THE IMPLEMENTATION OF CASCADING STYLE SHEETS (CSS). FOR SUGGESTED READING AND LINKS TO WEB SITES WITH MORE INFORMATION ABOUT CASCADING STYLE SHEETS VISIT WWW.DESIGNPRACTICE.COM.

Designing for the web requires an understanding of technology to implement a well-designed system, and to apply it to the elements in a way that eliminates ambiguity. Creating a system for the amount of text and images that make up a book takes an attention to detail and the discipline to create a system that, when implemented, allows the reader to navigate with ease.

Newspapers Have Hyperlinks Too

Not surprisingly the concept of the page and hyperlinks is not a new one. There is an older model we have all experienced—the newspaper. The decision points or menus use the same hierarchy of font sizes, styles, and column width. These sizes and styles indicate the level of importance of the story. A newspaper also has levels of importance from front to back, above or below the fold, number of pages back in the section, even the number of columns and lines. The sophisticated application of jump stories and continued headlines make newspapers resemble web sites more than any other familiar interface. The intricacies of creating a style manual and guide for a newspaper and a web site are very similar. (The style manual and production guide for the *Philadelphia Inquirer* is an 80-page document.) Figure 3.6 shows an example where a prestigious newspaper tries to carry the power and authority of its look to the Web.

www.nytimes.com

Figure 3.6

In the design of the New York Times web site, *the interface and look and feel of the site closely resemble the actual paper. When the visitors move to the story level however, the look and feel collapse into something that is entirely web.*

Screen versus Page

When speaking with a client they most often ask "Do you design web home pages?". We reply: "We design and construct Web sites." The word *page*, as in *home page*, is still used to describe the components of a site, although the parallel is insufficient in many ways. The page metaphor comes from the *original* web content, scientific and educational research material. These pages were defined by tags (HTML) that applied a visual hierarchy to the information, much like a book. Navigation was based on text links, often represented at the beginning of a document in the form of an outline or table of contents. References to other articles and information within or outside of the document or page were easily accessible by a *hot link* or *hyperlink*. Figure 3.7 shows two examples of first generation Web pages.

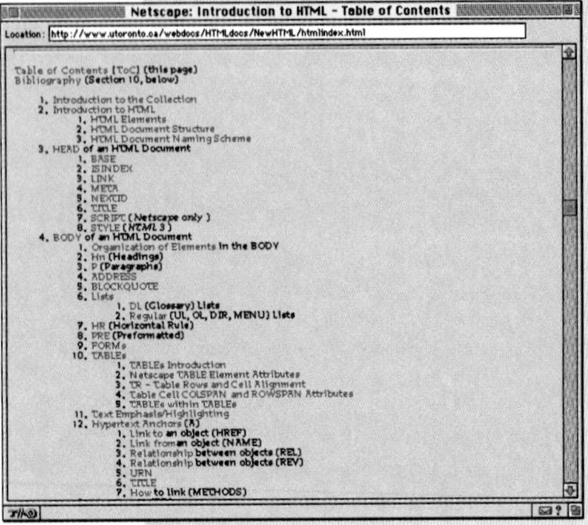

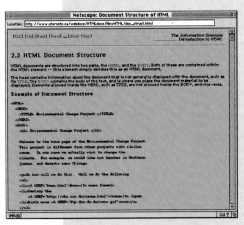

Those of us that have been designing for the web for a while have experienced the evolution of the technological solutions that can be implemented. We have watched the expectations of viewers increase. They want the immediacy of broadcast media with the depth of print. Viewers want the image capabilities of television on demand with the possibility of finding out more. As designers and developers, we have the responsibility to create something we haven't seen before and to make it accessible and valuable for all those who may use it.

Figure 3.7
A look at the original incarnations of HTML. A page with a hyperlink table of contents takes you to additional pages.

As the art of designing for the web evolves, and we find out more about how people react to the environment designed for them, we will see the new become old again. Until then, we will experiment with the hybrid of page and screen, taking advantage of scrolling or not, as the solution demands.

From Screen to Page

The original design of the Discovery Channel site, you may remember, was an image driven site that featured large photos, small snip-its of text as images—what one would call broadcast style. The large images and interface were exciting. The site had a consistent interface, and it was well-designed graphically and navigationally. The problem was more bandwidth than was the norm was needed to have an enjoyable experience. We recently visited the redesigned www.discovery.com. As you can see in the figures of the site today—the demands of the web have "redesigned" the site. The images and page layouts are still compelling, but the site is now much more text driven by than the original design (Figure 3.8).

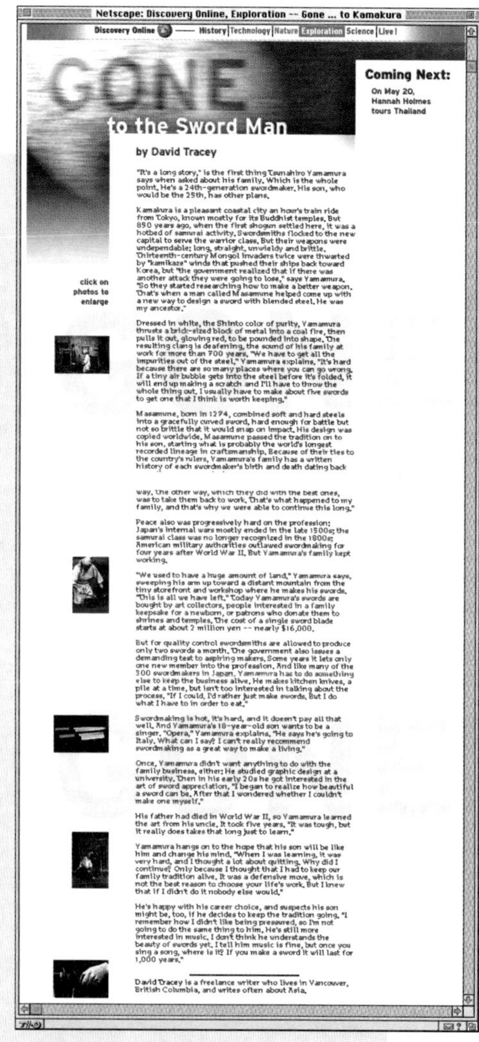

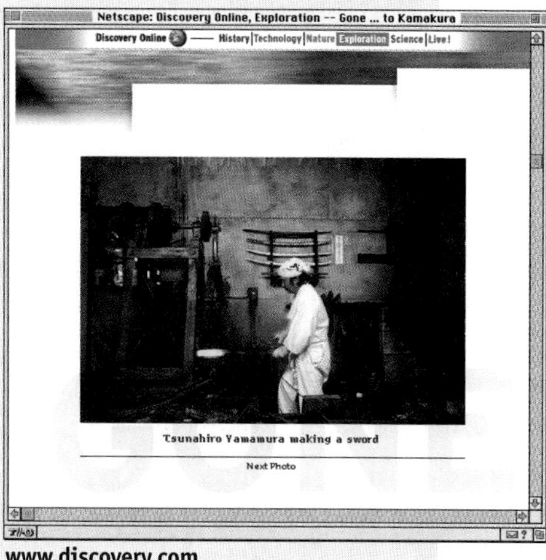

www.discovery.com

Figure 3.8

The current Discovery site (as of this writing). This is less a broadcast model (screen)—more like pages than its original design. The test of the story continues down one long scrolling page with walnut sized photos in the left margin. The loading time for this page is quick. Then, if the visitor is interested in the photos, a click on the image takes them to a larger version.

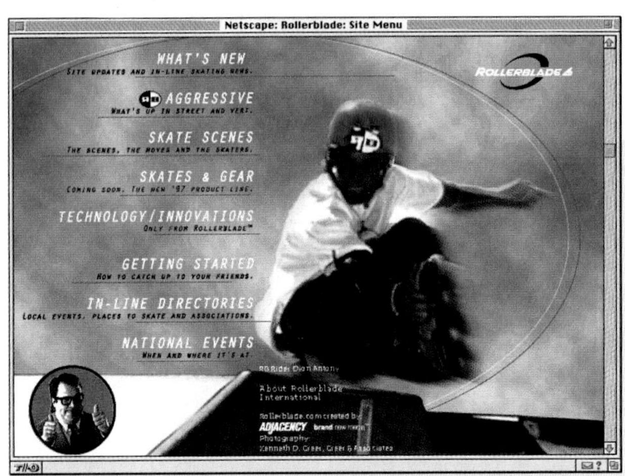

www.rollerblade.com

Figure 3.9
Rollerblade: *The personality of this site comes on strong and the look and feel is consistent with the brand print materials and TV advertising. You don't need any browser buttons to navigate at this site.*

From Page to Screen

The population of the web today is looking for a rich interactive experience that leaves them satisfied. The earlier generation of web sites are "flat" and have a closer relationship to a printed page than the new generation of web sites. Many marketing or exhibition sites show a strong preference for the screen model. These are sites that don't rely on any of the navigation tools of the browser itself; all of the navigation is accomplished within the viewing window. Clients and designers have greater expectations for what a site can be, that sometimes it can be like a cinema screen or a billboard, or an entire environment (Figures 3.9 and 3.10).

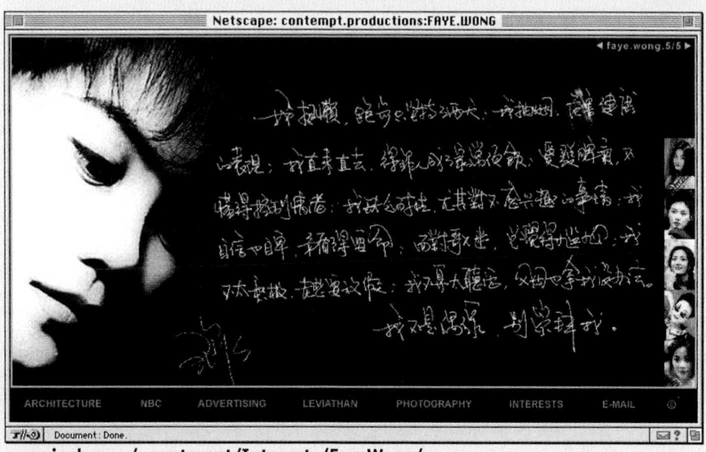

www.inch.com/~contempt/Interests/FayeWong/

Figure 3.10

These screen captures show three of the screens at ***Faye Wong****. Are you in a cinema or driving by a billboard? The scale is absolutely wonderful. The folks at Contempt Productions have a number of inspiring and interesting projects at their site. Be sure to stop by.*

NETOBJECTS FUSION'S OBJECT-BASED PAGE LAYOUT GIVES A DESIGNER THE ABILITY TO CREATE—ALMOST DUPLICATE—WHAT THEY CREATED IN PRINT FOR WEB DELIVERY. WE USED TO SWEAT ALL THE HTML AND CLEAR GIF FILE STUFF USING TEXT EDITORS AND APPLESCRIPT. NOT ANYMORE, NETOBJECTS FUSION DOES ALL THAT WORK.

Page to Page: Consistency

With all that hoopla we gave you about broadcast models let us tell you why in some cases the page model rules. A great deal of publishing is taking place on the web. Companies are supplementing their print vehicles whether catalog, manual, or handbook with a web presence. Along with all the hype surrounding the Internet is the new *branding* fanaticism. Everybody is talking about branding and how to maintain your brand identity in the international marketplace. (You'd think this idea was something new.) Figures 3.11 through 3.13 show extremely effective examples of carrying over the printed look and feel to the web.

The keystrokes and assets used to create print pieces are pretty easily transferable to the web. When we say *easy* we don't mean that it isn't time consuming. It's quite a task to re-express an entire print project, especially creating an architecture that takes advantage of the technology and doesn't just copy the print version. Before the implementation of tables in HTML, however, the kind of page control designers are accustomed to wasn't available.

Figure 3.11
This print catalog for the FontShop has a distinct identity. Its yellow and black stand out in any designer's office. And inside it is an information architect's dream come true thanks to the work of Erik Spiekermann of MetaDesign and his colleagues. This copy is from 1993 but we wouldn't ever through it out! Compare it to the web presence shown in Figure 3.12.

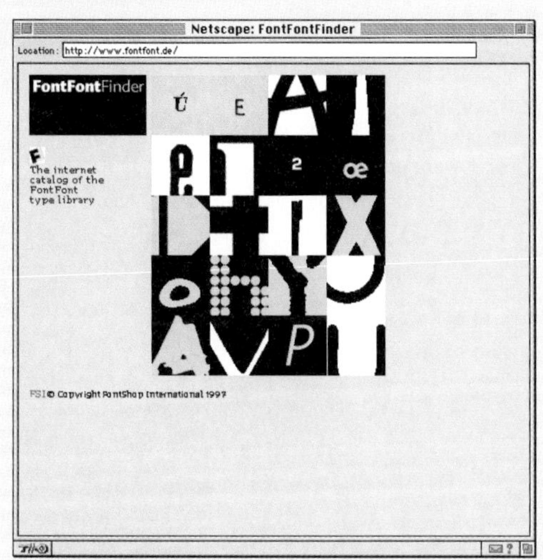

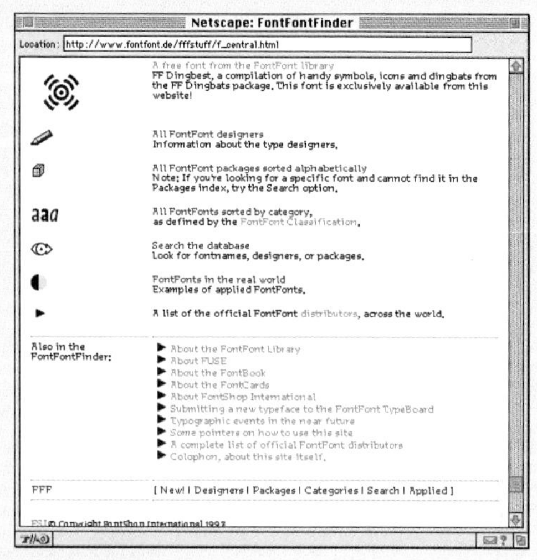

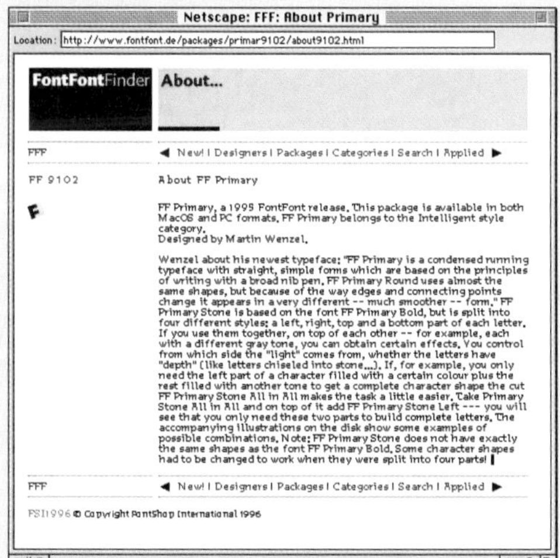

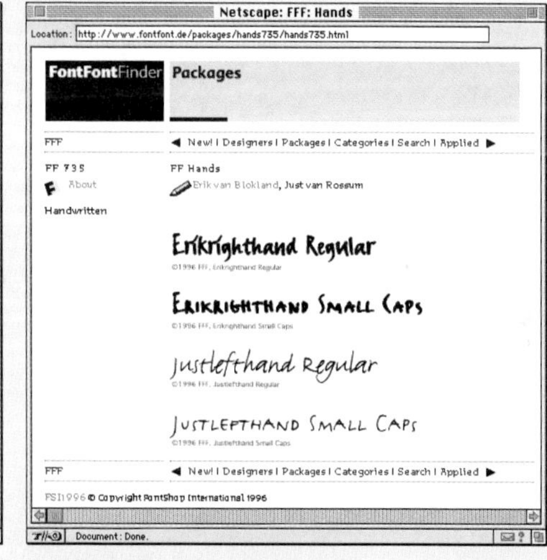

Figure 3.11

This is FontShop's FontFontFinder on the web. The brand is certain, the continuity holds across the print and Web versions. The advantages of hyperlinks and search engines add value to the system already created for print. Online you can experience the added dimension of expanded information about the font and its designers and examples of fonts in real life situations.

www.fontfont.de

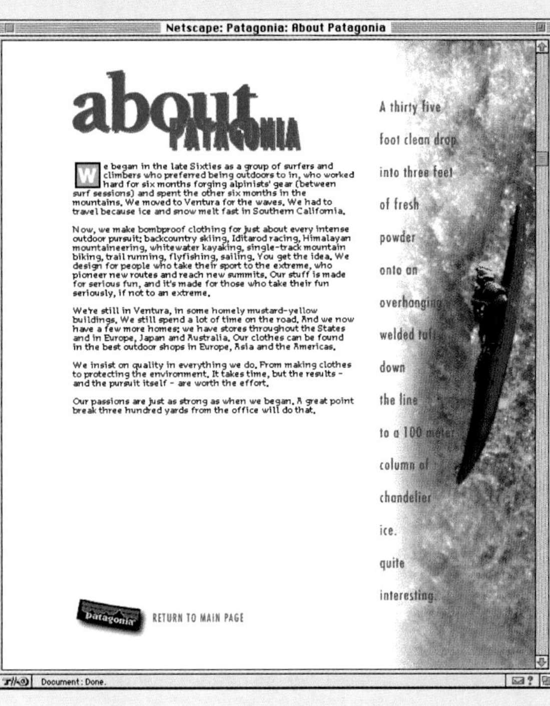

Figure 3.13

Patagonia (the company not the place), is one of our favorite companies for lots of reasons, not the least of which is their total commitment to design. From the climbing gear, to hiking shirts, luggage, and the label that adorns their products, Patagonia combines function and design. Their oversized mail order catalog was the first of its kind, breaking all rules, showing huge photos of the products and action photos of the product in the field often provided by Patagonia staff and customers. There is a direct relationship between the print and web image. Brand identity is carried from print to the web successfully. Drop by the site and request a print catalog to see for yourself.

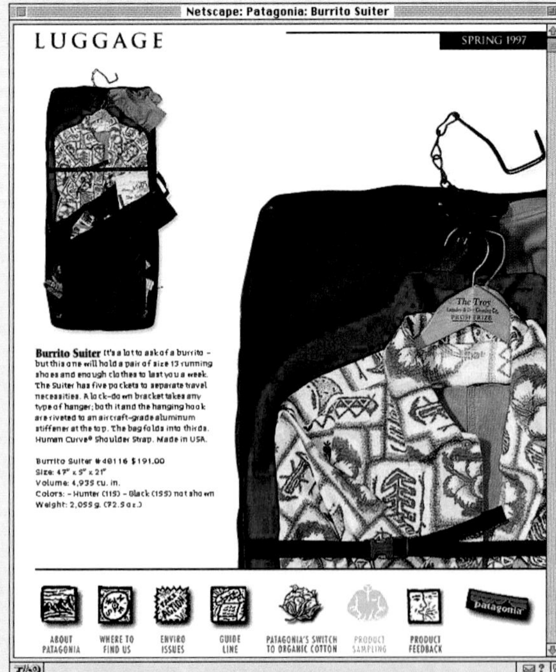

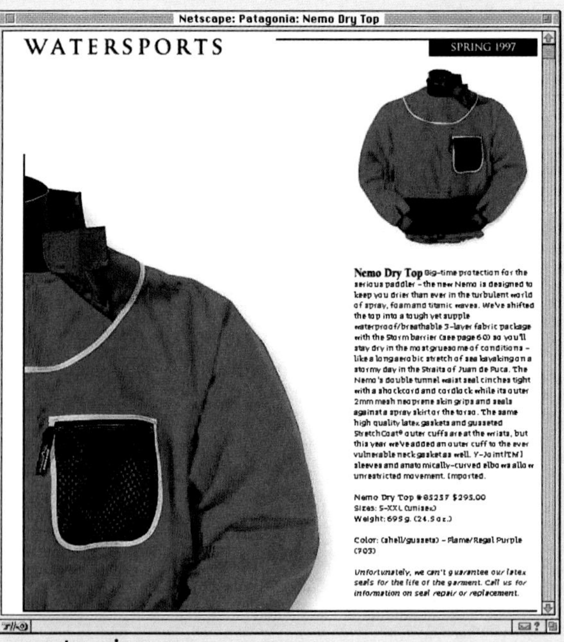

www.patagonia.com

It's a Hybrid

Earlier we spoke about how as designers we had the obligation to create something more than television and more than print for the web. We experienced something of what we had in mind just recently at www.us.chess.ibm.com. If you are a web surfer, chess player, or if you are just a technology junkie there has been plenty available at this site. The big media blitz "man against computer" Kasparov versus Deep Blue has been a huge media success for IBM. The intensity of a chess match was stoked by an interactive blitz. What kind of experience was it? We can tell you both the technology and the drama were huge, including the human drama of Kasparov's anger after his defeat.

ANOTHER ASPECT OF THE WEB IS ITS CAPABILITY TO HOST AN EXTENDED LIVE EVENT WORLDWIDE IN REAL TIME, WELL ALMOST REAL TIME. THE INTEREST IN THIS EVENT WAS SO OVERWHELMING THAT DURING A MATCH, IT WAS OFTEN DIFFICULT TO GET ACCESS TO THE SITE.

If you are a cave-dweller or a technophobe, allow us to explain some of the experience. The match site designed, developed and constructed by a formidable team including Studio Archetype had the best of radio, TV, print and the web. The technology included a Java viewer that displayed each move as sent from Deep Blue as the moves were made. Commentary was sent live as text onto the site, still images of the match were updated every 30 minutes, video highlights from the match were included, and a three-dimensional viewer of the site was available. Not to be outdone by technological wizardry, there was a considerable amount of *print* at the site too. It included in depth commentary by chess masters and columnists preceding the match, post game dissection, historical references, player overviews, interviews with Garry Kasparov, articles on other chess masters, and of course information on Deep Blue (Figure 3.14).

Along with all this technology and massive content was a sophisticated interface with an easily understandable metaphor of file folder tabs and expandable menus. A metaphor much like that of the Apple Macintosh Finder. It was easy to move through the site and find what you were looking for. This was not an easy feat when you look at the depth of information that was available.

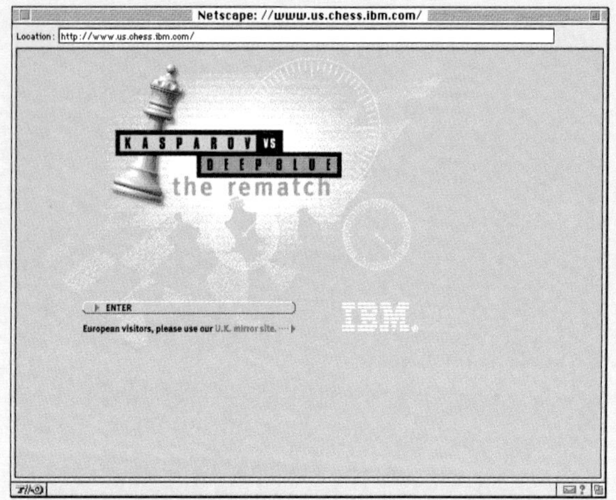

www.chess.ibm.com

3.14

Kasparov versus Deep Blue, an historic online event. Site design by Clement Mok's Studio Archetype.

Control Freak?

As an information architect you create the constraints that determine what choices a visitor is given. You decide what they will see first, and where they can go; you even control what they won't see at all. It is the designer's fault if a visitor can't access what he needs, or if a visitor has to work hard to find what he needs. This medium requires easy access. This does not mean that you are omnipotent. You'll be able to control certain aspects of your visitor's behavior, but you won't be able to control the variables in the technology. You can't control the speed at which the information is accessed, what typeface, monitor size or resolution, platform, or browser your viewer will choose. You don't have to give up all attempts at control but for now, (or at least until the technology changes) you have to learn to be flexible. Being flexible is the real challenge for designers. Those that are successful are open to change, and they are invigorated and inspired by the possibilities.

You may have noticed that many pages are getting more and more horizontal rather than vertical. One of the major factors driving this trend is consideration for the newbie using a web browser. The majority of people we know don't ever change the preferences in the application; they just live with the default settings including all those huge browser buttons. We equate this with getting into a friend's car to drive and not adjusting the seat and mirrors. In this case, less vertical space is available to the designer. The screen becomes even more horizontal on most monitors on the Wintel platform.

Some designers say viewers don't scroll. We disagree. We designed a screen for a client using an anchored link to pull a color bar to the top of the browser, simulating a color bleed at the top of the screen. When the client saw that the scroll bar indicated that the page didn't start at the top, he scrolled up. As a result, the color bar showed the browser offset. We find ourselves doing this often and we have observed in user tests that

AS DESIGNERS, WE LOOK FORWARD TO WHEN WE HAVE THE ABILITY TO DESIGN THE ENVIRONMENT THROUGH WHICH THE WEB SITE IS VIEWED. WHEN WE SAY THIS WE MEAN THAT THE LOOK AND FEEL OF THE WINDOW OR SCREEN IN WHICH THE VIEWER WILL EXPERIENCE THE SITE OR BROADCAST WILL BE CREATED BY US, NOT NETSCAPE OR MICROSOFT. THE ABILITIES A DESIGNER HAS TO CONTROL THE ENVIRONMENT USING JAVASCRIPT AND WITH THE AID OF A PROGRAMMER TO CREATE JAVA APPLICATIONS ARE ALREADY BEGINNING TO TAKE HOLD. DESIGNERS CAN DETERMINE WHETHER YOU WILL EXPERIENCE A SITE USING ONE OR MORE WINDOWS, AND WHETHER YOU WILL EXPERIENCE SOUND OR VIDEO.

others do it too. Visitors want to interact. They want to drive, so expect them to mess with the controls.

As a designer you have to be prepared for the loss of a good deal of screen real estate to navigational buttons at the top of the browser (Figure 3.15). You have probably noticed in our screen captures, we don't make the buttons or location visible. We use the key commands and contextual menus to go back and forward, along with the navigational features created by the site designer.

We recently attended a conference at Princeton University on The Human Side of Computing. One of the presenters explained how he was using a web site as a course online with resources and questions for in person discussions which would occur at a later date. The professor showed some simple page constructions with rather large, ugly shareware icons. He later created a revised site using frames and text instead of icons. He reasoned that this was because the icons took up considerable real estate. The fact that the icons took up more space than necessary was true, and the type treatment using a scrolling frame was much more efficient. However, the fact that the icons were poorly designed, magnified both the size and the problem.

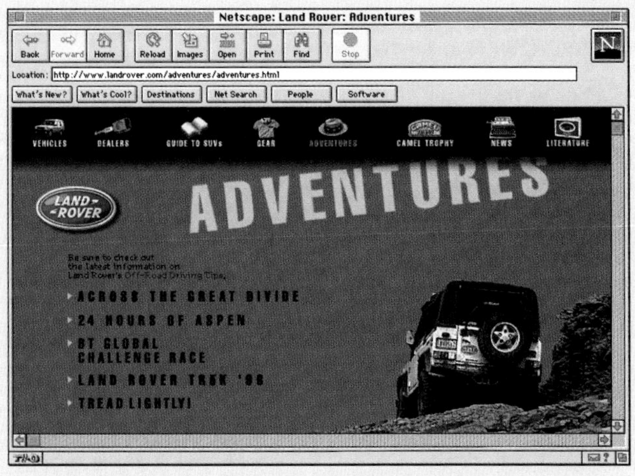

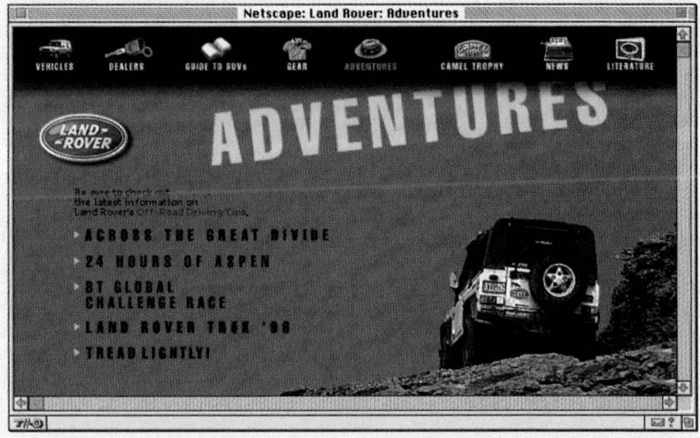

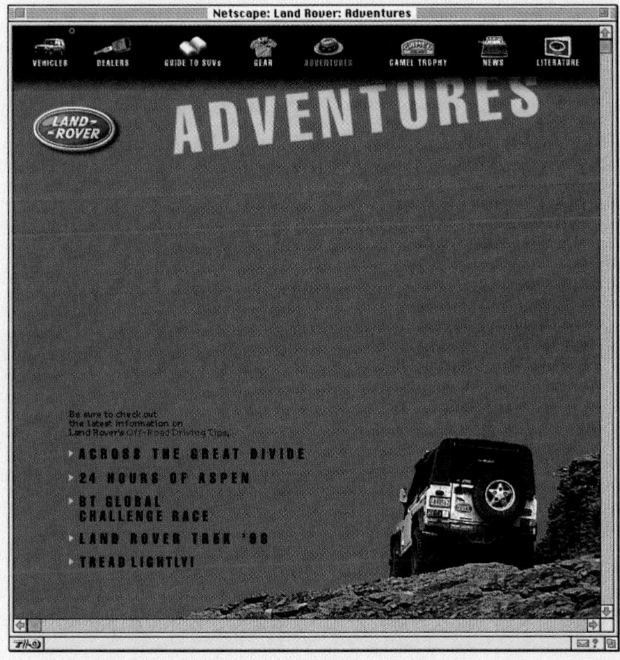

Figure 3.15

Let's experiment for a moment. Here are two screens using the default preferences. Just a bit of real estate can be taken up by browser control buttons. The new Netscape Communicator browser has toggle switches available so that you don't have to go into a pull down menu to adjust the window. Note the nifty HTML by the folks at Adjacency in the Land Rover screen. Setting the table data alignment in their HTML they assured a viewer of a well composed page independent of page depth.

part 2

a tool

NetObjects FUSION

Part 1 explored the design process, with discussion centered around Clement Mok's formulation of DADI—definition, architecture, design, implementation—and the specific challenges of web site and web page design. Although we saw some stunning results of good design, we stayed primarily in the fantasy-land of theory.

Part 3 will take you through the DADI process as it actually occurred for three sites. This reflects the day-to-day practice of designing web sites. These case-study sites were constructed using NetObjects Fusion, a web authoring environment that grew directly out of the theoretical DADI approach to web design.

Before jumping into the case studies, where you will see the software at work, certain aspects of designing with NetObjects Fusion deserve separate attention. As has been said, this is not a software manual; it assumes that you have, or can easily gain, a working knowledge of the software. Rather, this book attempts to focus on the process of design and how NetObjects Fusion has a unique set of characteristics that facilitates the design process.

4

Focus on the Entire Site:

Site View, Navigation, and SiteStyles

Figure 4.1
Did you ever wonder what .nod stood for? It is "NetObjects data." Fusion retains all of the information about your site in a database, which is infinitely more flexible than any expression in HTML.

The ancient "can't see the forest for the trees" trap is particularly dangerous when approaching a Web site. As we saw in Chapter 2, "Constructing Site Frameworks," the experience of a visitor is a product of the ease of traveling through a site and reaching the material that interests. However carefully we may design a particular page, the effort is wasted if a visitor never reaches it. Therefore, the focus must remain on the site as an entity, that responds to visitors with varying needs and interests.

Throughout this chapter features of NetObjects Fusion will be described, which most of you have probably already discovered (Figure 4.1). Sometimes the User Manual, however, describes a feature and leaves you thinking, "Why would I want to do that?" We talk about the situation, the goal or problem, and then describe how NetObjects Fusion can be helpful in reaching the goal or solving the problem. We will also be frank about the areas in which the program is *not* helpful (as of this writing, when it is in version 2.0).

UNLIKE ANY OTHER SOFTWARE PRODUCT ON THE MARKET TODAY, NETOBJECTS FUSION PRACTICALLY FORCES YOU TO CONSIDER A WEB SITE AS ONE ORGANIC WHOLE.

Although we will talk a great deal about how NetObjects Fusion can save you work, the main focus from a site design point of view is that the software addresses the site as a whole, and forces you to think that way also. The Site view is the centerpiece of this approach. Here we will consider how to visualize the site as a whole, and how the site structure is flexible and expandable, enabling revision without navigational nightmares. Because they also concern the unity of a site, we will briefly discuss SiteStyles, where you can automate visual continuity, to some degree.

The Site View: What You Can See

The most challenging aspect of focusing on the site is visualizing the site as a whole. Pages of pencil sketches on 11×14-inch layout pads, Post-its on the wall, or a binder of 8.5×11-inch printouts are all approaches that we have taken at our studio. Since we began using NetObjects Fusion, however, we have come to rely primarily on the Site view (Figure 4.2). We have found more and more ways to use the Site view: to view the actual site as it evolves, to create a quick "sketch" of a possible site structure, which can be used as a basis for discussion. Most of the examples in this section are from various stages of the structure of an intranet site for our book production division, containing training and reference material.

THE STRUCTURE SHOWN IN THE SITE VIEW IS NOT IN ANY WAY RELATED TO THE DIRECTORY OR FILE FOLDER STRUCTURE OF THE FINAL HTML FILES.

In Figure 4.2 we can see the five major sections of this site and their relative size, both in breadth (number of pages at any particular level) and depth (number of levels). We have color coded the pages to distinguish sections or substantive divisions within sections. One might think that such a visual representation would be a bonus feature, where activating a command would generate this picture of your site. On the contrary, the Site view is the core of the NetObjects Fusion application and most users bring it up on screen frequently—even if only to navigate quickly to another page. This means that even if your inclination is to focus on page design, the structure of your site is continually before you, demanding that you pay attention to it.

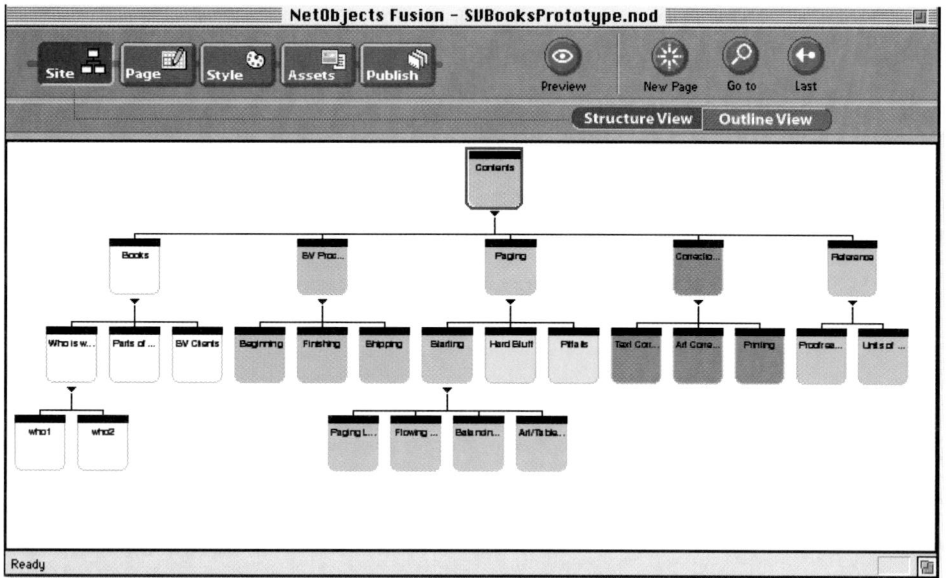

Figure 4.2

The Site view in NetObjects Fusion is an overall structural view of the site. For example, the page called Starting *has a parent called* Paging, *two siblings, and four children.*

NetObjects Fusion uses the metaphor of a family tree to describe how pages relate to each other within the site structure. Each page, except the home page, has a parent (the page directly above it), and it can have siblings (which share the same parent) and children. Note that these are *relationships*, not labels. In life, a person who is your parent is also the child of your grandparents. There is no such thing, then, as a parent page, or parent level, except in relationship to the page under discussion.

This is the extent of the use of the metaphor; there are no marriages or deaths and what would be generations on a family tree are simply called levels. Other conventions derive from the typical visual representation of the site: up goes to the parent page, and a right arrow or next goes to the sibling page immediately to the right; this applies whether you are talking about adding links or simply navigating within NetObjects Fusion.

Of course, the Site view is much more than a simple display of the site structure; it is an environment for building, reorganizing, and tracking the progress of your site. We will discuss all of this later in the chapter, but first we'll wrestle with the often underestimated challenge of viewing an entire site.

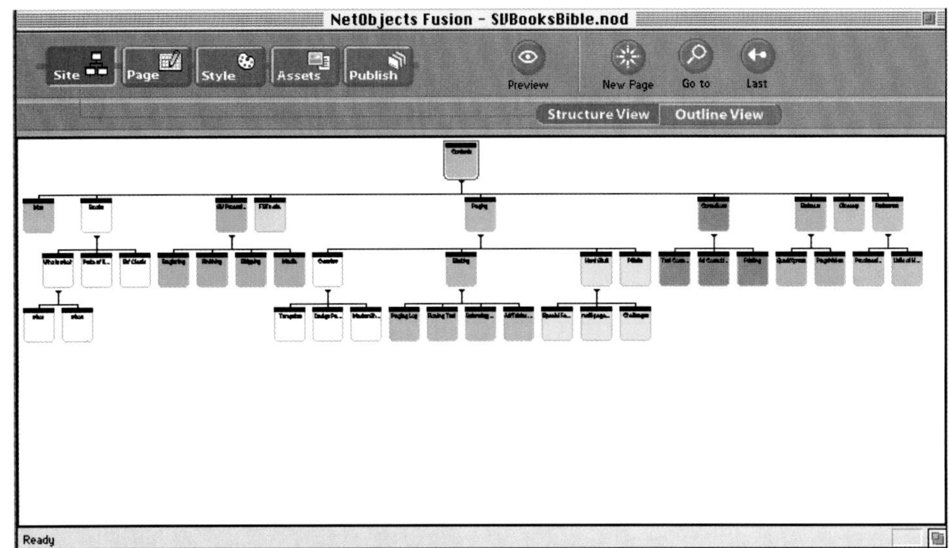

Figure 4.3
By reducing the magnification, using the familiar magnifying glass, this entire site is visible on screen at once.

Viewing a Site as It Evolves

One aspect of the Site view that aids in visualization is that you can enlarge and reduce the view on screen. By reducing the view you can see the structure of a rather large site, as seen in Figure 4.3. Conversely, you can also zoom in on one particular section of the site (Figure 4.4).

Sometimes the neat tree structure is disrupted by a section that has many pages on the same level (a large group of siblings), as is shown in Figure 4.5. Is this an inherently bad thing? Should they be subdivided just for the sake of a pleasing structure? No! In this case they are biographical sketches of staff members, and adding intermediary pages to subdivide the staff into groups merely adds a content-free level of unimportant choices. Remember the guiding principle from Chapter 2: the visitor should reach content as soon as possible.

Keeping a large number of pages as siblings is especially necessary if there is material that should be browsed directly from page to page without requiring a return to a menu. In order to use the convenient NetObjects Fusion smart links for next and previous pages, the pages *must* be siblings. These links and the special challenges of material that progresses from first to last is discussed further in the "Smart Links" section coming up.

In terms of viewing the site structure, however, these large sibling groups make it difficult to see the entire site except at an extremely reduced view. Luckily, NetObjects Fusion enables you to *collapse* any section of the

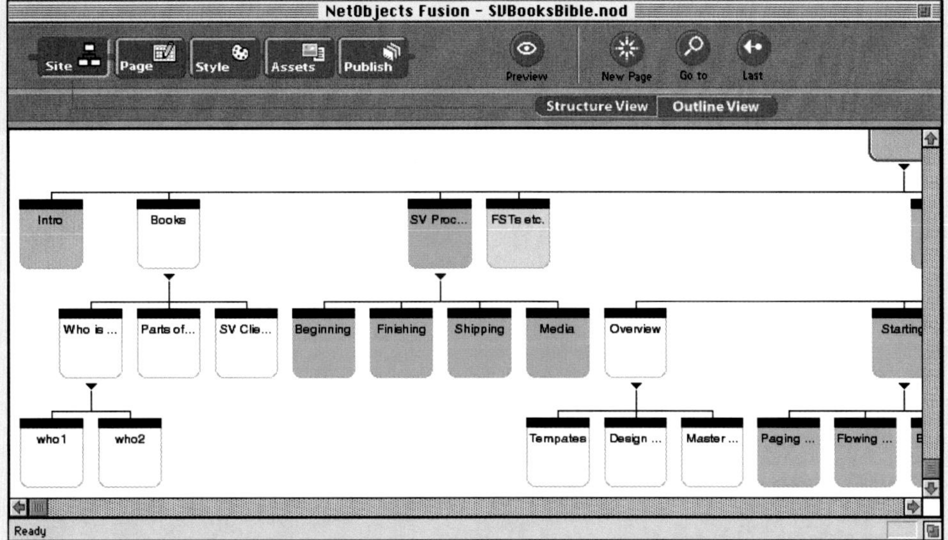

Figure 4.4
To consider a section of the site, you can enlarge the view so that you are able to read the page names.

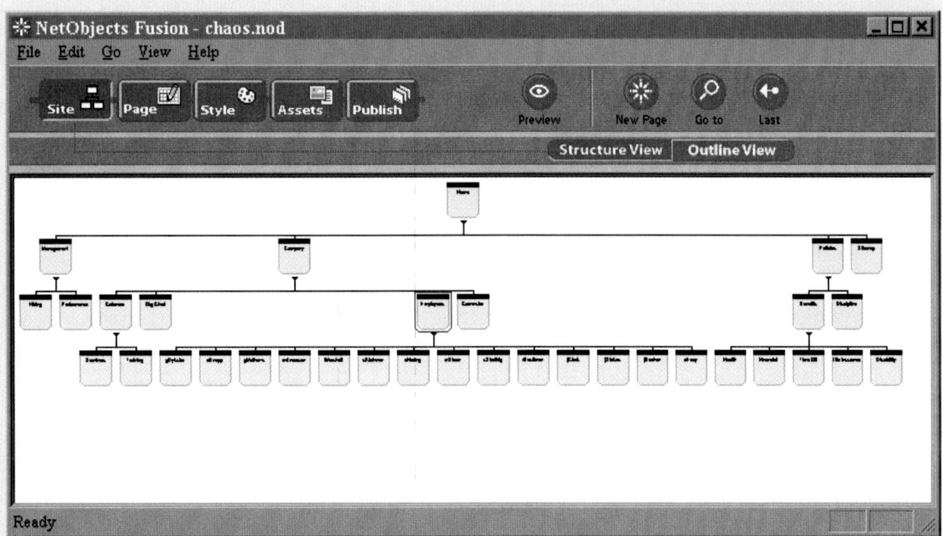

Figure 4.5
The 15 pages in a row are all siblings because they share a single parent page.

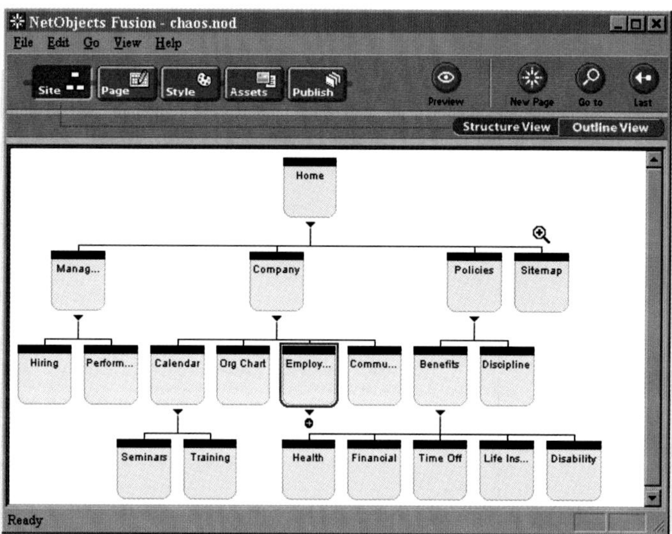

Figure 4.6
The plus in a circle below the page indicates that there are children (and perhaps grandchildren and great-grandchildren) of this page that are hidden from view.

site so that it is out of your way temporarily. Figure 4.6 shows the same site with the section collapsed.

We generally view sites in the default orientation, reading the hierarchy from top down, and the sequence within sibling groups from left to right. All of the figures thus far in the chapter have been oriented in this way, which NetObjects Fusion calls the *horizontal* orientation. You can change your view at any time, however, to what NetObjects Fusion calls the *vertical* orientation (Figure 4.7). To be honest, this has been most handy when printing out the site and writing comments next to sections. We found we were turning the printouts to make notes longer than a word or two and then realized that rather than turn the printout, we could re-orient the display in the Site view!

Sketching Site Structures

In the previous examples, the figures show the structure of actual sites as they were at one point in their evolution. We have seen how the Site view is powerful in simply *seeing* an entire site. It has many advantages over hand-drawn or computer-drawn diagrams, the primary one being that it is already done for you.

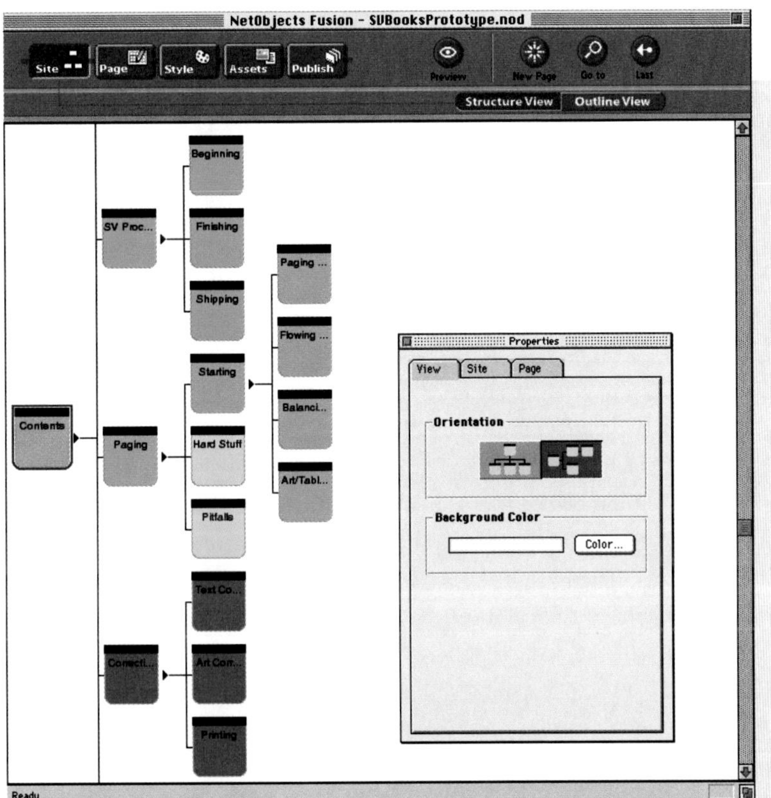

Figure 4.7
The children appear to the right of the parents in the vertical orientation display of the Site view.

What if you are in the architecture stage of the DADI process, however, and are beginning to conceptualize a site? Should you wait until this process is complete and you have a clear diagram for the site that you can then build in NetObjects Fusion? With previous web authoring tools, we didn't go into the web authoring environment until we were ready to generate HTML, the last stage of the process.

We have found, however, that sketching a structure in the Site view of NetObjects Fusion is a quick way to play around with alternate site structures. You can modify the structure easily by moving pages or entire trees of pages. To distinguish these files from actual sites, we usually call them Site.sketch.nod. It is neat and clean enough to print out to show a client.

Flexible, Expandable Structures

So far we have simply *looked* at sites in NetObjects Fusion, but the Site view is, of course, the environment in which you build and revise a site's structure. You can quickly and easily add, delete, rename, and move pages. When you move a page, all of its descendants come along with it. NetObjects Fusion assumes that you want to preserve the connection between a page and the pages that are subsidiary to it. You can, of course, move the secondary level pages individually if you do want to break this relationship. Also, when you delete a page, the application will warn you that the deletion will eradicate the page and its children—by which it means any subsidiary pages (grandchildren, great-grandchildren) not just immediate offspring. The basic idea is that pages have relationships to those around them; the graphical interface for playing around with these relationships makes the Site view in NetObjects Fusion an invaluable tool.

Revising Site Structure

SITES BUILT USING PAGES AND PAGES OF HTML INSTEAD OF A CENTRAL DATA REPOSITORY BECOME MORE AND MORE UNWIELDY TO WORK WITH UNTIL THE THOUGHT OF A STRUCTURAL REVISION SENDS THE TEAM INTO A COLLECTIVE ANXIETY ATTACK.

What happens if you are almost finished building a site and then realize that a different structure would be more effective? I remember in early 1996 we were meeting about a site and suddenly it became clear that certain problems would be solved if we reworked the site structure. The faces of certain team members went pale: "But all those links are already in the HTML! Arrgghh, the image maps!" So, schedule, budget, and morale had to be weighed against the advantages of the changed structure. It is as if a site gains weight as it grows, loses flexibility, and becomes difficult to shift.

Well, we did implement the revised structure. We went through the binder of printouts and circled all the links that needed to change (and missed a few). In a few instances, we could use a utility to globally change HTML footers, but in most places we had to both find and change the links individually. Then there was the issue of being sure that there were no old pages lurking on local or remote servers (because, of course, the file names must be the same).

NetObjects Fusion provides a system that saves all of that time and frustration and gives results that are virtually error-free. The impact on the design process is that there are no longer logistical pressures to retain a flawed navigational system simply because it is a *fait accompli*. In some ways it is parallel to the desktop publishing revolution, when revisions became possible which had been prohibitively expensive in the days of conventional prepress. As in that instance, it is important not to overuse this ability to revise simply because the freedom is there. Above all, *never* let the client or management know how quickly it can be done.

So, how would a structure be revised in NetObjects Fusion, and how would links and navigation be affected? Special situations require attention, but basically you can move the pages around in the Site view and all of your links will still work the way you intended. Of course, you should preview your site and double-check everything, but because of the software's system of relational navigation bars, internal and smart links, you will be in good shape.

Links and Navigation

We have seen that NetObjects Fusion thinks of pages as standing in relation to one another (parent, child, sibling). In addition, each page has an identity: a name. When you are setting up internal navigation for a site, you can either point to a *particular* page by name (an internal link), or point to a page in *relation* to the current page (a smart link). It is important that you choose correctly between the two choices when you are building the site. The automatic navigation bars that NetObjects Fusion offers can use either relational or position-specific links depending on the options you have chosen.

THE BIG EXCEPTION TO THIS EASY REVISION IS THAT YOU CANNOT CHANGE YOUR MIND ABOUT YOUR HOME PAGE. YOU CANNOT MOVE IT, REPLACE IT WITH ANOTHER PAGE, OR DELETE IT!

We made a point in Chapter 2 of differentiating between a site's organizational structure and navigational structure. Which is represented by the Site view? In general, it is simplest to construct the Site view to reflect the site's organizational structure. However, sometimes it is beneficial to

THE ONE PAGE THAT NEVER MOVES IS THE HOME PAGE, THEREFORE YOU CAN LINK TO IT BY NAME, AS YOU WOULD ANY OTHER PAGE, OR TO THE POSITION IT HOLDS. AS FAR AS NETOBJECTS FUSION IS CONCERNED "HOME" IS ALWAYS THE TOP PAGE IN THE SITE VIEW STRUCTURE.

position pages in the Site view specifically to take advantage of the easy automatic linking between adjacent pages. There are some examples of this in this chapter and in the case studies—times where some aspects of the Site view structure do not look neatly organized but make implementation of navigation easier.

Links to a Page

If there is a discussion of a particular topic and you want to link to a related page, you should point to that page by name (even if it is the next page). Then, if you move that page elsewhere in the structure, or you introduce other pages between the reference and the page, or even if you rename the page, NetObjects Fusion will make the link correctly.

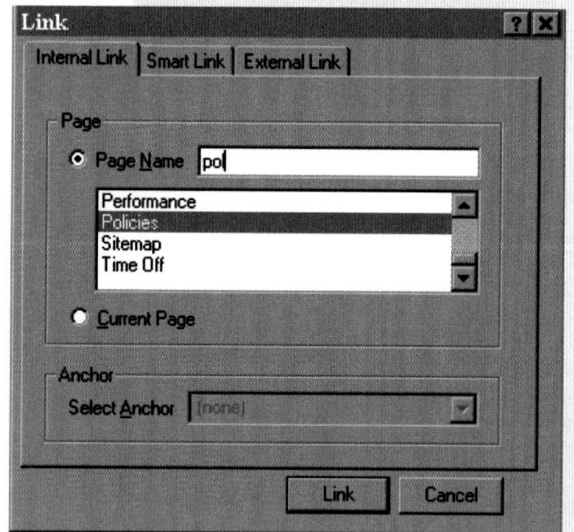

Figure 4.8
The Link dialog box showing the Internal Link tab, where you can specify the target page for the link. If you want a specific anchor on the page, you choose that from the lower section of the dialog box.

You create this link using the Link button on the Properties palette (under the tab of the text or image you want to link). This button brings up the dialog box that you see in Figure 4.8, and you choose the Internal Link tab (called a Page Link in version 1.0). One of the coolest interface features in NetObjects Fusion is that you don't have to memorize the exact page names to make the link; you can just choose from the displayed list of page names. If you hate to scroll, you can type the first few letters of the page name to automatically select the page.

Smart Links

The second kind of link does not point to a specific page (for example, Sale Items) but to a page in relation to the current page (for example, the page's parent). We call these links *relational* rather than *relative* to avoid confusion with relative URLs or links. Relative URLs specify the location of a file relative to a directory structure on a server; relational links in NetObjects Fusion are expressions of relationships within the Site view structure only. Most of the links available from automatic navigation bars in NetObjects Fusion, discussed in the next section, are relational in nature.

A relational link, outside of an automatic navigation bar, is called a smart link (Figure 4.9). There are two common scenarios in which a design might call for this: to browse a series of pages or to return to the previous level.

One navigational feature that is omitted from the navigation bars in NetObjects Fusion (to date) and is often omitted from otherwise carefully built sites is a way to go one page up the site tree (to the parent page). Sometimes it is assumed that you arrived at the page by proceeding sequentially down the site structure and can simply use the browser's Back button to return to the parent page. But what if you came to the page from some other route and want to see an overview of the section? I have been to sites where I can't even find the section again from the main site divisions.

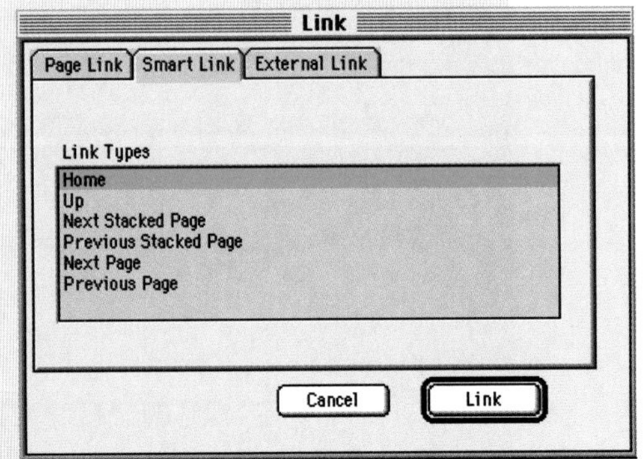

Figure 4.9
The Smart Link tab.

If you decide to designate an up arrow or a link that serves this function, you can use the Up Smart Link. If you use text or a graphic that specifically refers to the content of the parent page, however, you should use an Internal Link to the page instead of a smart link. Otherwise, a change in site structure could result in the link pointing to a page that no longer has the desired content. We generally mark any smart links on the printouts of our sites with arrows (up, left, right) so we know which kind they are without opening up the .nod file.

The other kind of smart links are Previous Page and Next Page links. (We'll leave the stacked page options for our discussion of databases in Chapter 6.) Looking at the Site view, the "next" link takes you to the sibling page immediately to the right. If there are no more pages it takes you back to the first sibling (the leftmost page). In other words, it takes you around in a circle through the pages in that section of the site. This can be used, for example, for a series of job listings so that wherever the visitor began she could click through the listings until she realized, "I've already seen this one!"

Unfortunately, if the material is truly sequential, such as a lesson or story, you do not want this circular effect, which would be extremely confusing. This happened to us when we were putting a chapter of our book *Designing Multimedia Web Sites* online (Figure 4.10). We had very large sibling groups to take advantage of the next and previous options. It would have been easiest to literally have one huge sibling group, but that was so difficult to navigate through in NetObjects Fusion that we did make some basic section divisions. If you browse the chapter at www.vizbyte.com/dmwsintro.html you will see that all the pages of the chapter have identical back and forward arrows at the bottom (or refer back to Figure 2.10).

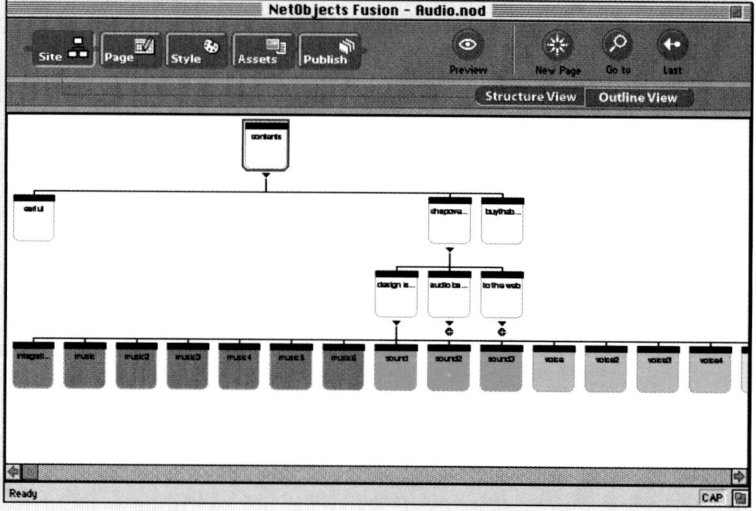

Figure 4.10
The extremely horizontal structure of a series of sequential pages, 64 total. Only one of the sections is expanded (the others are collapsed) and still it will not fit onscreen.

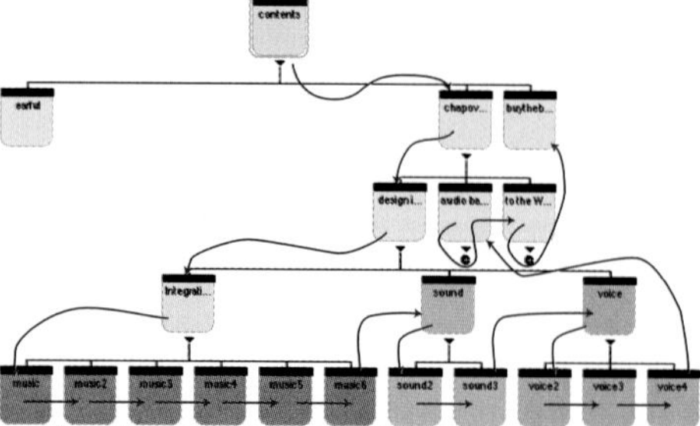

Figure 4.11
Here instead of many siblings at one level the pages have been subdivided. Although this looks easier to manage than the large sibling groups the navigation is much more difficult to implement. The arrows show the path a visitor would take to see all the pages in sequence

For each group, however, we had to modify the navigation of the final page so that the forward option was not a smart link but a page link to the next section opener (an aunt). A parallel modification was made to the previous arrow of the first page of the new section. This involved creating a new MasterBorder for the first and final pages of every section even though they seem identical in appearance and function to the visitor. Figure

OBJECTS ON MASTERBORDERS ARE NOT UNLIKE OBJECTS ON MASTER PAGES IN A PAGE LAYOUT PROGRAM, SUCH AS QUARKXPRESS OR ADOBE PAGEMAKER, BUT THERE ARE MORE LIMITATIONS IN THEIR USE. THERE WILL BE MUCH MORE ABOUT THESE LATER IN THE CHAPTER.

4.11 shows the principle here but with many fewer pages so that we can fit the illustration on the page!

Navigation Bars

One of the most amazing features of NetObjects Fusion is the ability to create automatic navigation bars. Most of the links in a Nav Bar (as it is called in the Properties palette) are relational in nature. The bar could be a simple line of text at the bottom of a page or an elaborate display of buttons across the top or down the side. They are usually contained in the MasterBorder area of a page so that they can be shared by several pages. The same navigation bar, however, on the same MasterBorder, will manifest itself differently depending on the *context*, the position of the page on which it is displayed relative to other pages in the site.

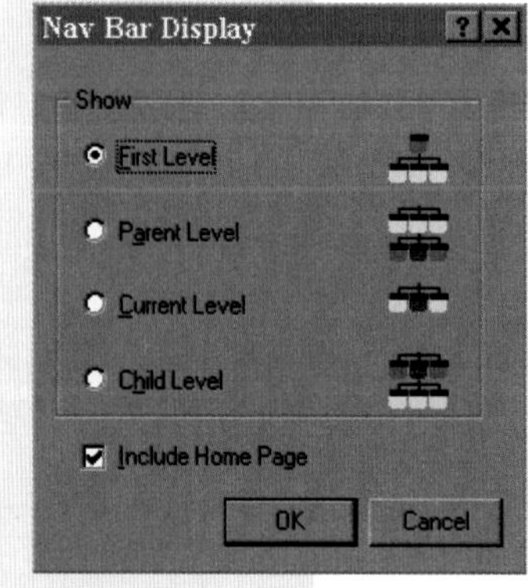

Figure 4.12
The Nav Bar Display dialog box is accessed through the Nav Bar tab in the Properties palette. Here you determine the pages the bar will point to such as the First Level pages. Note that the other three choices are relative to the position of the current page.

IN THIS SECTION OF THE CHAPTER WE ARE ONLY TALKING ABOUT THE NAVIGATIONAL ASPECTS OF THESE NAV BARS. AT THE END OF THE CHAPTER WE WILL DISCUSS THE AUTOMATED SYSTEMS FOR DISPLAYING GRAPHICS IN THE NAVIGATION BARS.

To take the simplest situation first, suppose you want to have the main sections of the site available at all times. You would select the First Level option in the Nav Bar Display dialog box (Figure 4.12). This and home are the only selections that are *not* based on position relative to the current page. This option will lead to the First Level pages from any page in the site on which the navigation bar appears. If you change the number or name of the pages at the first level of your site, the navigation bar will automatically update to the latest structure. As we mentioned before, Home is always the top page in the structure (sometimes called the node); First Level is the level immediately below the node

The real magic of the automatic navigation bars comes into play when you choose any other option from the dialog box in Figure 4.12: Parent Level, Current Level, or Child Level. If you choose the Parent Level, the navigation bar will display the names of the parent page and its siblings (uncles or aunts to the current

SOMETIMES PAGES, SUCH AS HELP, DO NOT BELONG IN ANY SUBSECTION, BUT YOU DO NOT WANT TO INCLUDE THEM IN THE MAIN NAVIGATION BAR. INSTEAD OF PUTTING THESE PAGES AT THE FIRST LEVEL, YOU CAN "TUCK" THESE PAGES IN A SECTION AND COLOR CODE THEM TO REMIND YOURSELF THAT THEY AREN'T REALLY PART OF THE SECTION. YOU CAN THEN PUT A SMALL HELP ICON ON EVERY PAGE AND LINK TO THE HELP PAGE RATHER THAN GIVE IT EQUAL WEIGHT WITH THE MAJOR CONTENT SECTIONS OF THE SITE.

page). Parent Level does not include other pages at the same level that are not siblings to the parent page. Similarly, Current Level includes only the page's immediate siblings (not cousins), and *includes the current page*. Child Level will cause the navigation bar to point to all pages that are offspring of the current page. If you use these automatic bars to guide a visitor's path down into a site, revisions to the site will not disrupt access in any way.

Think you understand all this? Try this little test, and if you are confused by it, review the material above once more. This concept is critical to take full advantage of NetObjects Fusion! Here is a scenario from a prototype for our internal training site. Okay, here is the test: compare Figures 4.13, 4.14, and 4.15. Two of these figures have the same navigation bar (shared in a MasterBorder area) and one has a bar that was defined differently. The position of the three pages and the pages referred to can be seen in Figure 4.16. Did you guess that 4.13 and 4.14 were the same? Wrong! They display navigation to the same three pages (Text, Art, and Printing), but in 4.13 these are *children* of the current page, whereas in Figure 4.14 they are *siblings* of the current page. Figure 4.13 and Figure 4.15 share the same navigation bar: displaying Child Level.

MasterBorders

MasterBorders, as we have said, display elements that are common to a number of pages. We will talk more about how MasterBorders are used to design pages in the next chapter, Chapter 5, but here we take note of how MasterBorders help keep a site design (and structure) flexible and easy to revise and maintain.

When building a site in HTML, it was not difficult to make many pages starting from the same header and footer (in a template HTML document), so that certain copyright information and logos were consistent. Inevitably, however, changes would be made to that material that was on each and every page. Utilities like HTML Grinder can make global changes within specific limited parameters, but something like changing the position of a graphic had to be done on every single page.

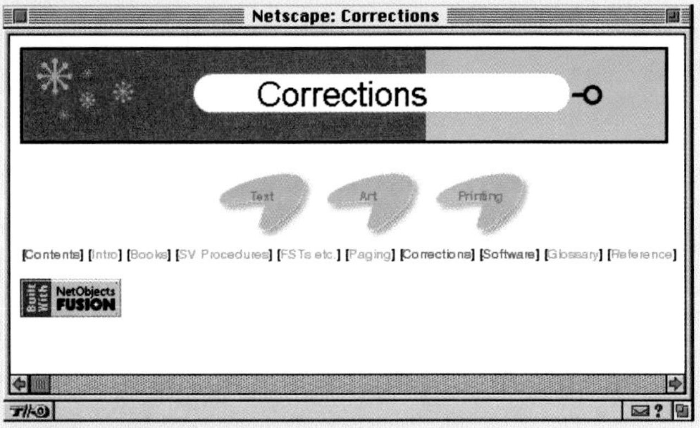

Figure 4.13
The Corrections page (the opener to the Corrections section) has links to its three children.

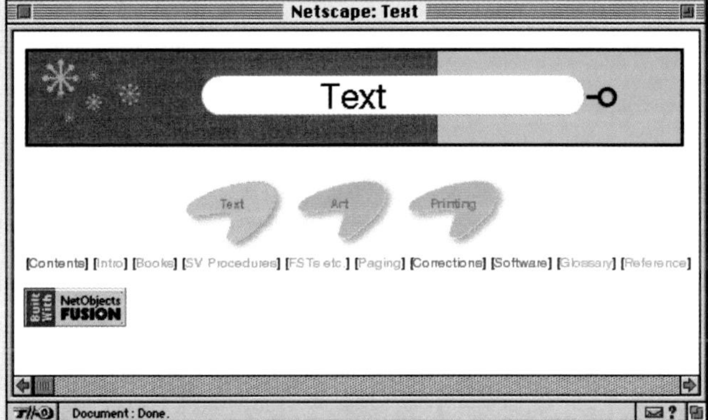

Figure 4.14
The Text (corrections) page also shows the same three page choices as Figure 4.13, including the current page, which is highlighted.

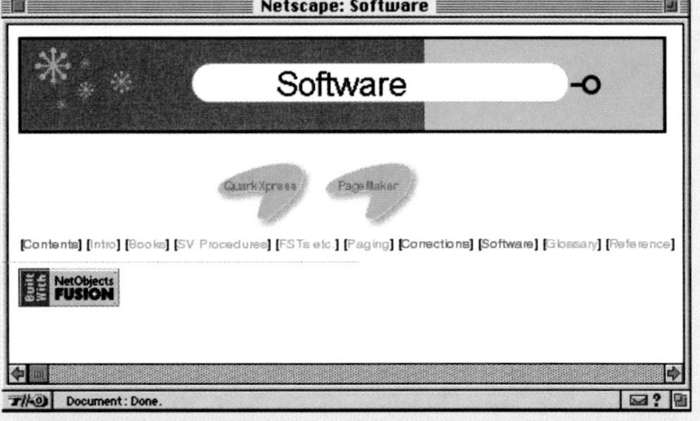

Figure 4.15
The Software page uses the same navigation bar as the Corrections page (using the same MasterBorder), displaying buttons for its two children.

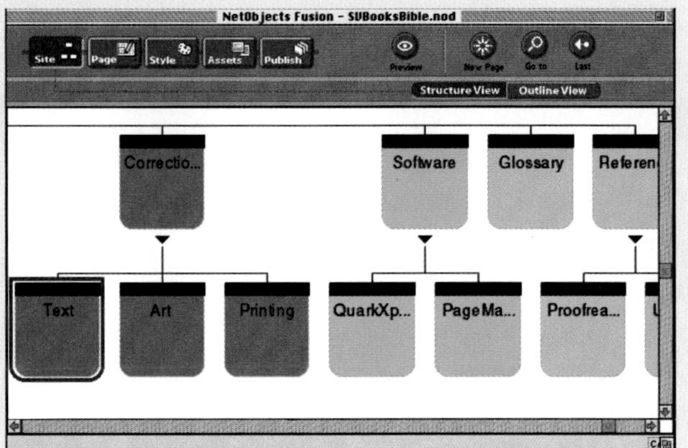

Figure 4.16
Here you see the Corrections and Software sections of the site with the subsidiary pages in each section.

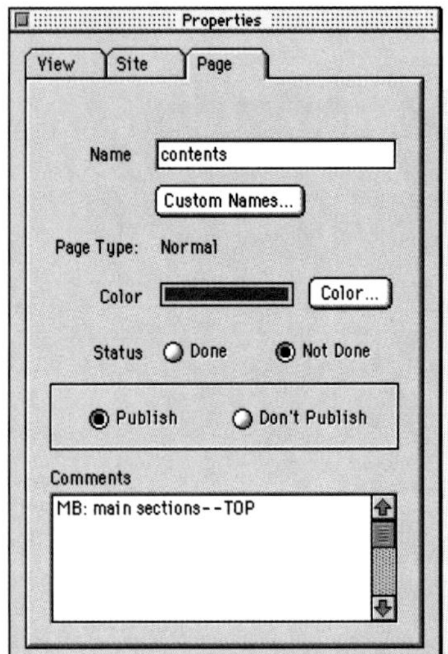

Figure 4.17
The Page tab shows up in the Properties palette from either Site view or Page view. Here we record which MasterBorder is used in the comments section.

Again, Web publishers felt "stuck" with a situation just because it would be too much work to implement an improved solution. MasterBorders in NetObjects Fusion give you a way to update and revise the repeating elements of a site very quickly. When you move a graphic on a MasterBorder, it is moved on all pages that share that MasterBorder. Constant navigational elements, logos, and page banners are items that are typically placed at the top, left or bottom of a page and can thus be easily included in a MasterBorder.

Because MasterBorders must be completely identical—top, left, right and bottom—you often have MasterBorders with identical footers and a slight variation, for example, the header. Be careful in your planning, however, that you do not create too many variations on a MasterBorder, where each only serves two or three pages. If you decide to move an element that is common to several MasterBorders you will have to move the graphic manually on each one.

We often make a note of what MasterBorder is used by a page in the comments field in the Page tab (Figure 4.17), so we can get access to that information directly from the Site view. This also means if you look at the outline display of the Site view you can read all the comments at once and see where the various MasterBorders are used. The more information that is kept available from the Site view, the more the focus remains on the site: what pages are finished, what pages should be published, color coding of pages, and so on.

Site Styles

The concept of a Site Style also ensures that decisions that are made (this time visual decisions) are applied consistently throughout the site. If images are put together into a systematic style, and if personnel on the project changes, the personality of the site will be carried through. Alternatively, if there is a decision to rework the look of a site, this can be changed without having to redo the site from the bottom up.

The graphics for the buttons in the automatic navigation bars are drawn from the Site Style. You can choose from two sets of buttons (primary and secondary) and choose to use a highlighted button to identify the current page. Some Site Styles have primary buttons set up for horizontal navigation bars and secondary buttons set up for vertical navigation bars. Button graphics can also be brought in independently for use elsewhere on the pages, which reinforces the consistent look of the site. However, if you bring an element of a Site Style in as an independent graphic it is not controlled by the style, and will not change if you choose to change Site Styles.

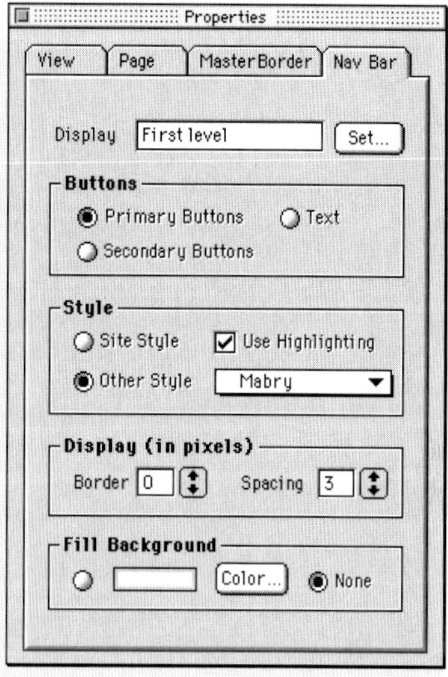

Figure 4.18
Here the Style Mabry has been selected instead of the Site Style for buttons.

IF YOU WANT TO CREATE YOUR OWN STYLE IT IS A GOOD IDEA TO GO THROUGH THE FULL GALLERY OF PROVIDED STYLES FOR INSPIRATION AND TO GET IDEAS FOR "TRICKS" USING STYLES. SOME OF THESE TRICKS CANNOT BE SEEN FROM THE STYLE VIEW. IT IS A GOOD IDEA TO BUILD A PROTOTYPE SITE AND APPLY MANY SITESTYLES TO SEE THE EFFECT. BE SURE NOT TO USE THIS .NOD FILE FOR ANY OTHER PURPOSE AS THE ACT OF BROWSING THROUGH MANY STYLES CAN CLUTTER THE .NOD WITH UNNECESSARY INFORMATION.

If you want navigation bars with different buttons in a specific section of a site, you can choose to call upon a different Site Style for those navigation bars (Figure 4.18). This innovation in version 2.0 has led to some confusion about the correct answer to the question, "Can you use more than one Site Style at a site?". The answer is that you can draw upon more than one Site Style for the background, Nav Bars or banners of any page or MasterBorder. This enables you to have different sections with very distinct looks if you need to. However, there is only one Site Style that is designated as the controlling style for the site—only one that you can change in the Style view. All of the places where you choose to draw upon other Site Styles cannot be managed from the Style view. You must return to the dialog box shown in Figure 4.18 to change your mind about the style.

The ideal situation is to create a unique style that suits the specific site. This is an excellent role for a consultant graphic artist who can provide sophisticated graphics that reflect the image of your organization. The style can then be implemented by the production staff and consistency is ensured. This way, you won't see the exact same navigational graphics used at other sites! The styles that come packaged with NetObjects Fuson give you a good idea of the range of possibilities. Many of them were designed by top studios throughout the country. However, if you use them you do run the risk of seeing the same graphics many other places on the Web.

The components of the Site Style, like the web of navigational options, are all related to each other. This reinforces the vision of the site as an organic whole, that is expressed in units of pages, but has an existence as an entity.

5

The Interface Factor:

WYSIWYG Page Design

Figure 5.1
This tool palette looks familiar to anyone with design or desktop publishing experience.

Recently, we were chatting with a colleague who teaches web design at a local art school and she was not familiar with NetObjects Fusion. We briefly described the interface and she said, "Oh, you mean it's what we've been waiting for!"

The manual for NetObjects Fusion gives clear instructions about how to use the various tools and palettes and this chapter is not meant to replace those explanations. We will highlight some features we have found especially helpful in the design process, or describe a particular way that we have discovered of working in the Page view.

Although NetObjects Fusion is young and has many areas in which it can grow and improve, its foundation and strength is an interface that is a substantial improvement over earlier options. The interface echoes the tools with which graphic designers and desktop publishers are most familiar (Figure 5.1). This presages the shift in web publishing, from the domain of HTML specialists and tech gurus to those in business communications.

Many businesses struggle with who should take the lead in setting up their web presence, but recently the communications professionals have been asserting themselves more vigorously. A couple of years ago, many did not even have Internet connections in their offices to see what was on the web, much less understand how to approach publishing a site. Many sites throughout 1996 were put up quickly to "have a presence," and may have been done by a young HTML-savvy employee over several weekends. Now most of these are being revisited because they do not meet the design standard that is expected in the company's other materials. Generally, in 1997, communications professionals are setting the goals for the sites and reviewing the implementation.

In terms of getting involved in hands-on design and implementation of sites, designers had two choices up until now:

- Learn the intricacies of HTML to create pages with the desired results (a small but brave percentage succeed)
- Use software with a "friendly" (but unfamiliar) interface that still seriously restricts your layout options

WORKING WITH HTML DIRECTLY, EVEN WITH THE ASSISTANCE OF A GOOD HTML EDITOR, REQUIRES CONSTANT PREVIEWING IN THE BROWSER TO HAVE ANY IDEA WHAT YOUR PAGE LOOKS LIKE. IT'S NOT UNLIKE SETTING TYPE IN THE OLD DAYS BEFORE WYSIWYG TYPE DISPLAY FOR PUBLISHING.

Designers have disliked working on web pages both because they do not want to learn HTML and because HTML has not given them the control that they are accustomed to having. Many applications claim to give control "within the limits of HTML." NetObjects Fusion has devised a system that pushes HTML further than it has gone before and gives serious pixel-level positioning control.

NetObjects has finally provided a tool that gives virtually complete control over layout, a familiar page-layout-style interface, and relief from the headaches of link and file management. Basically, NetObjects Fusion will spawn many more well-designed sites, not because of any magic associated with the software, but *because designers will be willing to use it.* The more closely those with design expertise are involved in the actual structuring, page design, production, and implementation of sites, the more obviously the quality of those sites will reflect their involvement. Figure 5.2 shows the Page view in NetObjects Fusion compared to the interface for three other applications: web, illustration and page layout.

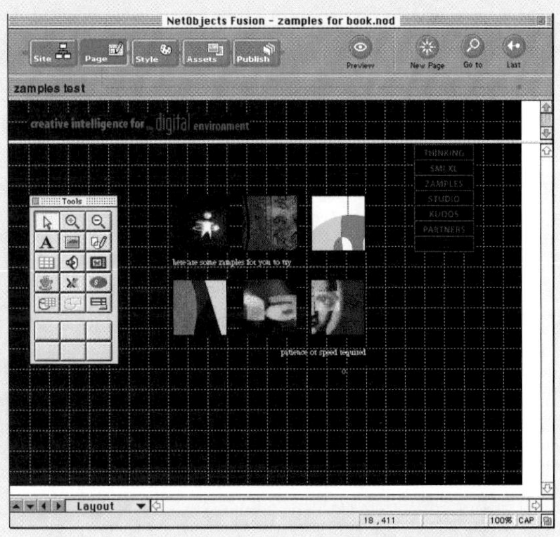

Figure 5.2

The Page view in NetObjects Fusion 2.0 (top), contrasted with the interfaces of Adobe PageMaker, Adobe Illustrator, and Adobe PageMill (from top to bottom). The Tools palette in NetObjects Fusion is quite similar to the illustration or page layout tools. Looking at the graphics themselves, virtually the same effect has been created in three out of the four.

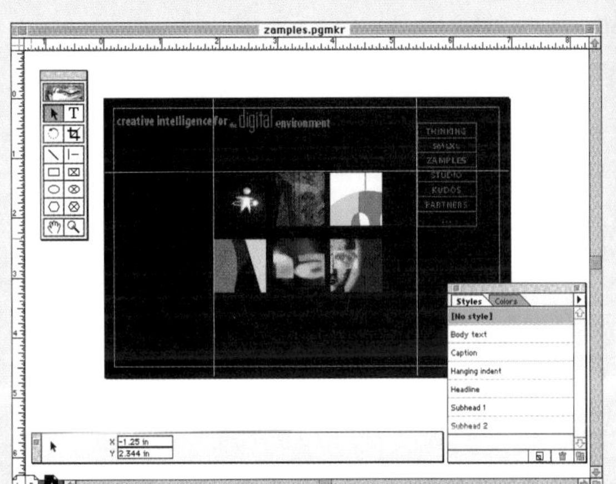

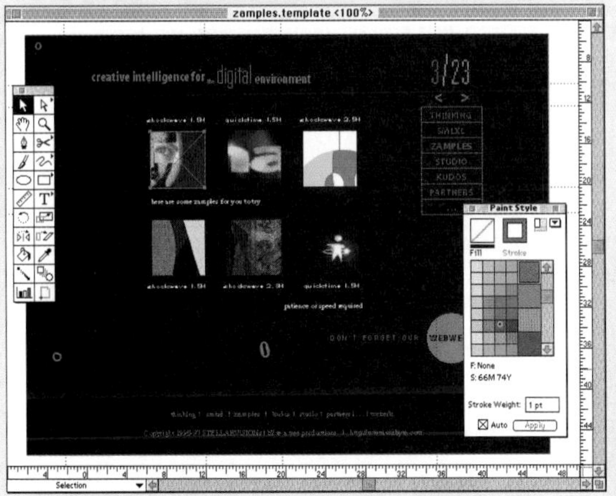

Page View: WYSIWYG

When you work in the Page view in NetObjects Fusion, it contains the familiar players of any page layout application. It includes a tool palette with the typical selection arrow, text tool, drawing tools, and magnifying glass, as well as more specialized tools. There is a grid or guides (at last in version 2.0) and on the page, there are boxes to hold images and boxes to hold text. Page view also includes elements that are specific to the Web or unique to NetObjects Fusion, such as the navigation bar/banner tool, but the *interface* is familiar. Of course, it is not as sophisticated in dealing with substantial amounts of text as a page layout application is. Page view is more reminiscent of working with text boxes in something like Adobe Illustrator (Figure 5.2).

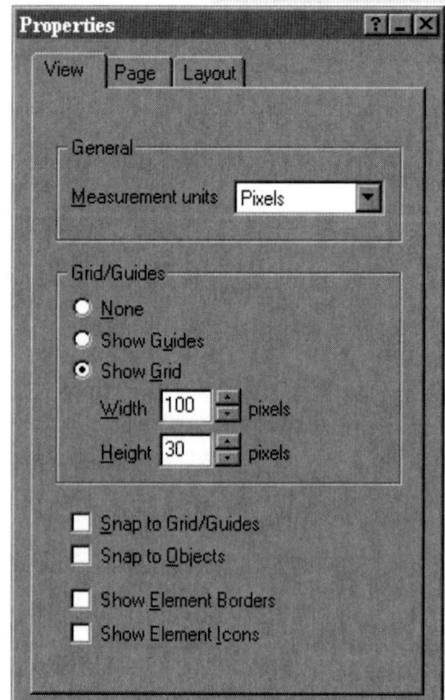

Figure 5.3
The View tab in the Properties palette in Page view. You cannot choose both guides and grid.

Positioning Elements

The biggest shock in working with NetObjects Fusion, if you have been working with other editors, is that you can literally position elements to pixel-level accuracy. NetObjects Fusion provides several aids to help you arrange your layout precisely: the grid, guides, Snap to options, the Align Elements command, and the nudge keys. You control most of these from the View tab of the Properties palette (Figure 5.3).

The grid is especially helpful because you can change the units that are used. The standard grid of squares that NetObjects Fusion gives you by default is 25×25 pixels. Figure 5.4 shows a page that was set up for a three-column layout, with horizontal rectangular grid units 50×25 pixels. The dark blue area at the left is five units across, the navigation can extend up to three units in from the left and the vertical type centers in the last two units. In the right column, the vertical divisions are helpful to space the elements evenly. The Snap to Grid option does not disrupt your current layout; you can turn it on to position one or two elements and then turn it off.

Figure 5.4
Creating a custom grid is a good idea to make it easier to conform to a set of complex design specifications.

The guides are a new feature in version 2.0. You cannot have both the grid and the guides; you must choose one. Guides, of course, make it easy to align elements. It appears as if there is only one vertical and one horizontal guide, but presto! If you hold down Control (Windows) or Option (Macintosh) and drag the guide you get another guide! You can have as many as you need. Guides' most useful application is to position objects from page to page in the same position, because the position of the guides does not change as you change pages. Therefore, you can set a guide where an object should appear, change pages, and position a different object in the same position. This kind of constant position helps a visitor feel a sense of continuity when browsing through the site.

NETOBJECTS FUSION ENABLES YOU TO MEASURE IN UNITS OF CENTIMETERS, INCHES, OR POINTS IF YOU PREFER THEM TO PIXELS. THIS, HOWEVER, IS A SIMPLE CONVERSION FROM PIXELS USING THE 72-PIXEL-PER-INCH STANDARD, BUT THE WEB IS ALWAYS DISPLAYED IN PIXELS. HTML DOESN'T DO INCHES!

New with version 2.0 is the option for Snap to Object. In version 1.0, it was difficult to get objects to align against each without either leaving a small gap or overlapping slightly. NetObjects Fusion (actually, HTML) does not permit any overlapping elements; if you do have elements overlapping and then preview the page in the browser, the WYSIWYG effect is destroyed and all the elements shift to avoid the overlap. The application highlights overlapped areas by reversing the display, so it is obvious that you must adjust the layout. By using Snap to Objects, you can align two elements quickly and easily without overlap. Also, in the Page menu is a feature that will select (highlight)

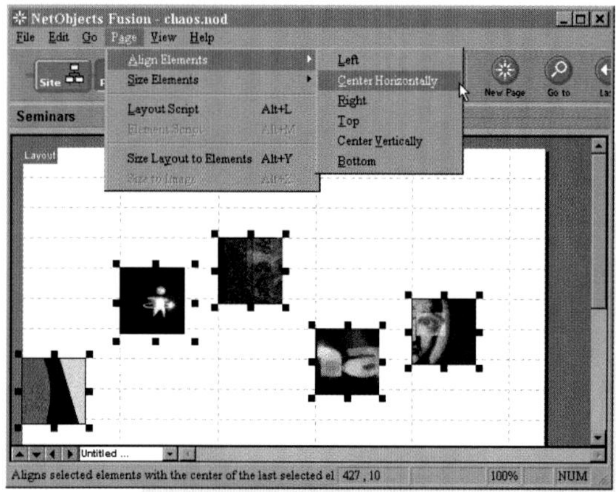

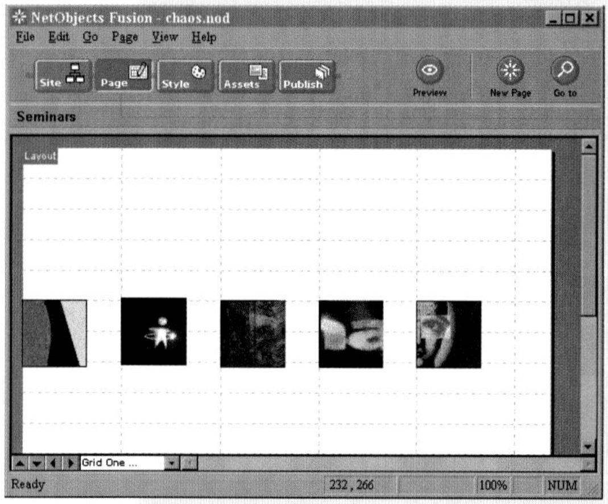

Figure 5.5

The Align Elements command from the Page menu with Center Horizontally chosen. The bottom screen is result of the command: the objects form a horizontal row aligned at top/bottom rather than aligning left/right as in most applications.

all overlapping elements. This is a useful quality control mechanism to use before publishing a site.

A somewhat hidden option is to use the Align Elements command in the Page menu. NetObjects Fusion makes such extensive use of tabs on palettes that it is easy to overlook features that are accessible only from the menu. Also, because the manual is organized around palettes and menus, this feature is not discussed in the same section as the features above, which also pertain to positioning elements precisely.

The Align Elements command is convenient for aligning a series of elements (see Figure 5.5). It does not, however, work the way that one would expect. Most applications use the terms "vertical" and "horizontal" to refer to the axis along which the elements are moved. Moving elements up and down to align them in a row across the page is generally called vertical alignment. NetObjects Fusion, however, considers the result of the alignment; the result of Center Horizontally is a *horizontal row* of elements. This is especially confusing because the two other alignment options that result in a horizontal row, Top and Bottom, are grouped around the Center Vertically command. The objects align with the last element you selected.

The nudge keys (←, →, ↓, ↑) on the keyboard are, it seems, an undocumented feature of NetObjects Fusion. If you select an object you can move it one pixel using the nudge keys. For a text box if you want to move the box be sure to click and hold for a moment (the highlight boxes should stay black, not switch to hollow). If you just click quickly on the box NetObjects Fusion assumes you want to enter or edit text and you get the text tool (with hollow highlights on the text box), and the nudge tool moves within the text itself as it would in any word processor.

The pixel-level control of position is implemented by NetObjects Fusion by creating complex HTML tables. The more complex the table structure, the longer the HTML takes to display in the browser. To be sure that the HTML table structure is no more complex than it needs to be to give you the results you want, use the Table Structure radio button in the Layout tab of the Properties palette. You can choose Columns or Rows. This tells NetObjects Fusion whether horizontal or vertical alignment is most critical to you so that when the application is building the HTML tables it makes the right decisions.

WHEN WE ARE TALKING ABOUT ALIGNING ELEMENTS, NETOBJECTS FUSION ACTUALLY ALIGNS THE BOXES THAT CONTAIN THE ELEMENTS. ELEMENT BORDERS ARE USUALLY HIDDEN AND SHOULD BE DISPLAYED ONLY WHEN THEY ARE HELPFUL.

Page Width and Text Column Width

The most obvious failing of many web pages is that the text is extremely tiring to read because it extends across the full width of the page. This is often true even at sites where elaborate artwork and multimedia elements have been added. As we discussed in Chapter 3, a column structure and controlled line length are crucial to a page that you expect anyone to actually read. Some determined designers discovered that the table element in HTML, originally intended to display simple tables of data, could be used to create page grids. This practice, while widely used, is tedious to implement. The more complex the layout, the more difficult and subject to error the table structure becomes.

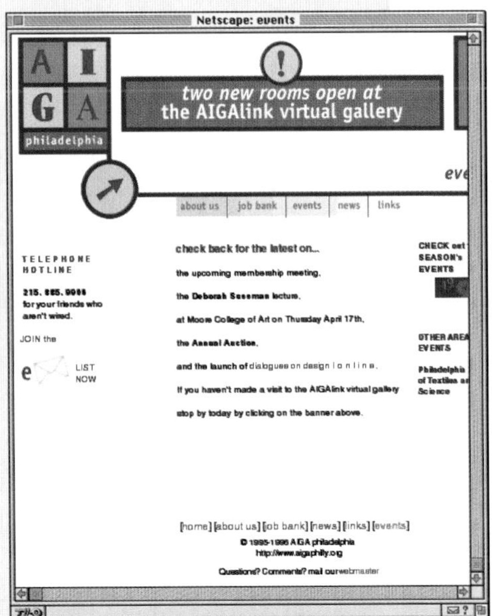

Figure 5.6

In this page from AIGAphilly.org the elements are cut off when the browser is made narrow. When fixed-width pages are not used, elements such as the word "events" would move down so that they were visible, the result is a disrupted layout.

NetObjects Fusion uses this table system to create columns. All you have to do is draw boxes the width that you want, just as you would in a page layout program, and the application will do the work to create the complex tables. As you can see in Figure 5.6, the pages are built to a fixed width, set by the page designer, and resizing the browser window will not cause elements to jump around or wrap to another line as often occurs on the web. The negative side of this is that if the browser window is set too narrow, elements are actually cut off and not visible to the viewer. Therefore, the issue of choosing a consistent page width (and depth) depending on the size monitor you are designing for, as discussed in Chapter 3, becomes even more critical.

Figure 5.7
The Layout tab of the Properties palette now shows both the layout width and the page width, which includes any MasterBorders. This tab is available only when you have clicked the Layout area of the page.

We have found that the information in the Layout tab of the Properties palette is extremely helpful in keeping the layout within the width you have determined (see Figure 5.7). The page width is displayed, which is the total of the layout width and the MasterBorder width. Here you can edit only the layout width; there is a separate tab for MasterBorders (see the next section). If you want to keep a constant page width and the MasterBorder width varies, you should modify the layout width so that the total page width is always constant and viewers will not need to resize their browsers to see all the information.

Unfortunately, if you paste something onto the page that extends beyond the page width, this number will change. You have to either keep an eye on the page width number or set a guide at the position. In version 1.0, the default page width of 800 pixels was too wide for sites geared to a consumer audience; in version 2.0, it has been decreased to 640 pixels. We generally use a page width of 600 pixels.

MasterBorders

As was mentioned in the previous chapter, MasterBorders are the area of the page where you position elements that will be identical on several pages. In terms of position on the page, they are like margins surrounding the layout area of the page. When you make a change in a MasterBorder, the change automatically applies to all pages that use that MasterBorder. In this way MasterBorders resemble master pages in page layout programs, but they differ in significant ways. Master pages apply to the entire page and page-specific material can be added anywhere on it,

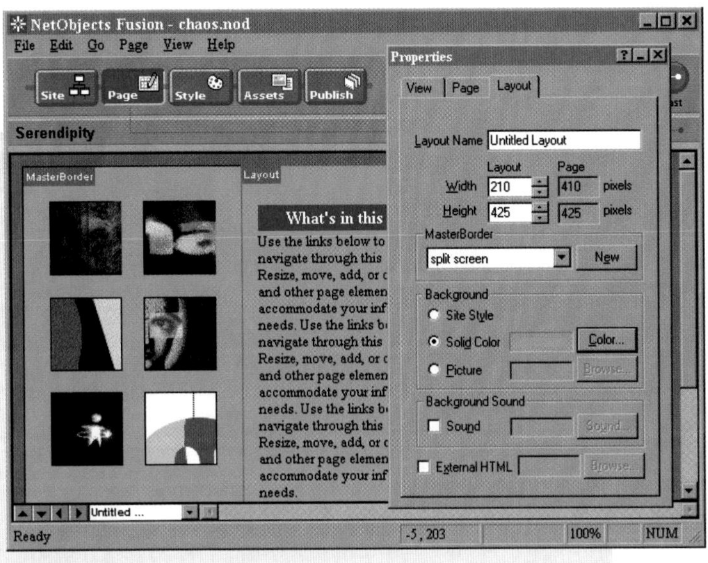

Figure 5.8
On this page the entire left side is the MasterBorder; all other dimensions for the MasterBorder are set to zero. The MasterBorder tab is available only after you click the MasterBorder area of the page.

including putting content into empty picture or text boxes. MasterBorders are a specific *area* of the page (contiguous with an edge of the page) and no page-specific material can appear in that area.

MasterBorders replaced the headers and footers that were available in version 1.0. With headers and footers (which do *not* correspond to the <head> element and the footer in an HTML document), you could specify a separate header and footer on a specific page. In other words, you could use the same footer throughout an entire site, with credits, email address, and copyright information. Even though you might use several headers, if you need to change something in the footer, you only had to change it once and the change applies to all the pages.

Headers and footers were very limiting because navigational devices placed down the side of a page could not be shared by multiple pages. MasterBorders, introduced in version 2.0, are a great improvement in that you can designate any area as a shared area, working from the edge of the page inward. The general idea is that a narrow area at the top, left, right, and bottom form a border and the middle contains page-specific content. Remember, however, that you can set the width of any of these areas to zero and dispense with the border except where you want it to appear. For example, you can split the page in half with the left half as a "border" and the right half as the Layout area (Figure 5.8).

Because it was considered too confusing for a developer to keep track of four separate borders, you can no longer apply them independently to various pages, as you could with headers and footers. Therefore, the top, bottom, left, and right of a given MasterBorder must always be applied together. This means that if you wish to change just one area of the MasterBorder and leave the others the same, you must create an entirely new MasterBorder and start from scratch. This involves removing the default navigation that appears, setting the sizes for each portion of the border, and copying and pasting the common material from your original MasterBorder. A feature that we have been advocating for future releases is the capability to duplicate a MasterBorder and then modify the duplicate as needed. Even when this becomes possible, however, any modification to shared elements, such as the footer, would have to be applied manually to each MasterBorder.

HERE WE ARE COMPLAINING ABOUT HAVING TO CHANGE MULTIPLE MASTERBORDERS. OF COURSE, WHEN WORKING WITH HTML, WE USED TO APPLY CHANGES LIKE THIS TO EVERY PAGE! THE HEADER/FOOTER SYSTEM IN NETOBJECTS FUSION 1.0 GOT US REALLY SPOILED IN TERMS OF EASY UPDATING.

MasterBorders are useful to ensure that there is continuity from page to page for things like navigation, logo position, and so on as we discussed in Chapter 4. They also make it easier for there to be a division of labor; the designer can set up the Site Style, several master borders, and a grid. Someone else charged with bringing content to the site can add a page, select the appropriate MasterBorder, and position the content on the grid following the designer's specifications.

Layouts

The concept of a layout is one of the most confusing aspects of the NetObjects Fusion interface because it is easily mixed up with the concept of a page. Think of a page as it is in the Site view, something that occupies a particular position in relation to other pages and has a particular name. When you go to Page view, you are seeing a particular layout of that page. If you never choose to employ multiple layouts, the pop-up menu at the bottom of the window will probably always read Untitled, the default.

The layout *area* of the page is everything but the MasterBorder. You can see this by choosing the Layout Only command from the View menu. The NetObjects Fusion manual explains that a Layout is "the arrangement of elements within the Layout area of a page." Different layouts, however, can have different MasterBorders and be different sizes. Layouts are specific to one page; you cannot set up a Layout and apply it to different pages

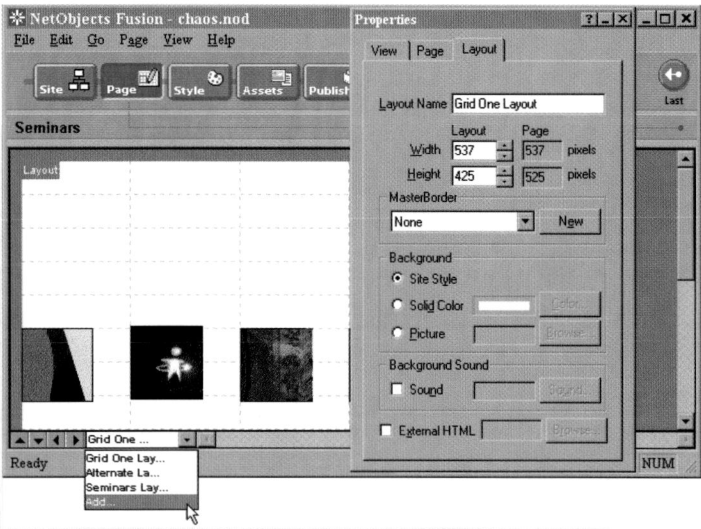

Figure 5.9
You cannot add new layouts from the palette as you do with MasterBorders. You must use the pop-up menu at the bottom of the NetObjects Fusion screen.

(wouldn't that be great?). So, multiple layouts for a page are basically different versions of a page that you can easily toggle between using the pop-up menu (Figure 5.9). These versions do not have to contain the same elements and changes made to elements on one layout do not affect others.

NEITHER THE MASTERBORDER OR THE LAYOUT CORRESPONDS TO ANYTHING IN WRITTEN HTML LIKE BODY OR HEAD. TECHNICALLY, THE MASTERBORDER AND LAYOUT ARE WITHIN THE BODY ELEMENT.

When we realized everything that layouts were not, we were left with the question: Why would you want multiple versions of a page? In the NetObjects Fusion manual, it suggests that you might want different versions for prototypes, for different languages, or for a text-only version. When you publish (or preview), the currently selected layout of each page is what is published. There is no way, at this time, to publish the French layouts and then the English layouts, for instance, without going to each page and changing the selected layout. This would be easier, however, than maintaining two separate parallel sites.

As with new MasterBorders, if you decide to build a new layout, you begin from an empty page. It would be convenient if you could duplicate a layout and make changes from there. In the example of different language versions, you would simply replace the text on the new layout. If you were wrestling with design issues, you might arrange the same elements differently. Unfortunately, if there is a text change (for example, in a heading), you have to make the change in *both* layouts.

As limited as they are, there are definite advantages to using a second layout rather than a second and separate .nod file. Any structural changes do not need to be made twice; the Site Style applies across both layouts and can be changed for both at once. If the layouts share MasterBorders, these can also be changed for both at once.

INDENTED PARAGRAPHS ARE NOT RELATED IN ANY WAY TO CASCADING STYLE SHEETS. THEY ARE NOT LOGICAL STYLES AT ALL, BUT A SIMPLE VISUAL INDENT.

One powerful way to prototype two versions of a site is to have two sets of MasterBorders, using different styles or position of navigation. You could apply MasterBorders A-1, A-2, A-3 to all the "A" layouts and MasterBorders B-1, B-2, B-3 to all the "B" layouts. At the prototype stage to determine the best navigation solution, when there is little content on the pages themselves, this would be a quick way to review two alternative approaches.

Treatment of Text

IF YOU WANT TO GET FANCY YOU CAN EDIT THE FONTMAP.TXT FILE THAT COMES WITH NETOBJECTS FUSION TO SPECIFY CUSTOM ALTERNATE FONTS. THE STANDARD ALTERNATES (ARIAL, HELVETICA) ARE ALREADY IN THE FILE. IF YOU ARE PRETTY SURE YOUR AUDIENCE HAS A SPECIFIC FONT, YOU CAN SPECIFY IT AND THEN GIVE AN ALTERNATE THAT IS MORE STANDARD.

In addition to positioning elements in HTML, the major difficulty designers have with web page design is the lack of control over type. Most page layout programs enable you with precise control over such things as kerning between individual letters, justified text, linked text boxes, and so on. None of this is possible given the current limits of HTML, but most browsers have instituted mechanisms to specify font size and even the typeface (provided it is available on the visitor's system). NetObjects Fusion takes full advantage of the control that is available and uses tables to give you additional control, such as indented paragraphs.

Specifying Type

Again, the interface for specifying type is close to that of a page layout program (Figure 5.10). Most of the choices are self-evident: alignment, character style, and so on. The size is relative to the size that the user has set in their browser for the base text size. The numbers in parentheses (0, +1, +2) will be familiar to anyone used to specifying relative typesize in HTML. The size 12 point is really an estimate based on an assumption that the user has their browser set to the default 12 point typesize.

The inset refers to how many pixels within the text box element will be left clear before the text begins. This is useful if you are putting a color behind the text, or if you want to align the text elements to a grid and use the inset to create gutters.

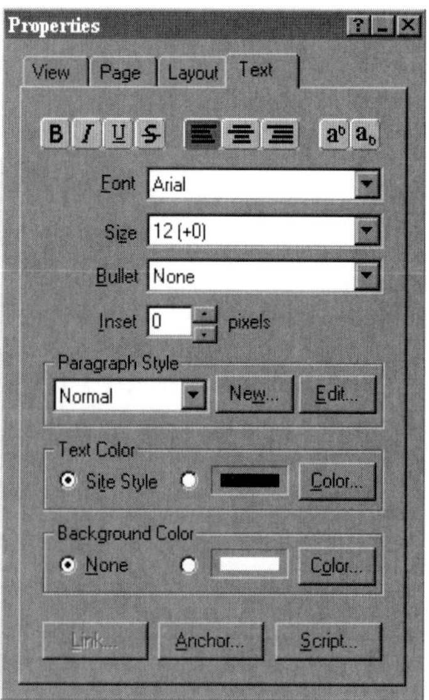

Figure 5.10

The Text tab in the Properties palette.

One note about specifying color for text: it overrides the link and visited link colors. The basic colors for text, links, and visited links are set up in the Site Style and let's say you have set these to black, red, and purple respectively. You then have a black background on a page and want to have a paragraph of white text, which contains some links. If you select the entire paragraph to be white, the links will not stand out (unless underlining is enabled in the browser). To keep the links as colors, select just the links and change their color back to Site Style. You could, of course, select another color (such as bright green) for the link, but the text would remain green even after the link was visited.

Using Paragraph Styles

One important aspect of continuity throughout a site is using text consistently. NetObjects Fusion helps by again drawing upon a desktop publishing convention. Our studio has extensive experience in book design and production, building templates with styles for every possible element that might appear in a book. Designers who don't usually lay out more than a three-fold brochure tend to ignore or underuse styles, but you can't afford to do that for long documents. Large web sites have more in common with text or reference books than they do with advertisements or brochures. To prevent having to specify attributes for each paragraph on every page, it is worth the time to set up custom paragraph styles for the text elements that will appear (Figure 5.11).

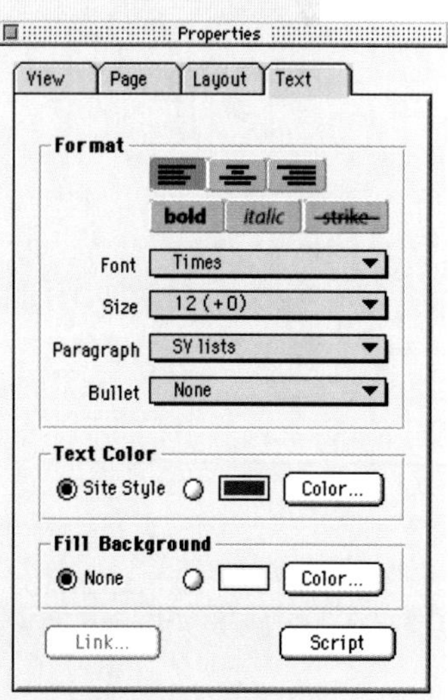

Figure 5.11

The Paragraph Style SV lists is a custom style we added to the pop-up palette.

As with page layout (or word processing) applications, you can change the definition of the style at any time and the change will apply throughout the site.

PARAGRAPH STYLES HAVE NOTHING TO DO WITH CASCADING STYLE SHEETS. NETOBJECTS FUSION PLANS TO SUPPORT CSS IN FUTURE VERSIONS.

In the Site Style, you can set the precise text attributes of the text that appears in the navigation bar. This automatically becomes a paragraph style that is called, appropriately enough, Nav Bar. This enables you to use the same text attributes in your headings or text navigation elements without referring back to the Site Style view. Assuming you have chosen commonly available font!

Images and Color

Graphics in NetObjects Fusion can be related to the Site Style, a shape drawn directly in Page view, a placed image, or a background image. You can specify the color for almost any part of an element, from the text to the background of the element (the color behind an imported graphic) to the arrowhead on a drawn line. It takes a bit of familiarity with the application and with Web design to begin to take full advantage of this bewildering array of capabilities.

Drawn Graphics

The drawing tool enables you to create simple shapes directly in NetObjects Fusion. Although this drawing capability is very basic, it is a breakthrough for web authoring environments that previously allowed only placed 72 ppi graphics. The explanation for how the application can achieve this is simply that the shapes are converted into GIF graphics when the HTML for the site is generated (upon preview, stage, or publish).

The subset of tools that appears when you select the drawing tool includes a line tool that looks like an arrow. You have a great deal of control over the line, and the various shapes you can add to each end of the line: squares, circles, and so on. You can specify the color separately for the line itself and the end elements in the Line tab of the Properties palette (see Figure 5.12).

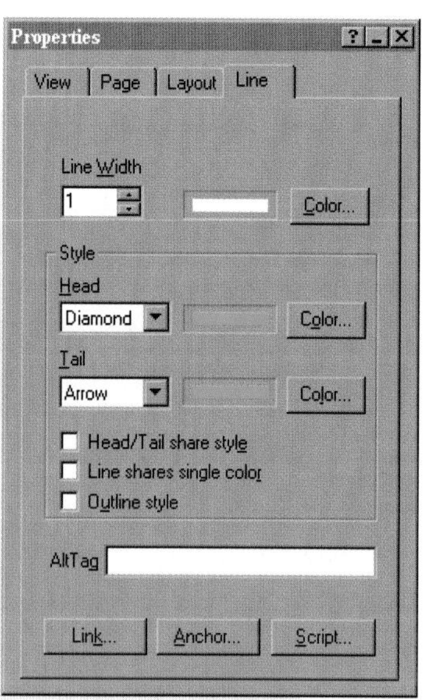

Figure 5.12

The Line tab of the Properties palette.

Drawn graphics, like other elements in NetObjects Fusion, cannot overlap other elements. So if you draw a circle or a square, you cannot then put HTML text or graphics within the square. Pixel-based graphics must be rectangular, even if part of the image is transparent so it appears *irregular* in shape. Although you can, for example, draw a line at an angle as in Figure 5.13, no other elements can be placed within the rectangular space as shown by the element border. You can, however, add text using the tricky Text in Element feature which is discussed below.

Placed Images

The interface to bring images into NetObjects Fusion does not need to be reviewed here; it is quite straightforward. We discovered one important lesson the hard way, however; the application remembers both the name of the image you place *and its location*. So, as with most page layout programs, it is not a good idea to change the name of an image after it has been placed. Also, if you move an image file (or other asset) after it has been placed in NetObjects Fusion, the application will not be able to find it and you will see an empty box in the Page view. Although you can point NetObjects Fusion to the new file name or location in the Assets view, this can be tedious. We have found that it is better to designate a folder (site.art) where all assets will be put before they are placed into NetObjects Fusion.

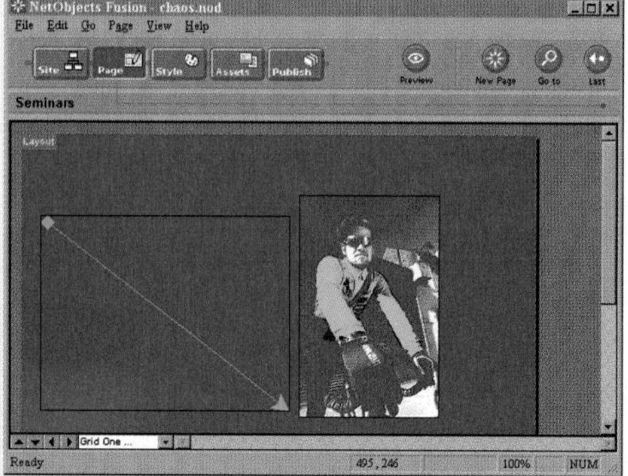

Figure 5.13

A diagonal line takes up a large rectangular space on the page.

The manual tells you that to allow a .nod file to be opened on another computer, you must save it as a Template. This requirement is cumbersome if you have a team working on a project. We have found that if you put your site.art folder on the your local server and place all the artwork from there, the .nod files can be traded back and forth successfully.

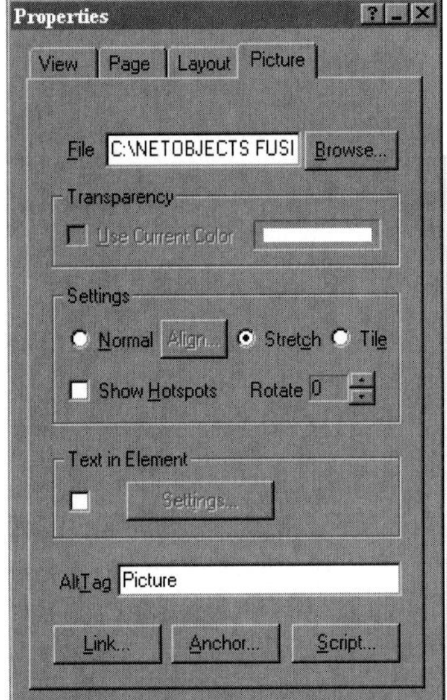

Figure 5.14
The Picture tab in the Properties palette. Here the Stretch option is selected under Settings to allow resizing.

The server must be available when the .nod is opened and remain available as you are working.

The Picture tab of the Properties pallette shows the options that are available to work with an image in the Page view (Figure 5.14). Cropping and resizing images directly in the Page view is a useful feature, especially in the design phase. When you crop, resize, or apply transparency to an image, however, NetObjects Fusion actually generates a new GIF file based on your original. We have found that some of our carefully optimized images, which may have been 9K, ended up with a larger file size when re-created by the application. For many situations, however, the auto-generated images are fine; we used them for the screen captures throughout our sample chapter of *Designing Multimedia Web Sites.*

To crop an image simply change the size of the element using the handles to crop out the portion you wish to eliminate. You can crop an image only from the lower left (no matter what alignment options are selected). To resize an image you must enable the Stretch radio button (Figure 5.14) and then resize the element. You cannot enter a specific percentage to resize precisely, you must just drag to the desired size. Unless you plan to resize an image, do not enable the Stretch option, so that you do not accidentally resize an image when you are merely selecting it—this would create an auto-generated image. Alignment of an image applies only to the position of the image within the element, which is most meaningful if there is a color applied to the element itself; otherwise, it is indistinguishable from the page background.

When we first saw the Text in Element feature, we thought that NetObjects Fusion had found some magical way to do the impossible: place HTML text on top of an image. What the software actually does is place the text you specify onto the GIF (or JPEG) image, and then generate a new image that includes the text. This is parallel to the process that it goes through to put text on the buttons in a navigation bar. The options for positioning the text are extensive, including rotating the text by any amount you specify (Figure 5.15).

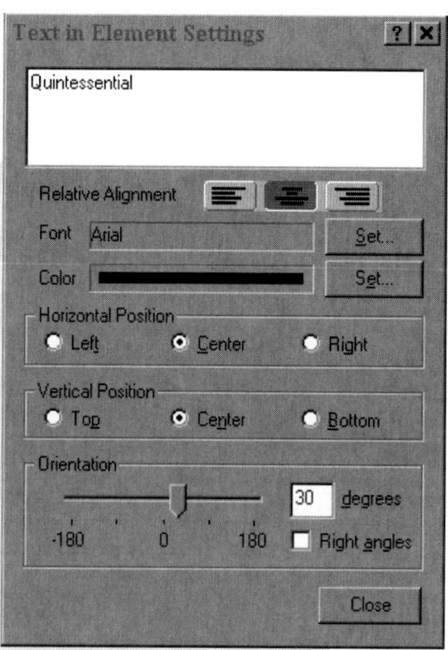

Figure 5.15

The Text in Element Settings dialog box.

Background Images

In the Layout tab of the Properties palette (refer to Figure 5.7), you can set up the background of the page. Each Site Style has a designated background, which you can use as is, or change in the Style view. Alternately, you can select a background from a different style from the pop-up menu of styles. If you choose None, you get a white background, not the default gray of most browsers. You can also select a specific color or image for the background. The best images to use for backgrounds are narrow horizontal images, containing only a few colors, which repeat to form a vertical pattern (or vice versa). You will find an example of how we created a background of a narrow vertical stripe so that it can load most efficiently in the case study of the AIGA Philadelphia site in Chapter 8.

Although the background is controlled from the Layout tab, it affects the entire page, not just the layout area. This means that you can apply different backgrounds to pages that share the same MasterBorder. If you do use a different color background from that in the style, check how the navigation bars, banners, and other images look on the different colors in the browser. When an irregularly shaped image is anti-aliased, it may have a halo effect that will show on backgrounds of different values (Figure 5.16).

Figure 5.16

Here an image has been prepared to go on a dark background, and when it is placed on a light background, there is a halo of dark around it.

It is difficult to align a background image precisely with images that are placed in the foreground in a way that will work across platforms and browsers. It's recommended that you leave an eight pixel range horizontally and vertically within which alignment is acceptable.

Elements with Color Backgrounds

In the Text tab of the Properties palette, you can designate a background color for the text element. It is important if you choose to do this, however, that you set an inset so that the text does not extend to the edge of the box. Otherwise the text will look like it is jammed up against the edge of the color and be slightly harder to read. These colored text elements are an incredibly quick and easy way to make a banner-like element that is HTML text, not a GIF (Figure 5.17).

Figure 5.17
The use of a background color with a text element. This actually uses a color in a table cell if you want to know the behind the scenes mechanism.

Color Specification

The topic of specifying colors for the web is discussed in Chapter 3, including choosing colors that will be consistent from platform to platform. To specify a color, NetObjects Fusion provides an interface that is shown in Figure 5.18. This palette is much improved on the Macintosh platform from version 1.0 to version 2.0 (the Windows palette was better to start with). A palette of basic colors to choose comes up as the default. If you wish to see the breakdown of any of these colors, choose the Define Custom Colors button. Now, on both platforms, you can see the RGB components as well as the HSL makeup of any color you select or you can define a new color. On the Macintosh, in version 2.0, you also can see the HSV Picker, the HTML Picker, and the CMYK picker. Another huge improvement is that now on both platforms the color of the currently select object is highlighted (as you can see in the top of Figure 5.18), which was not true in the Macintosh 2.0 version. We used to try swatch after swatch trying in vain to match an existing color! You can build a set of 16 custom colors, either from the basic colors or new ones that you define. These colors are set for the application, they will appear no matter what .nod file you open. While this is handy, it would be even nicer to be able to save a specific set of Custom Colors for each site you were working on.

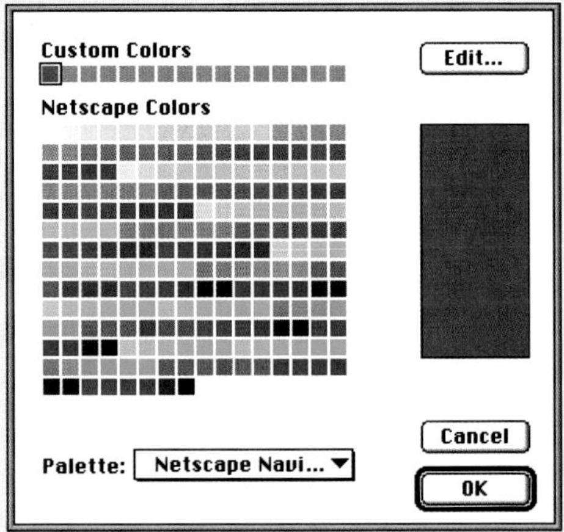

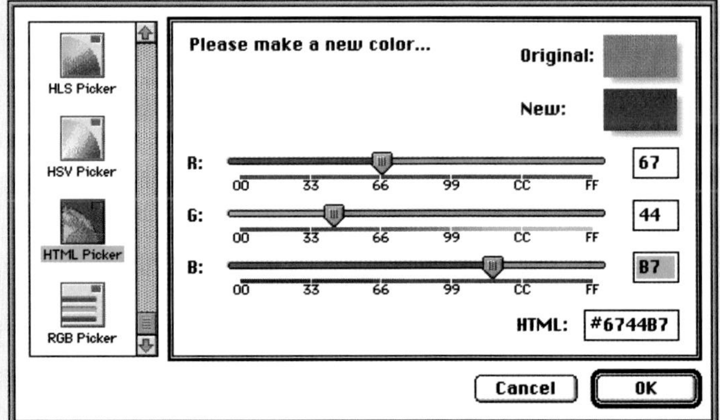

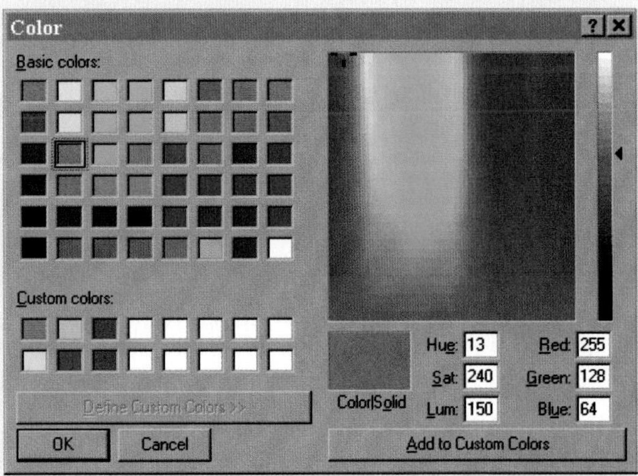

Figure 5.18

Here you see what happens when you edit a custom color on the Macintosh (the top two images) and Windows (lower image).

Behind the Scenes

One key difference between NetObjects Fusion and other web authoring applications is that no HTML is created as you work in the .nod file. The information about the site is stored in the .nod file (a database file). Each time you choose to preview, stage, or publish, the application generates fresh HTML for all the pages and generates any images that are needed. We have already discussed auto-generated images and how they permit more control over the images within the NetObjects Fusion application itself rather than in a separate imaging application (and the possible drawbacks in terms of file size).

Do You Know PostScript?

The parallel that we have been making between NetObjects Fusion and page layout programs brings to mind another parallel. The language that describes the elements on a page and determines how they appear on printed pages is called PostScript. The WYSIWYG interface, which allowed what you saw on screen to be displayed using PostScript, was a huge breakthrough that sparked the desktop publishing revolution. When PostScript was new, books on PostScript came with certain applications, such as Adobe Illustrator, so that you could create custom effects that weren't built into the application's interface. When you added actual PostScript code to the document, you would not be able to see the effect onscreen, only when printed to a PostScript printer. Although learning PostScript offered almost unlimited options, there weren't many takers. The market demanded WYSIWYG and that is how the applications have developed. You probably work with PostScript everyday and don't know anything about the coding.

The parallel we have in mind is obvious. At first, creating web pages required learning HTML tags. Gradually editors became helpful in automating applying these tags, but you still had to understand the effect of the tags to use them effectively.

As WYSIWYG environments begin to appear, you are limited to the effects that have been built into the interface of the application. With many applications, if you attempt to add additional HTML or script within the

HTML, you completely disrupt even the approximate WYSIWYG. Eventually, there will probably be as much need to know HTML as PostScript. This does not mean that you don't have to understand the current limits of the medium. You must understand the limits of HTML just as you have to understand what can be printed on a printing press and what cannot.

NetObjects Fusion provides an interface that is as close to WYSIWYG as possible. You also have the option of adding HTML (or scripts) that affect the interaction of the page and the browser (Figure 5.19). These snippets of HTML or scripts are both called "scripts" by NetObjects Fusion and are kept attached to the elements (or Layout) but are not displayed in the Page view. If you want to remember where you have added scripts, display the Element Icons in the View tab and a small icon appears next to all the objects that have scripts attached to them. Of course, if you call upon an image or something that takes up space on the page in the added HTML, the page in NetObjects Fusion will not reflect this. Generally, however, the script dialog box is used to add instructions that control the behavior of the browser in some way. For example additional parameters for multimedia (whether the control bar is displayed, whether an animation loops) or a JavaScript command to open a new browser window.

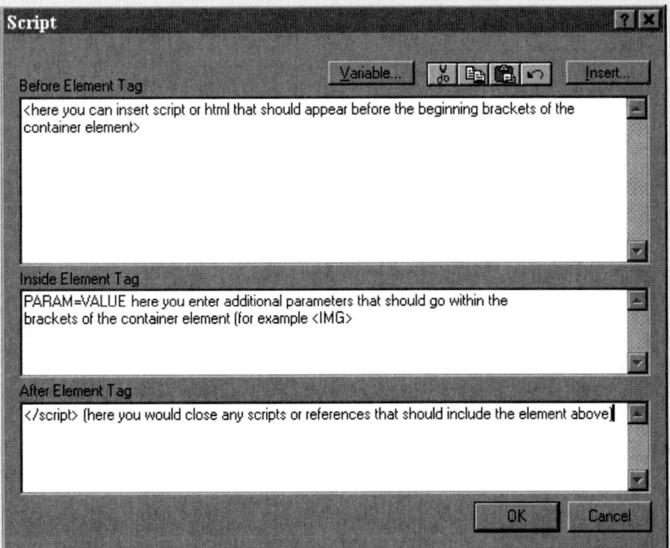

Figure 5.19
The Script dialog box, which can be accessed from the Properties palette when any element is selected.

File Organization

Although this may be a difficult adjustment for someone who already has a system in place to organize the files for the site, NetObjects Fusion will not be effective unless it is allowed to control the file organization. Once you give up this control, however, and understand how the application works, it will save a great deal of time that is usually devoted to file management.

Figure 5.20 shows the organization of a typical UserSite. The data is kept in the .nod file, but NetObjects Fusion makes one or more back-up copies of this file, appending dates to the file names, which is pretty convenient. The Assets folder is where the application stores building blocks for your site other than those associated with a SiteStyle. The Preview Folder parallels what a Staging Folder looks like, the my_html folder for pages you have created with other software, the index page loose, and then the assets and html. The NoMoreLinks.html page will appear when you only preview a single page and attempt to navigate in the browser!

When you use Preview to review your site, Stage to test your site on a local server, or Publish to a remote server, NetObjects Fusion accomplishes several tasks. It generates all necessary HTML, names the .html files

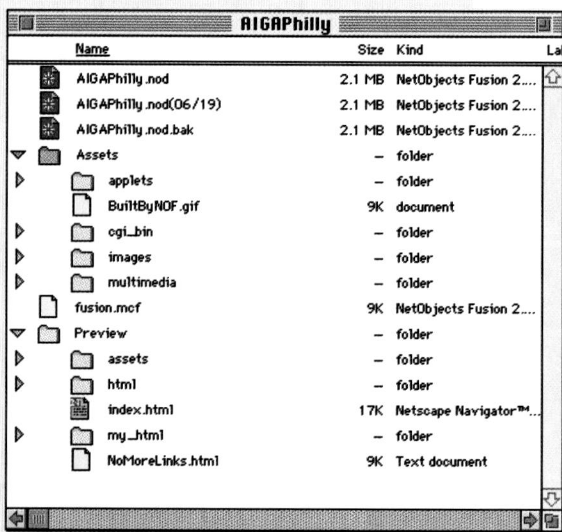

Figure 5.20

The file structure set up by NetObjects Fusion. Beware of renaming, moving, or adding things to these folders unless you are sure of what you are doing.

(the page name + suffix), copies placed images, and generates auto-generated images. Even if you publish to a remote server, NetObjects Fusion gathers all the files locally before uploading them. Because of the complexity of the relationships among these files, it is essential that you leave the structure as NetObjects Fusion establishes it.

In our studio, we direct Preview to the Preview directory within the User Sites directory. It is important to empty this folder periodically; a new preview will not empty the folder but will write over files of the same name. We direct Stage to a Staging folder on our local server and check the site on various monitors and platforms. If changes are needed, we empty the Staging folder and stage again after revisions. If the pages are ready to upload, we usually FTP manually from the Staging folder to the remote server and rename the folder Site.Mirror.Date (a reflection of what is live). We FTP manually because NetObjects Fusion sometimes puts some extra files loose in the Assets folder that are related to Site Styles (even a Style that was considered and not used) and these extra files simply take up space on the server. In this way, also, we can upload only those image files that have been revised. We always upload all the HTML!

6

Database Publishing:

Designing Information Delivery

NetObjects Fusion is designed for use by communication professionals, like ourselves, who care about the appearance and organization of material. This chapter is written for them (or rather *us*), and is being written with all the fervor of the newly converted. Many of us either panic or allow our eyes to glaze over when the word database is mentioned (Figure 6.1). We are thereby abdicating a crucial role in the most important development in web publishing since the introduction of graphics. We are also condemning ourselves (or the production and site maintenance staff) to tedious hours of site updates.

Figure 6.1
A designer's reaction to the thought of databases.

You should read this chapter for the following reasons:

- Understanding databases can save you hours of work
- Understanding databases can get you big accounts (if you are an independent designer), or make your boss love you (if you are in-house)

We will start from the beginning (what a database is), proceed to explain why it is significant for the web, and then discuss dynamic versus static database publishing. If you are already familiar and comfortable with databases, you may want to skip to the later part of the chapter to gain insight into how NetObjects Fusion works with databases.

Figure 6.2
A designer who has successfully published 100 revised pages after tweaking the layout of one.

The goal of this chapter is to inspire you to do one or both of the following:

- Build your own databases when multiple pages contain parallel information
- Insist on good interface design when giving access to large or dynamic databases at your site

To effectively do either, you must have a basic understanding of databases, what they are, what they can and cannot do, and why you should not be afraid of them. As designers we cannot allow database-driven pages to be considered outside of our scope, with their appearance dictated by the database.

THIS CANNOT BE STATED TOO FIRMLY: THE APPEARANCE OF THE INTERFACE SHOULD NOT BE CONTROLLED BY THE DEFAULTS OF THE DATABASE SOFTWARE OR LEFT TO THE DATABASE ENGINEER TO DESIGN.

This chapter is not a comprehensive step-by-step lesson in database publishing. Examples in this chapter and in the case studies, serve more as inspiration than models, because specific situations vary widely in terms of needs and capabilities. We simply want to persuade you that it is worth paying attention to this area, and maybe get you to jump in and manage some small-scale databases for publishing. Really, the rewards will be more exciting than you imagine (Figure 6.2).

The Opening Statement

Think of this as the opening statement by an attorney at a trial, "we intend to prove that the defendant, and so on." It is important that the jury understand where all this (sometimes tedious) evidence is leading. So before we get into the specific building blocks leading to an understanding of database publishing, we will restate the conclusion (slightly reworded):

- Database publishing gives you back your leisure time.
- Database publishing will make you rich and popular.

Okay, it sounds like an advertising pitch, but we're trying to get your attention!

Time Saving

Originally, building pages in HTML was a long, frustrating and error-ridden process. As products have emerged, the original building of pages has been streamlined, and the amount of actual HTML that you have to enter has been reduced. Especially if you begin with a template HTML document and insert the page-specific copy, you can generate a site fairly efficiently.

WE DISCUSS HOW YOU CAN CREATE A SERIES OF PAGES BASED ON THE SAME TEMPLATE PAGE USING NETOBJECTS FUSION'S IMPORT SECTION COMMAND IN THE CASE STUDY IN CHAPTER 10. IN THIS WAY YOU HAVE PAGES WITH DIFFERING CONTENT, BUT BEGINNING WITH THE SAME ARRANGEMENT OF ELEMENTS AND CONTAINERS. HOWEVER, ONCE THE PAGES ARE CREATED, CHANGES TO THE LAYOUT OF ONE PAGE DO NOT AFFECT THE OTHERS. WHAT IF YOU HAVE CREATED 30 PAGES OF PERSONNEL BIOGRAPHIES AND REALIZE YOU WANT TO MOVE THE TEXT TO THE RIGHT AND THE PHOTO TO THE LEFT?

The nightmare came with maintaining and revising the site. Although the pages were originally built based on a template, once built, they had no dynamic relationship with that template, and were all independent pages of HTML. In other words, an update to the template did not revise the pages you have already built. NetObjects Fusion revolutionized this (as discussed in Chapter 5), in that the HTML is generated on demand, and the revisions are made to the site where pages share common information. Changes to the MasterBorder areas, and updating links are painless revisions that affect the entire site.

Even if you use NetObjects Fusion, however, new information that falls in the body (or Layout area) of the page, must be manually placed on each page. What if prices have gone up? What if personnel has changed?

If you are producing a site for an established business, it is likely that much of the information that you want to put on the web already exists in database form. It may need some work before it is ready to publish, but once it is in the right form, it can be updated as the database is updated (as it would be in the normal course of business).

Publishing a database saves you time *creating* a site in two ways:

- Information that already exists in a database does not have to be keyed in (or even copied and pasted).
- The presentation of the information from the database (graphics, links, or text) can generally be determined once, and applied to all pages for that section of the site.

Similarly, database publishing saves you time *maintaining* a site in two ways:

- Information updated in the database (usually by clerical staff) will replace the old information on the pages automatically.
- You can alter the layout of one page in a section that serves database elements, and all the pages are revised.

For stacked pages in NetObjects Fusion, this second point applies to the formatting of text, position of elements, overall page size, background elements, and any common elements that appear on all pages (anywhere on the page, not just in the MasterBorder).

Riches and Popularity

As you can see from the points in the previous section, you will be popular with the production staff for lifting hours of tedious work from their shoulders. They might now have time for those great enhancement details that are usually put off in favor of mission critical (and boring) maintenance.

Many corporations that put up sites on the web relatively early are finding that maintenance is a nightmare. They know that database solutions are the answer. Porting your data to the Web or intranet is the current buzz in the corporate world. Many that have had experience with vendors that come from an engineering background, where the look and feel, and user interface is confusing or lacking in sophistication. If you talk about the importance of the visitor (customer) coming first, and the need to make the data serve the purpose of the site, not vice versa, you will establish your credentials and bias clearly.

Read the basic introduction in this chapter, and go on to read and learn more elsewhere about database publishing, interfaces, automating site production and upkeep. It is worth it. We will have updated resources and readings at our companion web site www.designpractice.com.

About Databases

What comes into your mind when you hear the word database? That great pool of information that has your mother's maiden name, your financial history and vehicle identification number? Actually a database could be as simple as a list, say a list of URLs. They can also be extremely complex with extensive inter-relationships among the data that they contain.

Many of the challenges of today's information managers are related to managing databases, and usually the problems are related to scale. The sheer size of the databases, and the number of records and fields, means that any manual scanning for accuracy or tweaking of exceptions is impossible. When the database is smaller, there is more room for an imperfect system that can be checked and corrected.

SUPPOSE A CLIENT TELLS YOU THAT THEY WANT TO PROVIDE COURSE LISTINGS ONLINE. YOU CONFIRM THAT THESE ARE CURRENTLY IN A DATABASE AND LAUNCH INTO A DISCUSSION OF PROS AND CONS OF STATIC VERSUS DYNAMIC SERVING OF THE DATABASE ON THE WEB, WHILE STILL FOCUSING ON THE EXPERIENCE OF THE VISITOR. BY DOING THIS, YOU'VE GOT THEM IN THE PALM OF YOUR HAND, BECAUSE THEY DON'T EXPECT YOU TO KNOW THIS STUFF.

For the purposes of this chapter there are two kinds of databases.

- Databases that due to their size or complexity must be managed by database professionals, and probably require specialized software and programming to bring it to the web
- Databases that can be managed by support staff, content developers, and even designers

If you turn to information about database publishing (for example, in the User Manual of NetObjects Fusion) it begins by using terms that might be unfamiliar or confusing: data field, data object, data list. These are all important terms, but they don't make sense unless you understand the need for them and understand the terms used to define these new terms. So to start at the beginning, as promised, we break down any database to its basic component parts: records, fields, and values. The discussion that follows may seem simplistic, because of the simple examples chosen, but the principles outlined are the key to successful work with databases.

The Simplest Database: A List

When you break the simplest database down it consists of records, fields, and values. In our example of a list of URLs, each URL is a record (let's say there are 75 URLs). There is only one field, the URL. The value, or contents of the field, in each record is the URL itself, such as http://www.vizbyte.com. A logical addition to this database would be to add the name of the site to which this URL would lead you. If we enter a site title on the same line as each URL, separated by a tab or comma, this would add a second field to the database (Figure 6.3). We now have:

- 75 data records
- 2 data fields: (URL and site title)
- 150 separate values, or pieces of data: 75 URLs and 75 site titles

links to sites

http://www.alberte.com the elements of einstein
http://www.panoptic.com Panoptic Communications
http://www.pcdir.com Philadelphia Creative Directory
http://www.id.iit.edu/~bmcgrath/site_4/almost.html Brian McGrath
http://www.hayden.com Hayden Books
http://www.workbook.com The Workbook
http://www.aigaphilly.org Philadelphia Chapter of AIGA
http://www.dol.com designOnline
http://www.phoenixnewtimes.com/ads/congo/ Club Congress
http://www.fontsonline.com fontsonline
http://www.timecycle.com TimeCycle Couriers
http://inclusion.org Inclusion Network
http://www.bsooy.com Brian Sooy and Company
http://www.commarts.com Communication Arts Magazine
http://www.viewsource.com viewSource Media
http://www.cow.com cow interactive communications
http://www.vizbyte.com STELLARViSIONs | bYte a tree

Figure 6.3

A list of URLs and site titles, where there is a tab after each URL and a return after each site title. Note that extra returns have not been added to align the columns visually.

This database is described as a list, and we mean just that, a typed list in a text document. We think of databases as synonymous with files in a database management application, but this example helps to point out that the database is independent of the management software.

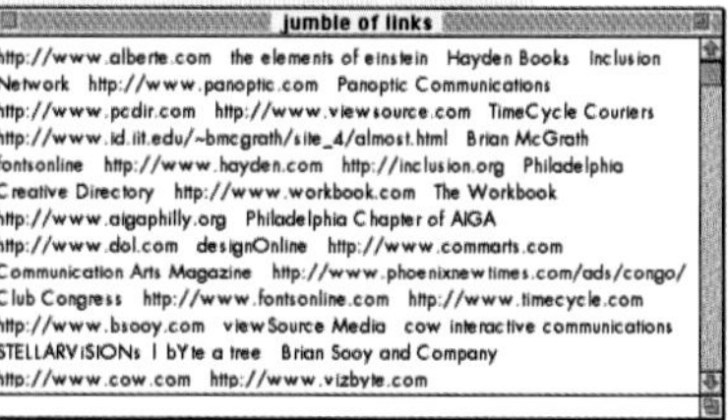

jumble of links

http://www.alberte.com the elements of einstein Hayden Books Inclusion
Network http://www.panoptic.com Panoptic Communications
http://www.pcdir.com http://www.viewsource.com TimeCycle Couriers
http://www.id.iit.edu/~bmcgrath/site_4/almost.html Brian McGrath
fontsonline http://www.hayden.com http://inclusion.org Philadelphia
Creative Directory http://www.workbook.com The Workbook
http://www.aigaphilly.org Philadelphia Chapter of AIGA
http://www.dol.com designOnline http://www.commarts.com
Communication Arts Magazine http://www.phoenixnewtimes.com/ads/congo/
Club Congress http://www.fontsonline.com http://www.timecycle.com
http://www.bsooy.com viewSource Media cow interactive communications
STELLARViSIONs | bYte a tree Brian Sooy and Company
http://www.cow.com http://www.vizbyte.com

Figure 6.4

Here the same text is shown in a random order, such that there is no longer any special relation between the URL and site title. This is not a database and is really not even raw data.

The 75 records, list of URLs, and site titles could be completely random. They do not have to be in order of any sort to form a database. However, if you had the 150 pieces of data jumbled together that would *not* be a database (Figure 6.4). The significant difference is that each URL corresponds to a specific site title. This is not a random correspondence, it has meaning. If you type the URL into a browser it will take you to a site having that title. No matter how random the records, this relationship is not broken, and must never be broken, for the database to serve its function.

Also, for each record, the two pieces of data always consist of a URL and a site title. If the URL is first and the site title second, this must be consistent. To suddenly put the site title first for some records would mix up the two fields. Even though each record would still have the two pieces of data, the data would be worthless.

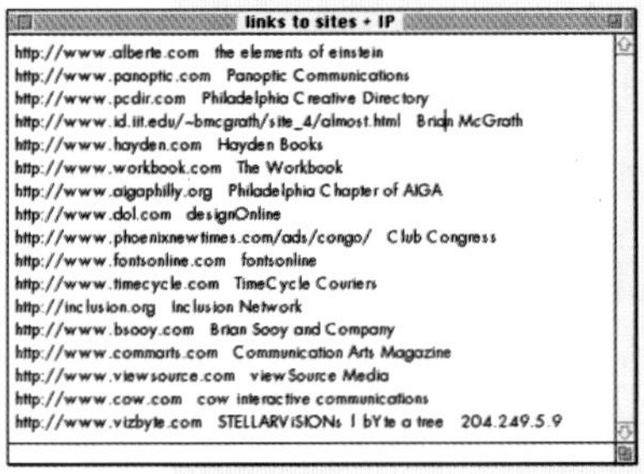

```
links to sites + IP
http://www.alberte.com   the elements of einstein
http://www.panoptic.com   Panoptic Communications
http://www.pcdir.com   Philadelphia Creative Directory
http://www.id.iit.edu/~bmcgrath/site_4/almost.html   Brian McGrath
http://www.hayden.com   Hayden Books
http://www.workbook.com   The Workbook
http://www.aigaphilly.org   Philadelphia Chapter of AIGA
http://www.dol.com   designOnline
http://www.phoenixnewtimes.com/ads/congo/   Club Congress
http://www.fontsonline.com   fontsonline
http://www.timecycle.com   TimeCycle Couriers
http://inclusion.org   Inclusion Network
http://www.bsooy.com   Brian Sooy and Company
http://www.commarts.com   Communication Arts Magazine
http://www.viewsource.com   viewSource Media
http://www.cow.com   cow interactive communications
http://www.vizbyte.com   STELLARViSIONs I bYte a tree   204.249.5.9
```

Figure 6.5

The addition of a third item on the last visible line (the IP address for vizbyte) essentially adds a field to all the records on the list. This field will be blank for all but vizbyte.

Similarly, introducing another element in place of the site title, for example the IP address, would corrupt the data. Even though the information is accurate (the correct IP) and meaningful (the numbers would take you to that URL) it is not of any value in the position that should be occupied by the site title. If we have an IP address that we want to add to the list, a third entry should be put on the line (adding a third field, as in Figure 6.5). The missing piece of information is not as problematic as misplaced information (with some exceptions), if the site name is not known it could simply be blank, or a generic entry such as title unknown be used. Because the IP address is only added on one line, for example, that field would be blank for all other records.

So we see that even a simple list of URLs and site titles, has several important properties:

- A meaningful correspondence between the values in every record—the URL http://www.alberte.com leads to site entitled "the elements of einstein".
- There is a consistent positioning, or field assignment in each record—the URL field always contains the URL, and the site title field always contains the site title (or "unknown") .
- For additional information (such as an IP address) to be added to even one record, a field must be added to all records. The information is of no value in the wrong field.

WHENEVER WE FIND SOMETHING CONFUSING OR DIFFICULT TO REMEMBER (LIKE HOW TO CALCULATE A PERCENTAGE) WE REMEMBER A SIMPLE EXAMPLE AND EXTRAPOLATE FROM THAT. IF YOU FIND YOURSELF CONFUSED ABOUT ANY OF THESE TERMS, REFERRING BACK TO THIS SIMPLE EXAMPLE MIGHT BE HELPFUL.

Database Records: Digital 3×5 cards

WHEN A HUGE PROJECT LIKE THE OXFORD ENGLISH DICTIONARY WAS UNDERTAKEN AROUND THE TURN OF THE CENTURY, ENTRIES CONCERNING WORD USAGE WERE RECORDED BY READERS AS THEY READ A WORK OF LITERATURE. THESE WERE THEN FILED IN CUBBIES, ALPHABETICALLY, UNTIL ENTIRE BUILDINGS HAD TO BE BUILT TO HOUSE THE SLIPS OF PAPER.

You can think of a database record as an old fashioned 3×5 index card. Remember how you were told to keep notes on index cards in school? Why was that? Because you could take the notes in the order you came across the information and then reorder the cards when you came to consider the structure of your school report. Unlike notes on sheets of paper, the cards can be easily grouped according to subject, and some set aside.

Not any group of index cards with information on them would be a database. There must be a relationship across at least two axes, something shared among the values on the card to make them a record, and a parallel structure among the records to make them a database. For the school report, each card would represent notes taken at a particular time from a particular source (Figure 6.6).

Therefore there are five fields on each note card. Again, it is not necessary for all the cards to have all of these pieces of data, but if this overall structure can be seen in the index cards then they are a database. We can extract all of the cards on one topic, or all of the cards from one author, or all of the cards written on a particular day— whatever is most useful.

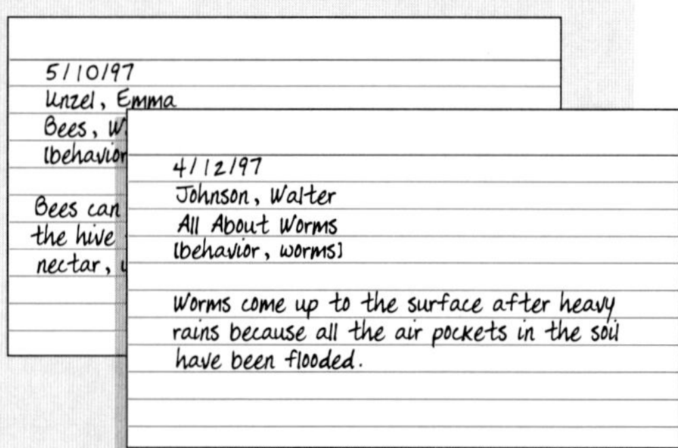

Figure 6.6
These cards for a biology research paper, show the parallel structure of the information on each card.

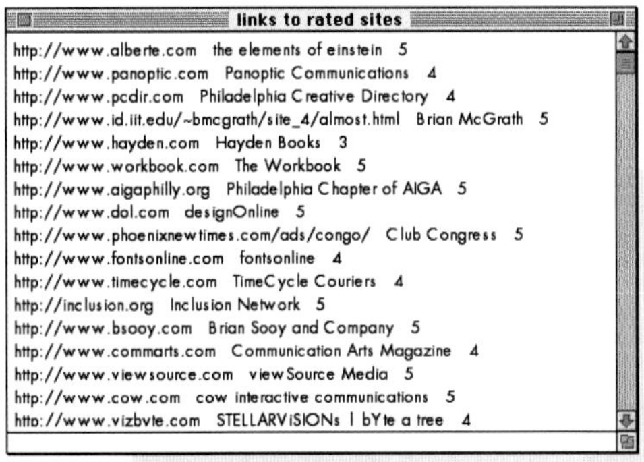

links to rated sites

http://www.alberte.com the elements of einstein 5
http://www.panoptic.com Panoptic Communications 4
http://www.pcdir.com Philadelphia Creative Directory 4
http://www.id.iit.edu/~bmcgrath/site_4/almost.html Brian McGrath 5
http://www.hayden.com Hayden Books 3
http://www.workbook.com The Workbook 5
http://www.aigaphilly.org Philadelphia Chapter of AIGA 5
http://www.dol.com designOnline 5
http://www.phoenixnewtimes.com/ads/congo/ Club Congress 5
http://www.fontsonline.com fontsonline 4
http://www.timecycle.com TimeCycle Couriers 4
http://inclusion.org Inclusion Network 5
http://www.bsooy.com Brian Sooy and Company 5
http://www.commarts.com Communication Arts Magazine 4
http://www.viewsource.com viewSource Media 5
http://www.cow.com cow interactive communications 5
http://www.vizbyte.com STELLARVISIONs I bYte a tree 4

Figure 6.7
Here numerals are added on each line, adding a new field. What do these numerals represent? Their meaning is not self-evident, we need an identifying element.

Field Names

In our simple example consisting of a list of URLs and site titles (Figure 6.3), notice that there are no column heads for the list. It is self-evident, from content, that the first column consists of URLs and the second is site titles. We have discovered that these represent two fields in the database.

What if there was another column consisting simply of numerals as in Figure 6.7? What do these numerals represent? It turns out that these are site ratings, on a scale of 1 to 5. This was *not* self-evident, we need an identifying element to tell us what the field represents. We therefore introduce the concept of field names. In Figure 6.8 you can see the same information brought into a database management application (Claris FileMaker Pro), and field names have been added. These are not pieces of data, per se, but identify the field for the purpose of managing the data more effectively. It would be as if the cards shown in Figure 6.6 had labels printed on them (Figure 6.9).

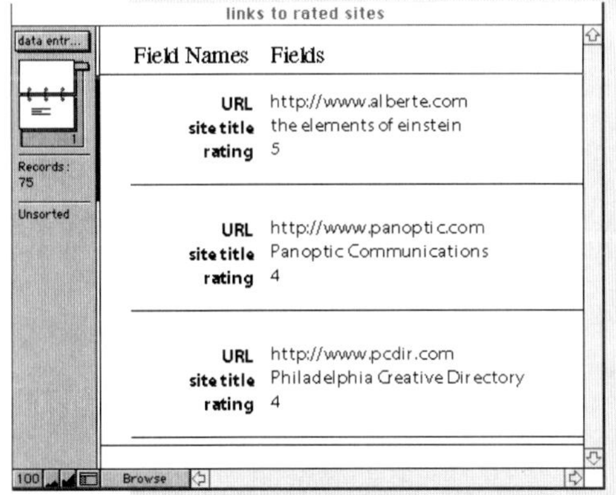

Figure 6.8
Here the data is displayed in FileMaker Pro. We set up and named three fields in the application and imported the records from the text file.

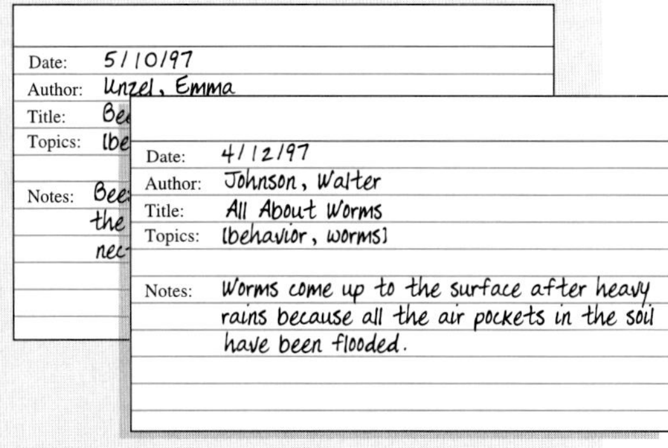

Figure 6.9
The printed labels such as "Author:" tell you where to put what information, and identify the data in a consistent manner. Field names do the same thing in a database.

In this way, the data would be recorded in a consistent fashion, and if a field was skipped, there would be no danger of wrong data being put in the field that should be empty.

Field names allow us to ask database software (such as Microsoft Access, Claris FileMaker, or dBase) to perform functions to certain fields (add fields A + B for each record, or give an average of field A over all records). The key thing to remember, however, is that they are a tool to manage the data, not data themselves.

WITHOUT FIELD NAMES, THERE IS A DANGER OF THE CORRESPONDENCE BEING OVERLOOKED AND, IF THERE IS NO AUTHOR, THE TITLE BEING ENTERED AS THE SECOND FIELD. THIS IS WHY PRINTED FORMS ARE SO POPULAR RATHER THAN JUST SAYING, "GIVE US YOUR NAME AND ADDRESS IN THE WHITE SPACE BELOW".

The Arrangement of Records: Sorting and Filtering

The concept of sorting records may seem self-evident, but there are some tricks to it. Database applications can sort by any field in ascending or descending alpha-numeric order. If you have had names entered as Mr. Smith and Joe Green, an alphabetical sort is not going to yield the results you want. Data entry must anticipate the sorting needs that are yet to come.

Database applications can also call up (or Find) records where a field meets certain criteria, or has any one of a list of particular values. An example of this is all the records where a particular field begins with R. When you want to select only certain records, such as eliminating those with empty fields, this is called filtering the records.

If you want to group records under general categories, say, design resource sites, technical resource sites, and inspirational sites, you cannot group the records manually and put the category at the top of the list. You must add a field (called site type, perhaps) and enter one of the three categories in that field for each record (see Figure 6.10). Database management applications have ways of doing this quickly. You could set up a pop-up choice to select a category for each site (which would not take much longer than deciding where it belonged). You can set up some required fields, optional fields, and so on. For this field there are only three possible values, all records must belong to one of the three. That way you know you will not leave any sites out when you separate by category.

You cannot sort or filter by a factor that is not part of the database. Obviously, you cannot sort our URL list by geographical location of the host server when that is not known and has not been entered. However, suppose you want a list of only those URLs that have been verified as up and running. You simply add a field to the database named "date verified" and enter the date as each URL is verified (Figure 6.10). Then you can call up all those that have been checked for your live list, sorting by that field. This will also prove useful to keep track of when you go back and verify the URLs again.

If you are working with a large existing database, verify exactly what fields are present and the capabilities of the management software. That way you will not count on being able to filter out old information (such as URLs not verified in the last month) when there is no date stamp on the records. Or you might want to sort the URLs by those that end in .com, .edu or .org. Be sure that the management software can search for a portion of a word and not just the beginning or entire word (a URL, because it contains no spaces, is considered a word).

The Layout and Hidden Fields

Generally, when you picture a database record you visualize a screen in FileMaker or Access, where you have a nice layout and fields are identified by labels (as we saw in Figure 6.10). By viewing this same screen in layout mode (Figure 6.11) we can clearly see what elements are drawn from the database and which elements are simply placed on the layout. This is a critical distinction. For convenience in managing the database, many applications will automatically create labels for the layout that reflect the field names, but this is for convenience only. You can put any words or graphics you like on the layout and it will not affect the data, or the field names. It will affect how the data is perceived by anyone looking at it.

The layout shown in Figure 6.12, for example, uses information from the database to fill in blanks in phrases. The layout in Figure 6.13 uses a list form where column heads are used. The column heads are not identical to the field names, as you can see, but are designed to present the material clearly to the viewer. Often databases are presented using the field names on the layouts as a default, even on the web. Question this! It does not have to be that way—the layout is your most powerful tool to give information the correct context so that it is useful.

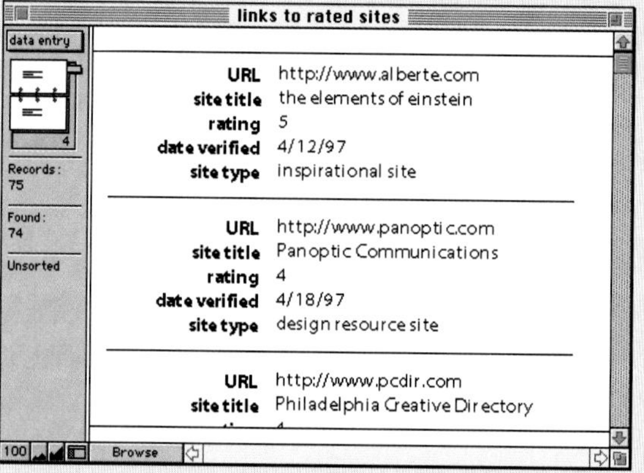

Figure 6.10
Here the fields for date verified and site type have been added.

Data is only typed once. All of the layouts you see in Figures 6.10 through 6.13 are simply different layouts of the same data. The relative order in which the elements are displayed (first to last), the arrangement (vertical, horizontal, columns) does not change the database in any way. The arrangement of elements should suit the purpose of the page; a default arrangement of fields will probably not be acceptable.

Not all of the fields must appear in all of the layouts. Suppose, instead of displaying the ratings 1-5, you simply wanted to list all the top sites on a page with a graphic of five stars at the top (with separate pages for the other rankings). The field ratings is essential to sort the records properly, but it is not displayed. Similarly the field that certifies that the URL is verified is essential, you might filter out those that are not, but it is not displayed. These are called hidden fields because they are not seen by the viewer. There is nothing more mysterious or difficult about hidden fields.

Obviously, there is a lot more that could be said about databases, like explaining intelligent data or relational databases, but that is really beyond the scope of this book. We will move on to how you can take this data and make it available to visitors to a web site.

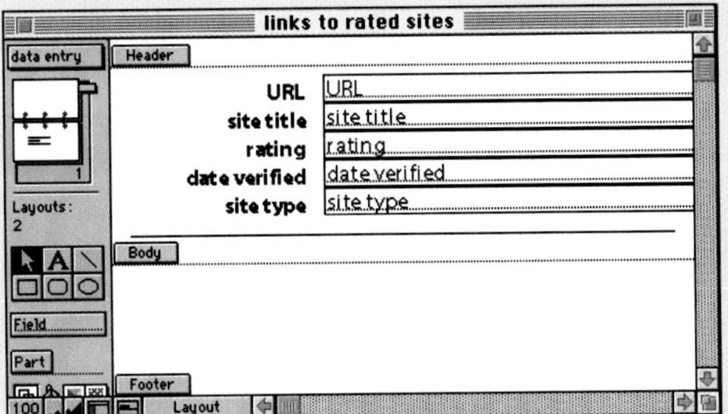

Figure 6.11

This shows the data fields, displaying the field names, not the values contained in any specific record (called layout view in FileMaker Pro). Although the same field names are shown as labels (for clarity of data entry) these labels do not affect the field in any way.

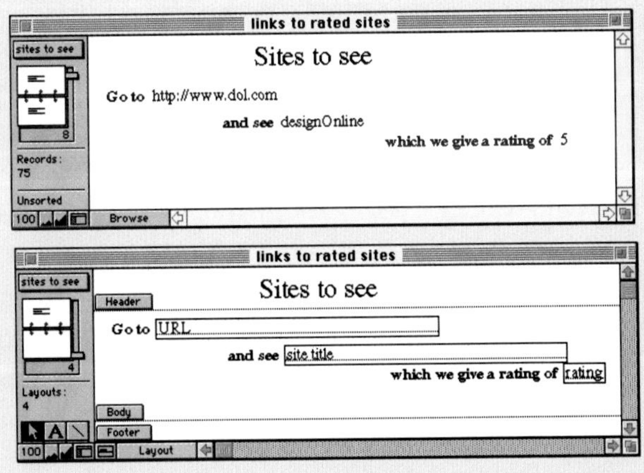

Figure 6.12

Here is a simple directive, where the blanks in the sentence are filled in from the database. In the layout view you can see the fields that are being called upon.

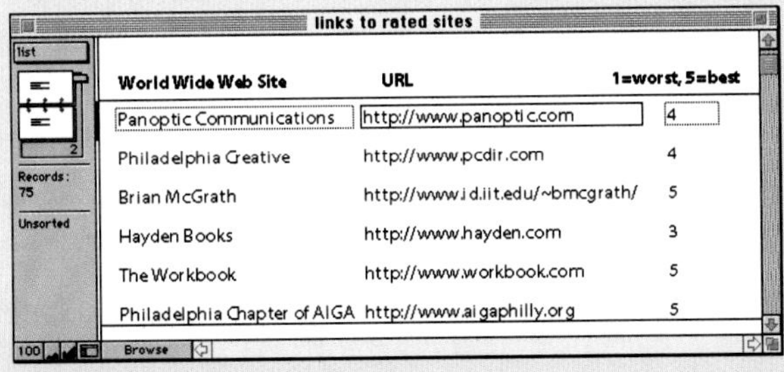

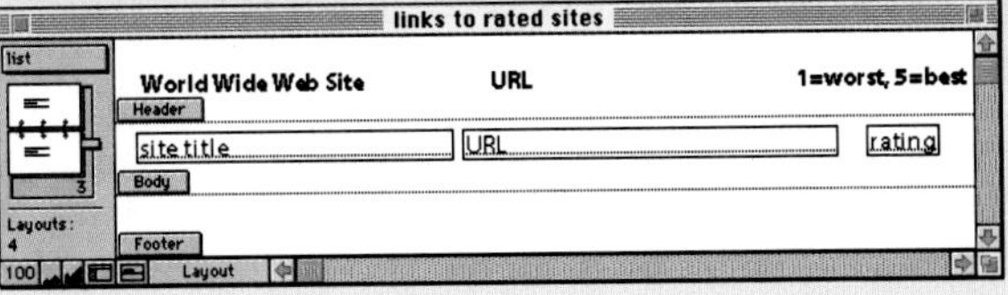

Figure 6.13

Here you see the design for the list (the layout) and the list with the data displayed (browsing). This list presents much more information at once, and the column headings avoid taking up space with repeating labels. The column heading for the ratings column doubles as a key to the ratings.

Databases on the Web

Most corporate sites have at least some sections of pages that are called *database-driven*. With tools made available by NetObjects Fusion, this capability does not have to be limited to sites with access to expensive consultants and specialized server software.

INTERESTINGLY, THE MOST SOPHISTICATED DATABASE SOLUTIONS ARE NOT ALWAYS THE MOST POWERFUL OR THE MOST EFFECTIVE. THE PROBLEM WITH ASSIGNING ALL TASKS THAT SEEM DATABASE RELATED TO SPECIALIZED PROFESSIONALS, WITHOUT BEING KNOWLEDGEABLE YOURSELF, IS THAT YOU SOMETIMES GET A SLEDGE HAMMER TO DRIVE A PUSHPIN.

There are two major ways to serve pages on the web based on database information. Both take values from a database, plug them into appropriate fields, combine them with layout elements, and translate the whole thing into HTML to be read by a web browser. The key difference between the two is when this takes place and who initiates it:

- Dynamically-built pages pull the data from the database and create HTML (or fill in blanks in HTML) upon a demand from a visitor at a site
- For static database pages, the Web publisher or author determines when the data is pulled from the database and the HTML created, these HTML pages then reside on a server and are browsed by visitors just like any other HTML pages.

THERE IS A THIRD WAY OF EXTRACTING DATA AND PUBLISHING IT WHERE NO ONGOING CONNECTION REMAINS BETWEEN THE TWO, AND WE CALL THIS DATABASE-ASSISTED PUBLISHING. IT ALSO CREATES STATIC HTML PAGES, BUT THEY CANNOT BE CALLED TRUE DATABASE PUBLISHING.

Dynamic pages must have a connection between the database and the web server. Stacked pages maintain a connection between the database and the web authoring application (NetObjects Fusion).

Dynamic Database Publishing

When you visit a search engine and enter your search criteria, you are taken to a page that displays the results of your search. A page such as this is built on-the-fly, and is called a dynamic page (Figure 6.14). It is parallel to the screen that you see when you ask a database application such as FileMaker to find records that contain a certain word in a particular field (Figure 6.15). When you are using the search engine, you are doing more than browsing on the web. You are entering a powerfully programmed

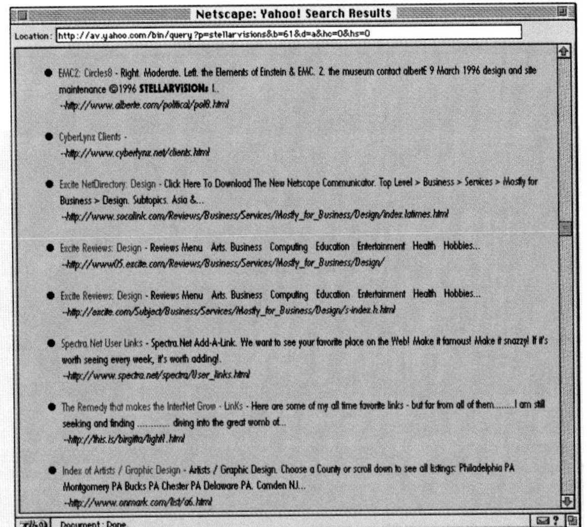

Figure 6.14

The results of a search at Yahoo!, where we were searching for STELLARVISIONs.

(and scripted) interface, and the process has more in common with using an application than passively viewing pages.

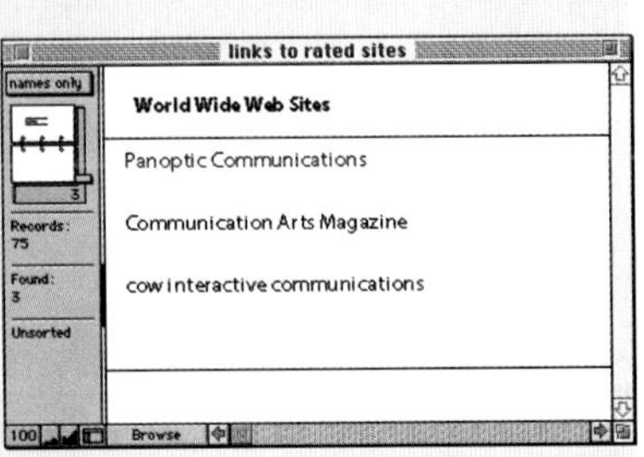

Figure 6.15

The results of a search in our database for the word "communication" in the site title field. You can see at the left that 3 records have been retrieved (Found) out of a total of 75.

The web is interactive by its nature, and subject to user control and decisions. With dynamically-built pages, the visitor's control extends beyond simply choosing what page to view next, into actually determining some aspects of the composition of that page. Does this mean the data is changed to fit the visitor? No, the data remains unchanged, but you pick and choose what data will be displayed.

If you go to a community college site and ask to see listings of Spanish courses held at night, the server will provide you will a listing based on searching those two fields. The layout and formatting of the page will (probably) remain the same no matter what the results of the query. But you, as the visitor, control which records are displayed (those that have a value of *Spanish* in the topic and evening in the class time). Because there would be no way to anticipate the exact combination of parameters of importance to each visitor, such pages could not be built in advance, but must be built on demand. If you have the capability to choose more than one field, you usually have a submission form to send a query to the database. This does not have to be the interface, however, you could simply choose from a list as you would to call up a conventional HTML page.

An example of a dynamic database on the web is the Philadelphia Creative Directory (PCD) Online. The PCD, in print form, holds over 6,000 listings of creative professionals and associated industries. When this was brought to the web, the designers at Panoptic Communications considered how they could best give easy access to these listings. In the printed book there are clear tabs for major divisions and headings for subsidiary divisions. This structure could have been followed using conventional HTML pages, but the visitor was given quicker access by using a dynamic interface. Of course even for the printed publication all of the entries were already in database form so it was logical to simply bring this to the web. Here radio buttons and pop-up choices are used so that a simple typing error or different phrasing of a category does not end in frustration (Figure 6.16). You are also able to enter the name of the creative professional or firm (if you know it) and bring up their listing immediately.

The positives of dynamic database publishing are:

- The capability to generate pages displaying a set of records that meet visitor-defined criteria
- Immediate access to relevant information from a submission form—no need to choose from multiple lists of topics
- The capability to search large databases for a specific item (such as a book by its title at www.amazon.com)
- When the database is updated with current information, that information is *immediately* available on the web

There are also drawbacks to this approach. We would love to give you the URL at amazon.com that sells this book, but the address is generated each time a visitor calls for a page. Therefore if you bookmark the page the browser remembers a long string like:

http://av.yahoo.com/bin/query?p=left-wingedduck&b=61 & d=a&hs=0

You cannot be sure this will work from a different browser or under different circumstances. Also, it can be frustrating to be faced with a submission form if you are not sure exactly what you are looking for, or how what you are looking for is spelled or expressed! The pop-up solution used

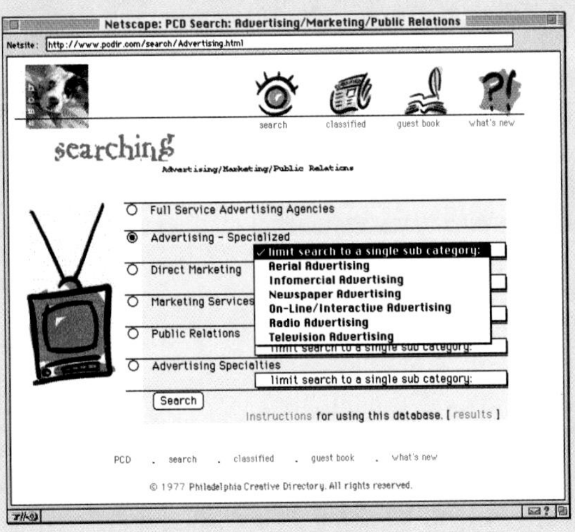

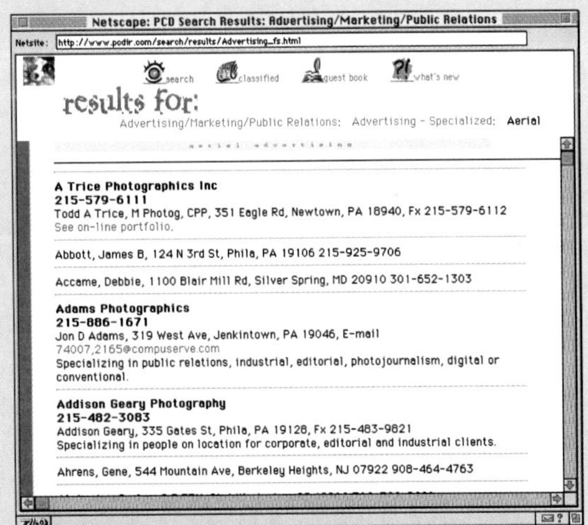

Figure 6.16

These pages are from the Philadelphia Creative Directory site_www.pcdir.com. First select a general category from the first page shown. You are then given the option of choosing any or all of the subcategorizes with radio buttons. You can even select a more specialized category using the pop-up menu, if you want to narrow your query. Finally you see the results of the search for aerial advertising (skywriting anyone?)

by PCD is only viable when you have a limited number of categories. Also, if you search for a specific entry you see it out of context.

The negative aspects of dynamic database publishing include:

- Specialized software and the involvement of database professionals is essential to make the system work
- The visitor must wait while the data is retrieved from the database and the page is built (much depends on the server and software delivering the pages and the complexity of the database)
- If you misspell or simply express a topic in different words than those known to the database, you will not have a successful result
- There is no true URL for the page that is generated.
- You cannot look at the context of the page you generate, to see what topics are near it that might be related (unless this is programmed in)

Dynamic database publishing is most effective where information is changing frequently, where the combination of variables required by a customer is unpredictable, where it is desirable to display multiple records at once and where resources are available to create a truly efficient delivery system with a well-designed interface and options.

Because specialized professionals will be involved when this kind of system is implemented, it is important that the interface issues be addressed from the beginning so that all work on the site is toward the same goal. Question assertions that have to do with the limitations of the existing database software. Remember that the database is a separate entity from the management software. Ask whether the data could be transferred to a more web-friendly or versatile system.

Static Database Pages on the Web

Many businesses are trying to get their print catalogs, or product description sheets available on the web. In these situations it is often desirable to display only one product on a page at a time, especially if a photo of the product is shown. This information changes occasionally—prices change, products are discontinued or added—but probably does not change on a daily basis. Obviously, building 50 catalog pages using traditional HTML is tedious, especially when it comes to revising them, or updating the look of the pages.

Because NetObjects Fusion generates new HTML each time a site is published, it is well-suited to periodic site updates. When you update your .nod file it does not magically update the live web site, that is only changed the next time you publish or manually FTP your files to the server. NetObjects Fusion provides a system, described in the next section, whereby you can either create a database internally within the application, or link to an existing database. Each time you re-publish the site, the data seen on the web is updated from the most current database.

From the point of view of the visitor to a site, this system has some advantages. The pages load just as any other HTML page would load. There is no waiting for a page to be built before it can be displayed. You can bookmark the page (although the page name is auto-generated and is something like Catalog 32).

A SITE USING STATIC DATABASE PAGES CAN PROVIDE A SEARCH ENGINE TO BRING A VISITOR DIRECTLY TO THE PAGE, IF DESIRED, BUT THE SEARCH ENGINE MERELY POINTS TO THE PAGE (IT DOES NOT BUILD A CUSTOM PAGE). ALSO, THE SEARCH ENGINE IS NOT PUTTING A QUERY TO THE DATABASE, AS HAPPENED IN THE DYNAMIC PAGES, IT IS SIMPLY SEARCHING THE SITE THE WAY ANY SITE SEARCH ENGINE DOES.

However, only one record is displayed per page (one product, one employee, and so on.) You cannot call up a long page with a series of records, and you cannot retrieve a custom group of pages that can be browsed as a unit (at least not without some tricky scripting). The fields that are displayed are set by the web designer, they cannot be customized upon viewer request. However, once you reach a page, you can see the preceding and following pages and get some idea of the context of the page (for example, other employees in the department).

There are some other limitations with the way NetObjects Fusion treats its stacked pages that may just be temporary limitations of the software. For example, you access the pages from a list on a contents page, and there cannot be multiple versions of that list (sorted differently) leading to the same pages.

Publishing Databases with NetObjects Fusion

By providing a dynamic connection between a database and the web authoring software, NetObjects has provided an incredibly powerful tool for small-scale database publishing. The system for publishing databases in NetObjects Fusion can be easily handled internally at a small business or communications firm. Although there are some serious limitations to this system, as it is currently implemented in NetObjects Fusion, it is still a wonderful boon to publishers.

IF YOU ARE INTERESTED IN OUR UNIQUE DATABASE-ASSISTED PUBLISHING SYSTEM, VISIT WWW.DESIGNPRACTICE.COM. IT CAN SAVE HOURS OF CUT AND PASTE IF YOU ARE NOT AFRAID OF DATABASES, SPREADSHEETS, OR APPLESCRIPT.

The information in the User Manual takes you step-by-step through the process of data publishing with NetObjects Fusion. Here, we will do the reverse and look at the results that are possible. It is important to start off with what you want the result to be and work backwards. Build and test a prototype before the database is complete (or even started). Consider all the decisions you make along the way and be sure they will permit the desired final outcome.

One Layout Creates an Entire Stack of Pages

Database publishing in NetObjects Fusion creates stacked pages. These are unlike any other kind of page in the application and are represented by a stack (Figure 6.17). There could be one or 100 pages in that stack, one for each record in the database. There is only one page name for the entire stack, the pages have no separate identity of their own.

When you go to the Page view for the stack you see one of the records displayed (Figure 6.18). There is no way to display the layout without showing the contents of a specific record; you cannot display the field names in their positions. The layouts for all the stacked pages are identical. If you change any aspect of this page (except the data itself) the change will immediately affect all pages in the stack. Really, when you go to a new stacked page in NetObjects Fusion you are not seeing a different page but merely calling up data from a different record to fill the fields.

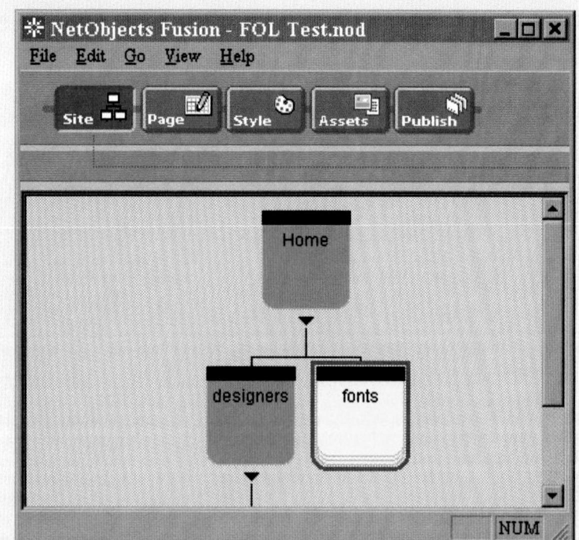

Figure 6.17

Stacked pages in the Site view.

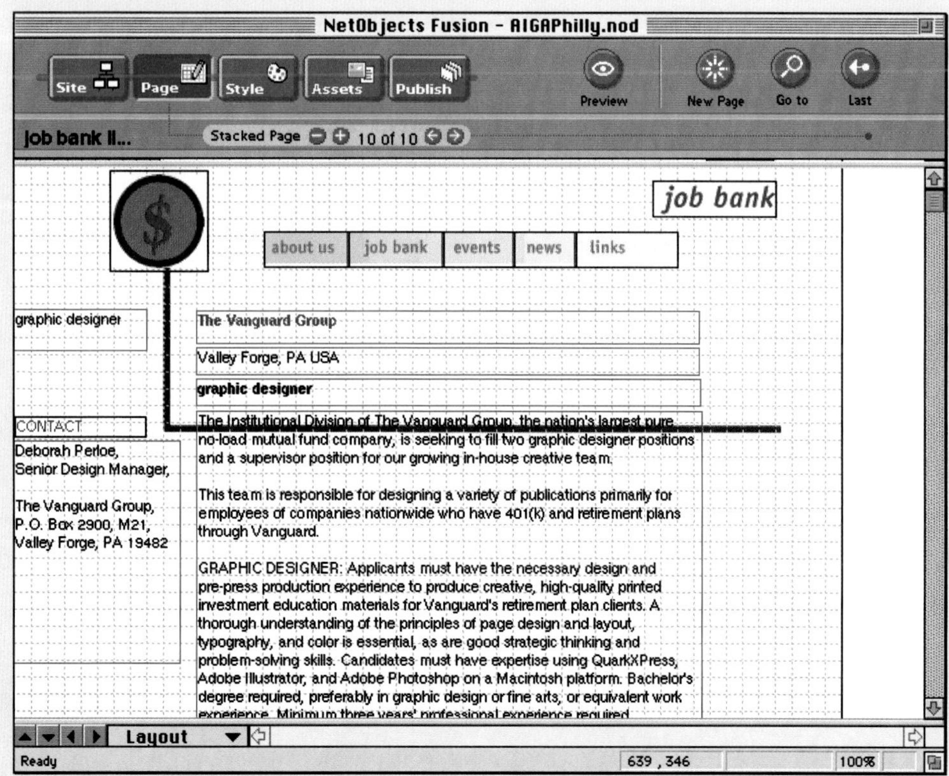

Figure 6.18

A stacked database page from the AIGAphilly.org site. The fields from the database are outlined in red. To navigate to other stacked pages you do not use the usual navigational devices but special arrows in the top submenu.

When HTML is generated and you browse, the pages are indeed separate pages. All the blanks have been filled in the publishing (staging or previewing) process. The HTML files have been named by adding a number to the name of the page stack (catalog_0.html, catalog_1.html, catalog_2.html, and so forth). You can page from one stacked page to the next (or previous) using an automatic smart link button. You cannot, however, link to an individual stacked page from a related part of the site unless you enter it as an external link to that filename.

The Table of Contents: The Data List

Figure 6.19
The Data List tool is selected here, and by default the internal source option from the submenu. Select the external source only to introduce a new external database.

Obviously there must be a way to access these stacked pages. NetObjects Fusion provides an automatically generated entry to these pages, a table of contents to your catalog, job listings, and so on. This is called a *data list*. Indeed, the way you initiate generating a stack of pages is to introduce a data list element to a page, and presto! There will be a stack of pages added as children of that page. Figure 6.19 shows the tool that adds the data list to the page. The submenu appears with internal and external sources. The internal (default) refers to any data object that is already included in the .nod file.

Figure 6.20 shows the data list for fontsOnline (or part of it!). However, as you can see in Figure 6.21 the list works well for short lists. You can format a list to have bullets, or not, borders, or not, and so on using the Properties Palette. For the bullets in the data list there is a separate image in the SiteStyle. These are different than the bullets used in text. In Chapter 8, "A Community Site," we discuss how this list was created and formatted to appear as it does (without borders or bullets).

HERE IS AN EXAMPLE OF THE BACKWARD-THINKING WE REFERRED TO EARLIER. IN THE JOB BANK FOR THE AIGA PHILADELPHIA SITE NONE OF THE FIELDS SEEMED APPROPRIATE FOR THE LIST. WE HAD TO GO BACK AND ADD A NEW FIELD IN THE DATABASE THAT WAS A BRIEF JOB TITLE JUST FOR THE PURPOSES OF THE LISTING ON THE OPENING PAGE.

In setting up a data list you must choose which fields you want to appear on this list (usually only one). If you do choose more than one, you can use the Up and Down arrows to reorder the fields for display.

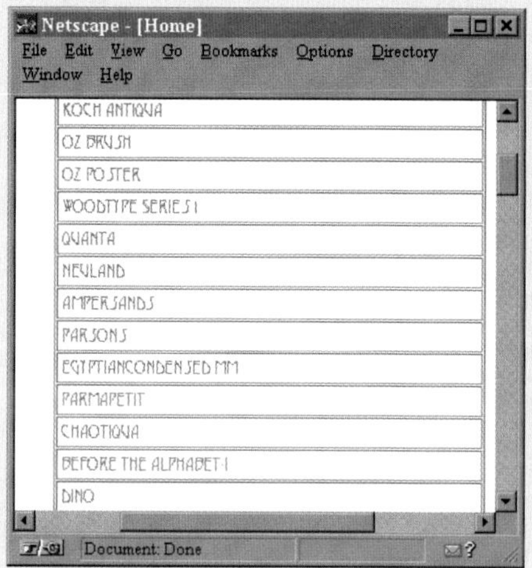

Figure 6.20
The data list generated for the fontsOnline site (see Chapter 9). There are 91 records in this database.

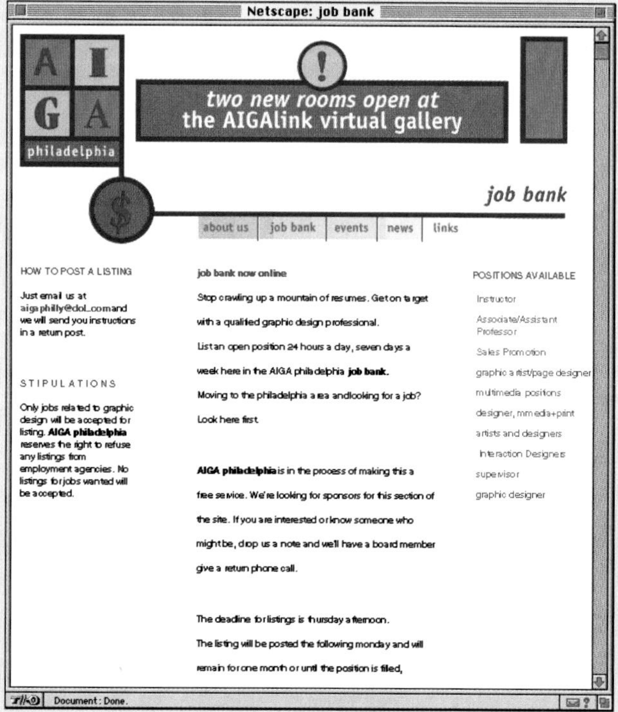

Figure 6.21
Chapter 8 discusses the building of these stacked pages. A data list does not need to take an entire page, here it is conveniently placed to the right beside the explanation of the job bank.

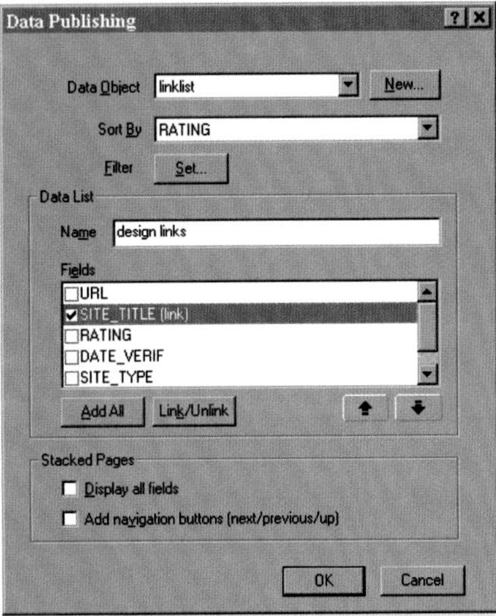

Figure 6.22
Here the Site Title is chosen to be listed, and it is a link (the word link should appear next to the field name). You can see the data is sorted by rating.

You must also choose by which field to sort the data. The sort field does not need to be the displayed field. The job listings, for example, might be listed with the most recent (or oldest) first. If you want to group by category you might have to add a new field that gives each category a number for correct sort order (that is, red=1, blue=2, green=3, and so on). You can almost always achieve the results you want if you are creative about adding useful fields in this way.

The default result of creating a data list, believe it or not, is that the listings are NOT links to the pages (the data list bullets beside them are). We strongly recommend that you always check the link option when you choose a field to be listed (see Figure 6.22). We really dislike lists on the web where the text is not a link.

You can choose to filter the data that will appear on the list that is essentially sending a query to the database (note the dialog box name in Figure 6.23). For example you can eliminate expired products (remember to enter an expiration date for each record). A filter could also be used to separate the 91 fonts into four pages (text, display, fonts, or script fonts). A list can be set up on four separate pages, each list filtering out all but the fonts that fall into that category. Unfortunately, the benefit of having just one layout has now been diluted because you will now have four stacks of pages using four layouts. These pages can share a MasterBorder, but to keep the internal arrangement identical, you must be sure to make all modifications to the four pages.

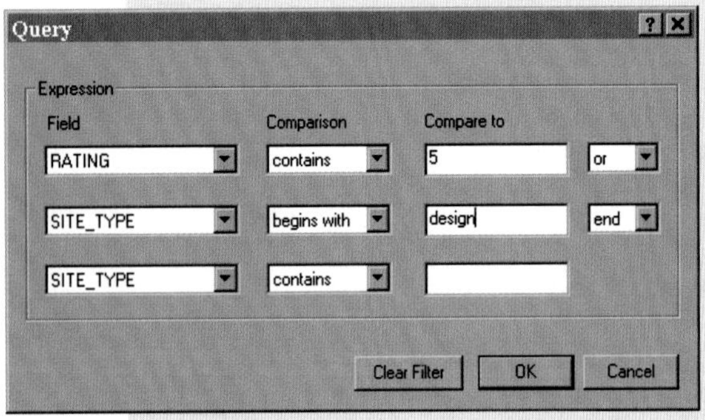

Figure 6.23
The filter dialog box. Here we want only sites that have a rating of 5 and are design resource sites.

Data Objects

Data objects are a collection of data fields. Basically this is the database, in the form that it has been brought into NetObjects Fusion. The data object gets its information from an internal database (you actually enter the data on the stacked pages) or from an external source. You cannot delete data objects from the .nod file. If you are conducting testing do not use the actual .nod file you will want to use later for production. Multiple data lists can draw upon data in the same data object (as we saw above). Also, data objects can contain variables that will not be displayed but be called upon in scripts associated with objects on the page (such as URLs for links).

External Data Objects

From the Windows version of NetObjects Fusion you can either link directly to a compatible database application (such as Microsoft Access) or you can export your database as .dbf and use that file as the external source. This is not available on the Macintosh platform, you can only build an internal data object. You can also use .tab or .csv files but the field names are lost, so it is confusing to set up your fields for sorting, and so on.

The export process is often seen as an irritating extra step, but in a way it can transfer some of the responsibility for the data to another department, or to your client. Suppose you are publishing a catalog. You agree with your client to update the pages every month. Perhaps you are on a Macintosh system and they are on a Windows system. No problem, the simply export the appropriate records as .dbf. They certify that any record they export and send to you is ready for web publication (correct prices, and so on) and they have done all the filtering and sorting.

AN INTERNAL DATA OBJECT USES THE STACKED PAGES IN NETOBJECTS FUSION AS THE INTERFACE TO ENTER THE DATA. THERE IS THE ADVANTAGE OF ONE LAYOUT CONTROLLING MANY PAGES, BUT THE STACKED PAGES ARE NOT EASY TO WORK IN AND ENTERING THE DATA IS TEDIOUS. WE USE OUR COMPAQ TO PRODUCE THE STACKED PAGES AND JOIN THEM TOGETHER WITH THE REST OF THE SITE THAT HAS BEEN PRODUCED ON THE MACINTOSH.

Variables

Variables are wonderful things, and apply to more than just stacked pages, check them out in the User Manual. The way they apply to database publishing is that you can call upon a field in the database as a variable in the Script dialog box. This is a bit hard to understand, and might be most clear through a specific example.

Suppose we were making stacked pages using the site titles from our earlier example of a database. We want these site titles to link to the external site, and we want to automate that process. Instead of placing the site title on the page as a data field you would do the following:

1. Draw a text box large enough to contain the longest title.
2. Click the script button to attach script to the element.
3. Open the reference by typing <A HREF=".
4. Click the variable button to bring up the Insert Variable box (see Figure 6.24.)
5. Choose Data Object from the Type pop-up menu. This will only be available on stacked pages from an external database.
6. Choose the URL as the variable (this will be entered as the destination of the A HREF.)
7. Close the quotes and brackets.
8. Insert the site title as a variable (this text will appear on the page in the browser and will be an active link.)
9. Close the reference by typing </A>.
10. Insert any formatting commands you want (see Figure 6.25).

You will not see any data on the stacked pages, but when you browse the generated HTML the correct site name will appear and it will be a live link.

You can do the same thing to bring images in if you don't have database software (compatible with NetObjects Fusion) that can handle images. Simply make a field in the database for the filename (there is an AppleScript on the CD that will generate a list, ready to insert into your database, from your filenames in Finder on the Mac). If the image is to be a link, also have a field for the destination URL. Then insert the variable as described previously choosing the image file name. You can insert the path to where your images are kept in the script dialog box.

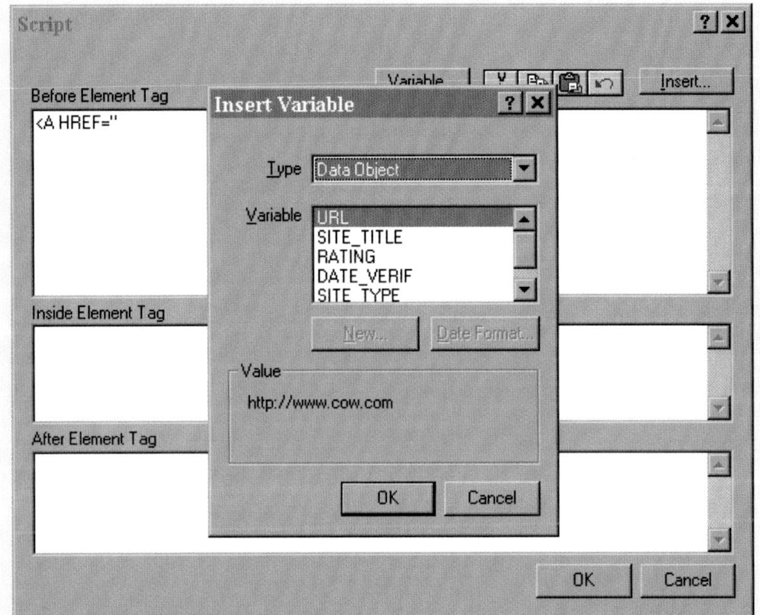

Figure 6.24
The Insert Variable dialog box where you choose Data Object and then see a list of fields that are available.

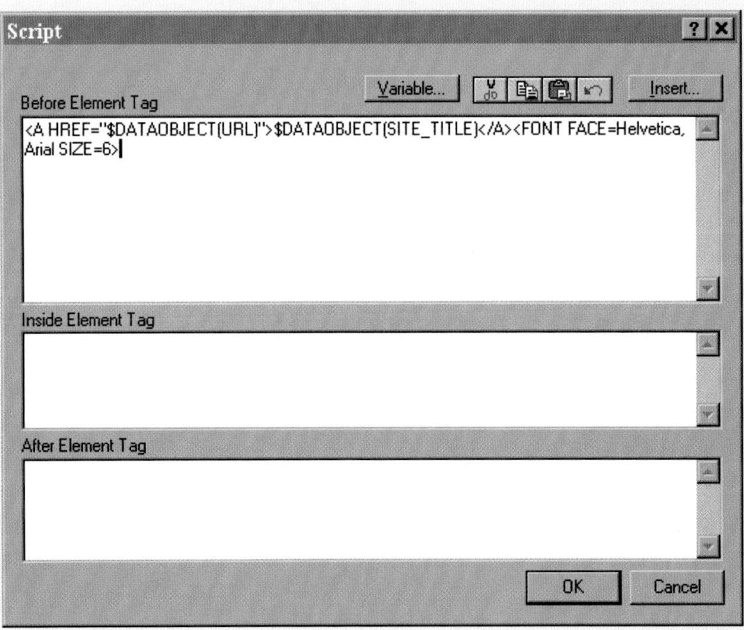

Figure 6.25
The Script dialog box, you can see the Variable button at the top of the box. Here we have entered code that calls will display the site title (in Helvetica or Arial) which will be a link to the URL.

7

Multimedia Enhancements

Figure 7.1
Multimedia can enhance a site in many ways. This icon is one option provided by NetObjects Fusion to point visitors to a video file.

bYte a tree productions began in 1994 as a multimedia studio, a new division of our established graphic design studio. We eagerly began creating interactive experiences that involved text, music, sound, animation, and video. As we were drawn into the web (so to speak) we applied what we had learned about user interfaces, navigation, and testing to building sites. Naturally, we also looked for places to show off our talents in other aspects of multimedia design, where appropriate.

The term *enhancement* is deliberately chosen, because it implies two things:

- Something is added, and the visitor's experience is enhanced by the addition
- The basic site exists and serves a purpose, with or without the enhancement

SOME INTERACTIVE EXPERIENCES, SUCH AS DYNAMICALLY SERVED DATABASE PAGES, ARE NOT CONSIDERED IN THIS CHAPTER BECAUSE THEY ARE A BASIC TECHNOLOGY THROUGH WHICH CONTENT OF THE SITE IS SERVED, NOT AN ENHANCEMENT.

Usually, discussion of multimedia is divided by the type of medium (sound, video) or by the type of technology used to deliver it (Shockwave, Java). Here we discuss the various purposes served by enhancements, and give a few examples, and then discuss the way that these enhancements are incorporated into NetObjects Fusion (Figure 7.1).

TYPES OF MULTIMEDIA ON THE WEB

Audio
- Music (mood music, sample clips, sound tracks)
- Sound Effects
- Voice (interview clips, voice over, narrative story)
- Radio on the Web

Video
- Live Action Footage
- Text, graphics and live images combined in video

Animation
- A series of still graphics that simulates motion
- A deliberately abrupt change in graphics

Interactivity
- Rollovers
- Forms
- Threaded Discussions, Chat Rooms
- Games, Contests, Surveys
- Virtual Reality
- Responsive access to information

Included in multimedia enhancements are audio, video, animation, and interactive elements (where the visitor's input makes a change to the appearance or content of the page). You can find current books that we recommend on incorporating multimedia in a site (some in this same *Killer Web Design* series) at www.designpractice.com. Also, our earlier book *Designing Multimedia Web Sites* goes into the topics of audio, video, animation, and interactivity in detail and gives some ideas about tools and techniques to create these enhancements.

One way in which the web is different from a printed catalog, brochure, or advertisement is that you can add sound and motion. The Web is different from television or video because the visitor can interact with what is happening on the screen. And although you can choose when to turn on your television, you cannot choose when Sunday Night at the Movies begins. A key attribute of the web (as with videos on tape) is that the content is available on demand, at your convenience. This is also true of those phone numbers you call that give you access to a voice-mail system of information on many topics—an example is the IRS information line. This is the kind of information-on-demand system that many commercial Web sites want to provide for their customers, but the web allows you to give much more dimension to the information you provide.

Figure 7.2 shows the medium of the web as primarily at the intersection of the two attributes of interactivity and the availability of on-demand content, with a small overlap with moving images (video and animation) and audio. There are many things left off this diagram, like CD-ROMs for example. It is not meant to be an exhaustive catalog of media, but simply to show where the web falls in terms of these attributes. Figure 7.3 breaks down the area covered by the web in more detail, again just showing some examples in each overlap.

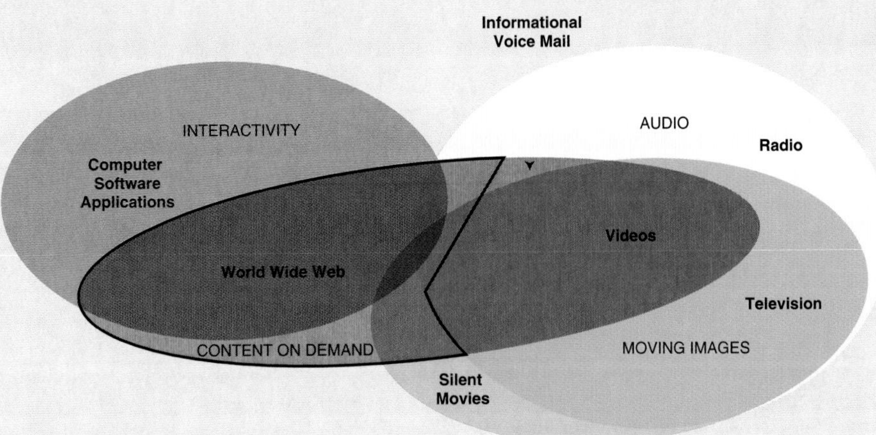

Figure 7.2

Here the four ovals represent four attributes of a medium: Interactivity, Audio, Moving Images (animation or video), and content on demand. A few examples of other media are shown as well. The area represented by the web is outlined in black (mostly, but not entirely interactive). The oval for content on demand is gray, which you don't see alone, but only mixed in with the other colors.

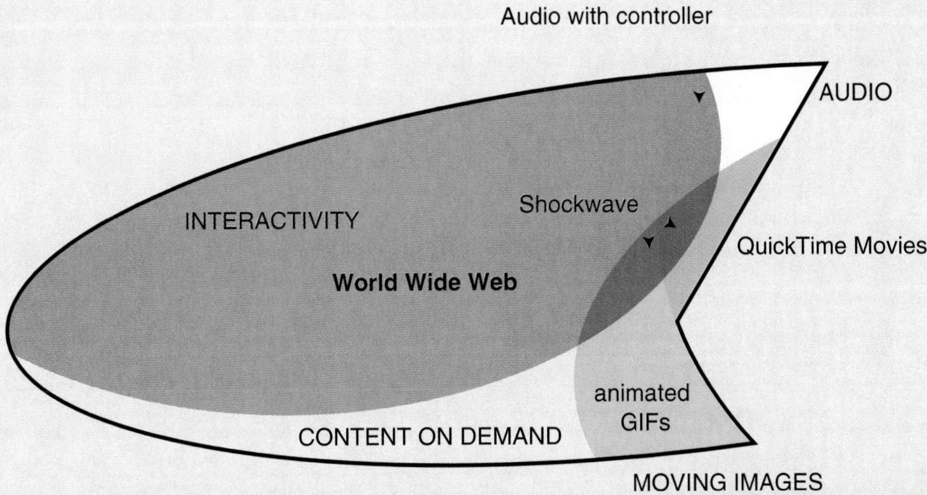

Figure 7.3

Here is a detail of just the web area (with the gray color deleted because it is all content on demand). Examples of a few technologies are positioned according to which attributes they involve: sound or motion (with or without interactivity).

How Can Multimedia Enhance a Site?

The following are the steps that we follow when introducing multimedia or other enhancements to a web site:

1. Clarify how the use of multimedia or other features will serve the goal of the site.
2. Choose where it should be introduced.
3. Decide what delivery system you will use to serve the multimedia element (Plug-ins, Java, JavaScript, and so on).
4. Design and build the enhancement.
5. Test and implement across different platforms and browsers.

These steps are not accomplished once and then over. Step one is constantly revisited each time someone has a *cool* idea for an enhancement to the site. The delivery system choice is put before the design and building because the choice of delivery system will usually affect how the piece is built. However, you may have a piece already built and decide to change your delivery system due to other considerations. Similarly the method of bringing the effect to the web has repercussions with regard to site goals—will the need for plug-ins turn off certain visitors?

Common web site objectives include:

- Providing information about products and services
- Delivering key messages, that is, we are international
- Increasing name recognition of the product or company
- Increasing customer involvement and connection to the product or company

In addition to these objectives, you have the goals of the web site design, which might be enhanced by adding multimedia:

- To direct visitors to particular promotional pages
- To delight and charm visitors so that the web spread-the-word phenomenon promotes traffic to the site

- To explain concepts effectively by involving the learner as more than a passive recipient

Use these lists as a starting point, make the points more specific to your site, and add additional points not included here.

Figure 7.4

At www.motorola.com, *these are three stages of the smooth opening and closing motion of the flip-phone.*

Providing Information

The ways in which companies have been accustomed to communicating information to their customers has been primarily through print with the occasional promotional video or informational voice mail. Television and radio commercials use other media to promote a product or service, but are not usually very informative. Reproducing a commercial online—unless it is an award-winning stunner—does not generally meet the *worth the bandwidth* test. The web is about information. The following sections are examples of ways in which sites can use multimedia enhancements to deliver more information.

Showing Additional Aspects of a Product

Suppose what you are trying to convey about your product simply does not come across in still images? At the Motorola site they show a flip phone opening and closing using a quick-loading animated GIF (Figure 7.4). The most compelling feature of the product is dramatically evident as you watch it open to reveal the controls, and close into a small smooth compact unit. At the Land Rover site, you can see all the different colors and external accessories for your chosen model, adding and changing them with a click. This is a really impressive example of interactivity using Java, where the image changes almost instantly without refreshing the entire photo (Figure 7.5).

Figure 7.5
This brilliant site by Adjacency allows you to visualize your custom vehicle in the Outfit Your Land Rover section.

When the Product is Media

A flip-phone is an example of a physical product where adding another dimension (motion) does a better job of presenting the product. What about something even more obvious like a music CD or a movie? There are really great examples of audio and video online at the music label and Hollywood studio web sites. A visitor can sample the merchandise before buying it.

A more specialized group of sites are those where the information is the product, as is the case in journalism. Interview clips (audio and/or video) of world leaders making significant anouncements are popular. Here the on demand aspect of the web is significant: a major event occurs but you have missed the news, you can just go on the web read the stories and see or hear the video and sound bytes! These are generally options, so that those with smaller bandwidth connections read the print and skip the multimedia experience.

The Web is a gathering place for those who share a particular passion or interest. They frequent sites that give current information that is relevant to them, but is not carried on the nightly news. For example, the latest announcements from MacWorld are always online, with

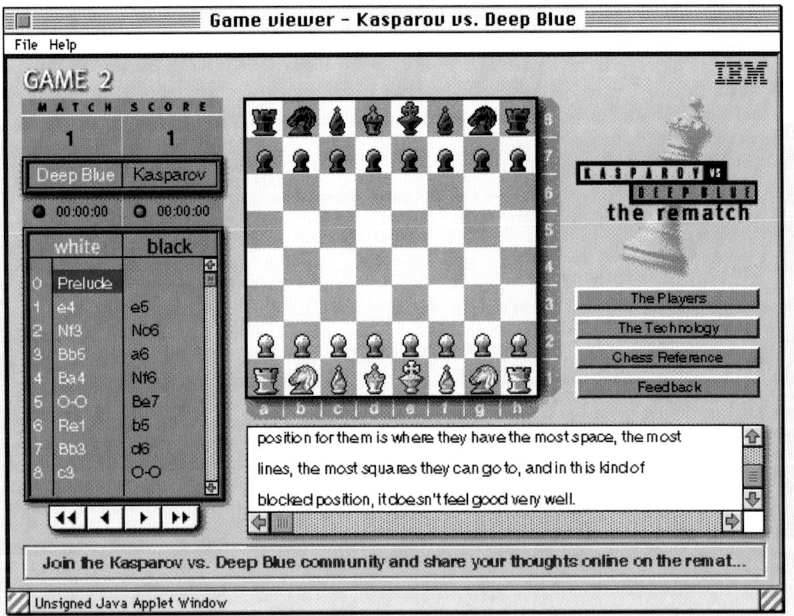

www.chess.ibm.com

Figure 7.6

This Java Applet, the Game Viewer, allows visitors to see the position of the pieces at any point in the game, and to read commentary by chess experts (that was given live during the match).

the option of live feed video for significant events. The Kasparov versus Deep Blue chess match was followed by millions of people, visiting the IBM site or chess club sites. IBM provided many enhanced ways of seeing the information: live feed of moves, the capability to replay the moves and see commentary, and photos updated every 30 minutes (Figure 7.6).

Conveying Concepts, Teaching

Often sites attempt to educate visitors in some way, either as a public service (or to increase traffic to the site), or to create more demand for their product or service. Some concepts are difficult to convey in static images and text, and there is a body of research that shows that the more senses involved in learning the more likely it is that the information will stick. Font designer Brian Sooy created an interactive slider to explain how multiple master fonts function (Figure 7.7).

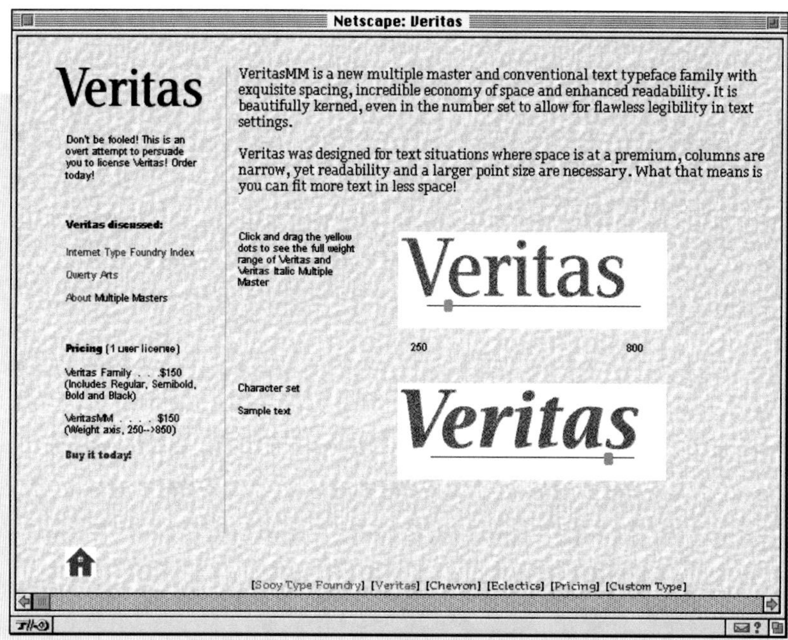

Figure 7.7 *You click the yellow dot and drag it to see the full range of weight of Veritas MM (font designed by Brian Sooy).*

Sometimes complex charts and graphs can be made more understandable through the addition of interactivity or motion. This is a challenge for the information architect—the enhancement is almost as likely to be a distraction as a clarification, but in some situations it can be helpful. If you have a map with many overlays, for example, it can be helpful to add the overlays one at a time and take in each piece of information before comparing it with another. Voice-over can also be useful in explaining a process or concept.

Animate Key Messages

Often there are one or two messages that a client feels are key to get across to an audience. They may be key because they represent a change (Now available for Macintosh!), because they contradict assumptions (or suspicions) visitors might hold (No hidden charges), or they may simply be the central message. Adding some multimedia elements to the message can help draw attention or generate surprise.

A Text Message

Many web publishers despair when they learn through experience that putting words on a page does not guarantee that they will be read. Animated text, however, demands the eye's attention. It must be paced correctly—not too fast to read, and not too slow to lose attention. Words can be much larger onscreen if they follow one another in the same space than if they all had to share the space simultaneously. The Philadelphia Creative Directory, when it came onto the web, announced on the splash screen "The most comprehensive directory of creative services in Pennsylvania, Delaware, and New Jersey, now available around the world." Figure 7.8 shows how large we can make the type in the Flash animation, later the letters circle around for the last phrase. For those who do not have the relatively new Flash plug-in, JavaScript detects this and serves them a slightly simpler animated GIF.

Figure 7.8
The splashy opening to the Philadelphia Creative Directory Web site www.pcdir.com. *Site design by Panoptic Communications, animation by bYte a tree productions multimedia.*

Increasing Name Recognition

Probably the most popular (and overused) multimedia element is the animated logo. Here the message is simple and often repeated, "Acme Advertising, Acme Advertising, Acme Advertising." It will be interesting when there are results of research, as the web ages, to see if all these distracting spinning and jumping logos actually accomplish their goal. Our preference is to accomplish an interesting entrance for the logo, preferably on the splash screen that is only visited once. After it has been introduced, we retire it to a static presence in the same location on every page (usually also a link to the core page). For example the heavy type Anvil Systems (shown in Figure 7.9) drops in from above and lands with a definite thunk sound and slight vibration before sitting peacefully from then on.

Guide Visitor Within the Site

Roll-over highlight buttons are increasingly popular on the web. NetObjects Fusion has a convenient component, DynaButtons, that uses a Java Applet to swap the highlighted button for the standard button in a navigation bar. Even more valuable is a roll-over where additional information about the destination is provided so that the visitor can consider whether or not to click and travel to the next page. This permits you to have blocks of explanatory text when needed, but only one block of text shows at once that helps keep an uncluttered page. At the site for Anvil Systems the reverse is true, instead of rolling over an icon and getting words, you roll over text and get an illustration (Figure 7.9).

Navigational aids do not need to be neutral, they can steer you toward pages at the site that are particularly important (items on sale, recent news, and so on.) In Chapter 3, "Web Page Design," we discussed how using a metaphor can help visitors understand a navigational system. Sounds

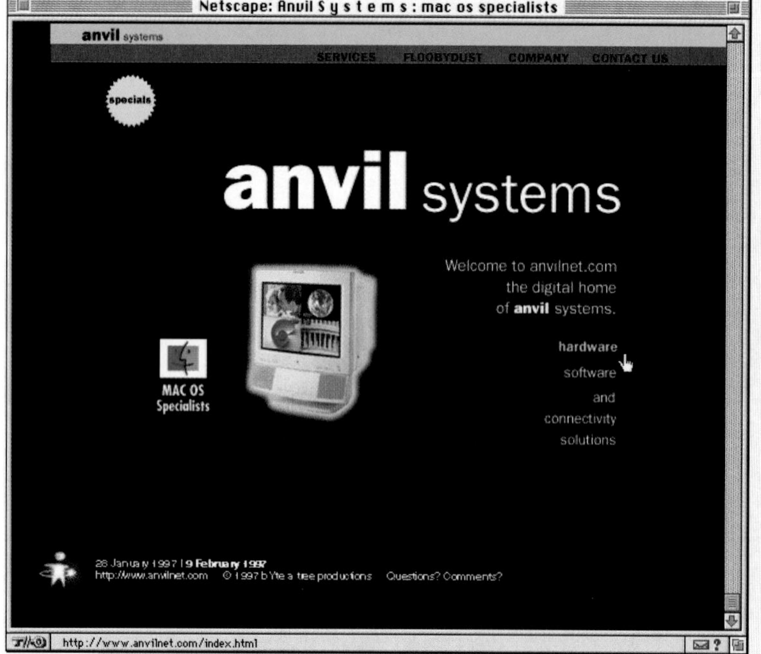

Figure 7.9

A JavaScript controls the rollover at www.anvilnet.com. *Here an illustration appears when the mouse is over the word networking. The logo drops in from above with a thunk, and then the word systems appears.*

and animations can help support the metaphor that you are using. The illusion that you have pushed something is supported by the shadows on the image changing, and by the sound of a click.

Developing a Connection

As we have discussed many places in this book, the web is a personal experience, visitors to a site want to feel part of things, and you want them to leave in a glow of positive feeling. Anything that enhances the experience or involves the visitor in a significant way contributes to this effect.

Enhancing the Experience

At Sotheby's (www.sotheby.com) you can go to catalogs of past shows and go, for example, to the Einstein Manuscripts. As you look at the pages you begin to hear classical music in the background (a quickly downloaded MIDI file). At www.cow.com, the wooden blocks come apart and reform into various forms in a delightful manner. Think of your favorite sites, and the impressions they made on you during your first visit. Often multimedia enhancements contribute to that impression.

Visitor Involvement

It is one thing to give experiences to a visitor, it is another to accept input in return. Forms for feedback, discussion threads, games, surveys, contests—all of these are popular at web sites. The capability of a visitor to make a contribution to the site is a powerful force for forming a connection.

The absolute minimum requirement is a form that enables visitors to tell you what they think: of your product, site, and your company. Set up automatic acknowledgments of email so that there is an immediate response. Be sure that resources are allocated to allow individual responses to the mail as appropriate. NetObjects Fusion, and some help from the professional configuring your server, make forms extremely easy. The best

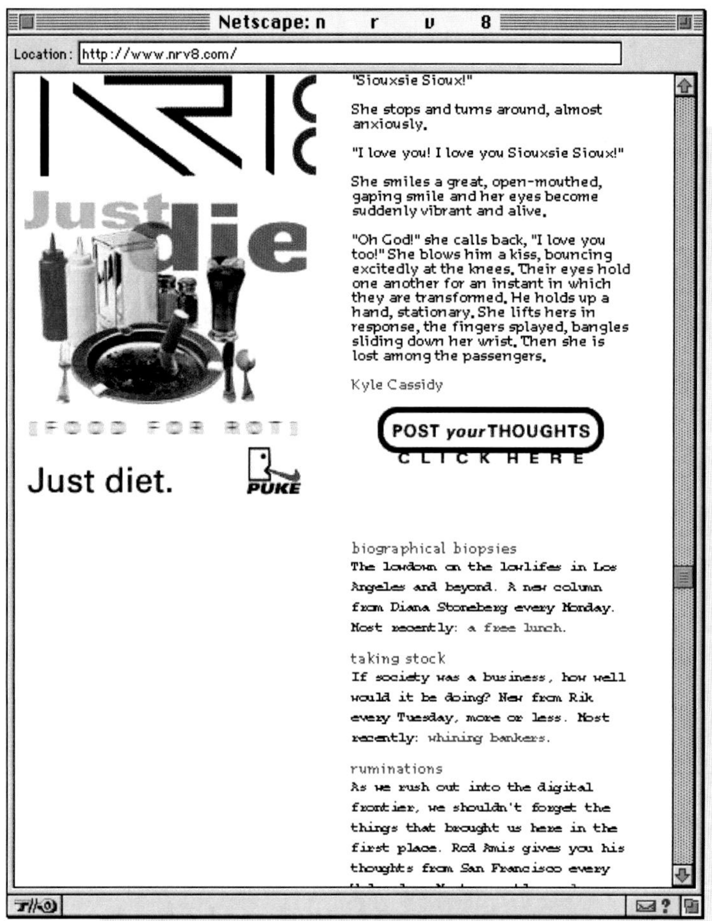

Figure 7.10
www.nrv8.com. *The article text is in a narrow scrolling column on the right (a frame) and at the bottom of the article is the section "Give us your thoughts".*

aspect of creating forms in this application is that you can design an interface for the form that matches your specific needs and works with the rest of your site. Often forms are the worst looking pages at an otherwise well-designed site, and if they are confusing or frustrating it is even worse.

Threaded discussions allow a true contribution from a visitor, they can return and see that their contributions have become a part of the site. At the site www.nrv8.com, each article invites feedback from readers (Figure 7.10). NetObjects Fusion has a built-in component that enables you to put up a BBS (bulletin board), and once more gives you full control over the look and feel of the interface. Figure 7.11 shows an example of a discussion area that uses the NetObjects Fusion BBS component.

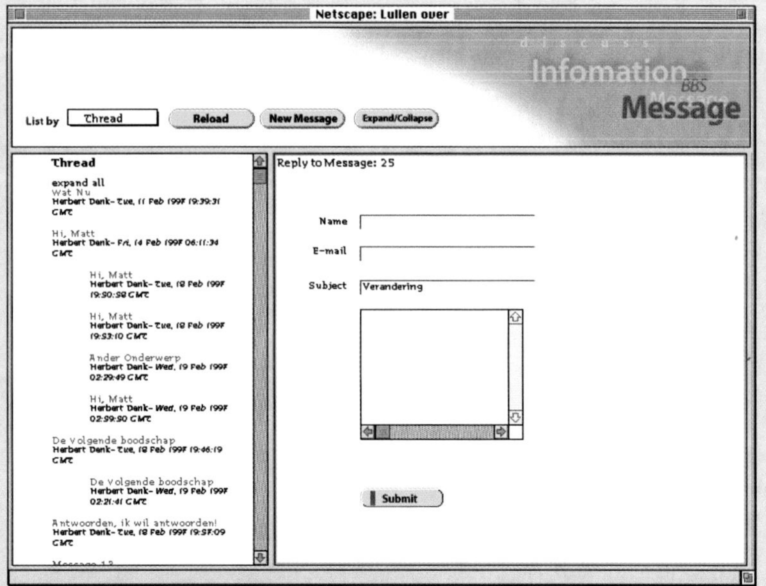

Figure 7.11

This is an implementation of NetObjects Fusion's BBS feature by Herbert Denk. In the left frame you choose which thread to read, and the messages appear in the right frame. When you wish to reply a form appears to submit your message.

Incorporating Multimedia with NetObjects Fusion

As you know, NetObjects Fusion retains the information about what objects you want placed where, and various attributes of the objects (links, colors, sizes, scripts). When you are ready to see the pages in a browser, the application generates the HTML to serve the pages you have designed. For the most part, multimedia enhancements (unlike text and images) cannot be seen (or heard) in the NetObjects Fusion interface, you only experience them through the browser.

The ways in which various browsers handle various kinds of media is a patchwork of plug-ins, built-in features, and helper applications. Even if a product is available there is no guarantee that your visitor is using it, or how they have instructed their browser to handle files such as PDF, WAV, and so on. Therefore, pity the developers at NetObjects, the only thing they can do is bring the files into the HTML in a manner that is most likely to work. As a publisher of multimedia you must be aware of how the elements work in the HTML and what attributes must be set—is the <EMBED> element used (or <OBJECT> for Explorer) or is it a simple <A HREF> that points to the file? Above all test the pages on multiple platforms, with older browsers, browsers lacking plug-ins, and so forth. You are trying to enhance the visitor's experience, not create a nightmare of broken puzzle pieces or blank pages.

There are several tools in the palette that are relevant to incorporating multimedia or other effects. If you understand the HTML, you can incorporate almost any type of media, including those developed since the release of the latest NetObjects Fusion. For example, the Shockwave tool simply puts the file into an <EMBED> tag. You can use this for other media that you want to insert using <EMBED> such as the new Flash animation.

JAVASCRIPT TO PROTECT THE INNOCENT

YOU CAN WRITE SCRIPTS THAT WILL SERVE YOUR ENHANCEMENT ONLY TO CERTAIN POPULATIONS, FOR EXAMPLE, TO THOSE VISITORS THAT HAVE NETSCAPE 3.0 WITH THE CORRECT PLUG-IN. ALL OTHER VISITORS WILL RECEIVE THE REPLACEMENT, USUALLY A STILL OR ANIMATED GIF. YOU CAN FIND EXAMPLES OF THESE SCRIPTS AT WWW.DESIGNPRACTICE.COM THE FIRST PORTION OF THE SCRIPT IS GENERAL AND SHOULD RESIDE IN THE HEAD ELEMENT, INSERTED IT AS A LAYOUT SCRIPT IN NETOBJECTS FUSION. IT CONTAINS NO INFORMATION SPECIFIC TO THE FILES YOU ARE USING. THEN WHERE YOU INSERT YOUR MULTIMEDIA YOU WILL INSERT ADDITIONAL SCRIPT REFERRING BACK TO THE FIRST!

Animated GIF files—place in Page view as an image
- motion without audio or interactivity
- can be seen by older browsers, no plug-in needed

Shockwave files—use Rich Media Shockwave Tool
- audio, animation and interactivity
- embedded file must be read by special plug-in

QuickTime movies—on Mac use QuickTime Tool (on Windows use Rich Media Video Tool)
- audio and video (or an animated sequence)
- viewer can start and stop by clicking

Active X—on Windows use Active X tool
- extensive effects including audio and video
- is not available for Macintosh platform

Java—use Java Tool
- extensive effects available, especially interactivity
- requires recent browser

Audio Files—use Rich Media Audio Tool
- All have plug-ins, some come built into browsers
- Real Audio requires special server configuration, does not work inline
- NetObjects Fusion also supports: .WAV, .AU, .AIFF and .MIDI

Video Files—use Rich Media Video Tool
- NetObjects Fusion supports .MOV, .MPG, .MPEG, .AVI
- All have plug-ins, some come built into browsers

JavaScript—insert into script dialog boxes
especially useful for controlling window size
can detect the presence of plug-ins
can receive keystroke input from visitors

This chapter will not take you through the palettes and choices for every type of media or component, it is not meant to replace the function of the User Guide. In general, the NetObjects Fusion interface attempts to do as much of the work for you as is possible.

Rich Media

This puzzle piece tool implies exactly what it is, a way to call upon Netscape Plug-ins. The secondary tools that appear when you select the Rich Media Tool are shown in Figure 7.12, and handle sound, video and Shockwave. It is a good idea to add script to any of these elements to hide them from visitors that do not have the plug-in, perhaps providing a still image instead. We have given you a bit of script that might be helpful. It is much more welcoming to let visitors know that enhancements are available and where to get the plug-ins, but still allow them to view the pages without the enhancements.

Figure 7.12
The Rich Media Secondary Tools, audio, video and Shockwave (from left to right, shown on the Windows Platform).

Figure 7.13 shows the Properties palette with the sound tab showing and there is a similar tab for video. Here you designate the visual that will appear on the page and activate the sound. If you designate a graphic that will appear on the page (one of the supplied icons or your own) that graphic will activate the sound or movie (the browser is pointed toward it using an <A HREF> element). What happens when the file is activated depends on the configuration of the browser—the file downloads or a new window appears, displays the file or controller.

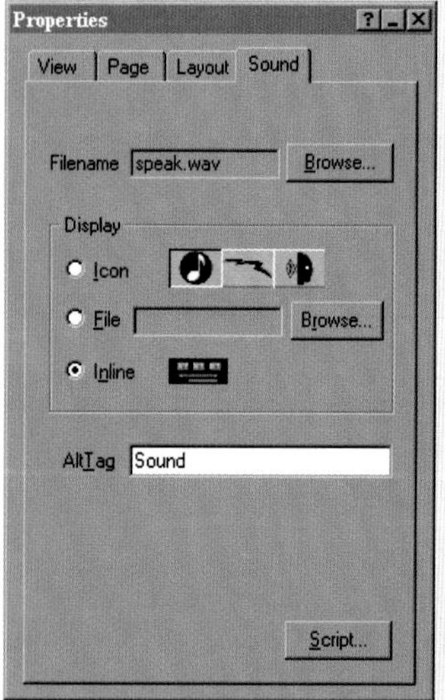

Figure 7.13
The Sound tab of the Properties palette, choosing inline uses the <EMBED> element.

REAL AUDIO CANNOT BE INSERTED USING THE INLINE OPTION.

If you choose the Inline option then the <EMBED> element is used and, if the browser will support it, the file will be played directly in the browser window. Be aware that the width and height of the graphic in NetObjects Fusion will supply the width and height parameters. The software cannot read the height and width automatically as it can with GIF and JPEG images, and you cannot simply add height and width parameters in the script dialog box. The easiest thing to do is to watch the width and height numbers that NetObjects Fusion displays for objects in the lower-left of the window and make these exactly the size of your element (Figure 7.14).

If you are going to set additional parameters in the script dialog box, check a sample HTML file that NetObjects Fusion generates to see what parameters are already set. For example, for Shockwave .DCR files the application inserts the parameter PALETTE=background (a good choice). Figure 7.15 shows a the script we added to the QuickTime movie that removes the controller (the visitor can be instructed that a click will stop and restart the movie), starts the movie automatically, and loops it continuously.

A great improvement over the 1.0 version of NetObjects Fusion is that they have a way for you to quickly

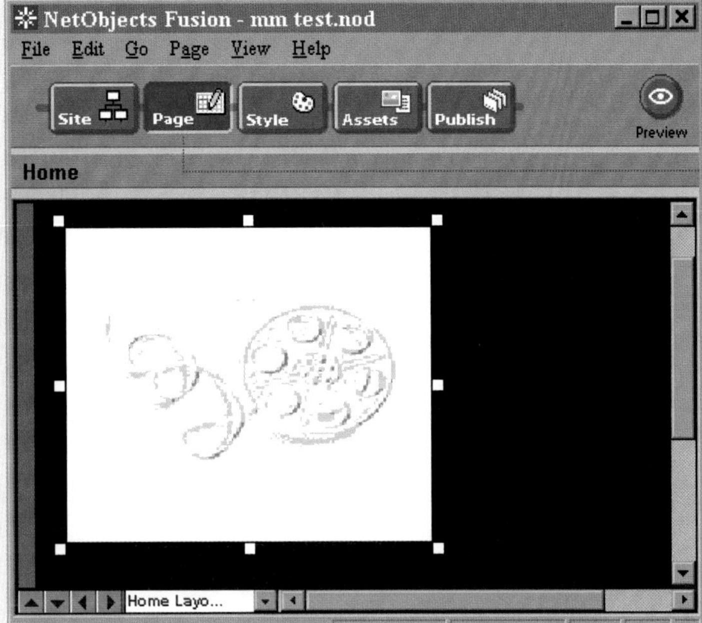

Figure 7.14

Here a QuickTime movie is placed on the page(Windows platform) using the Rich Media Video tool. The Inline option is checked and the graphic is made exactly 240 pixels wide and 202 pixels deep (the middle set of figures at the bottom of the window).

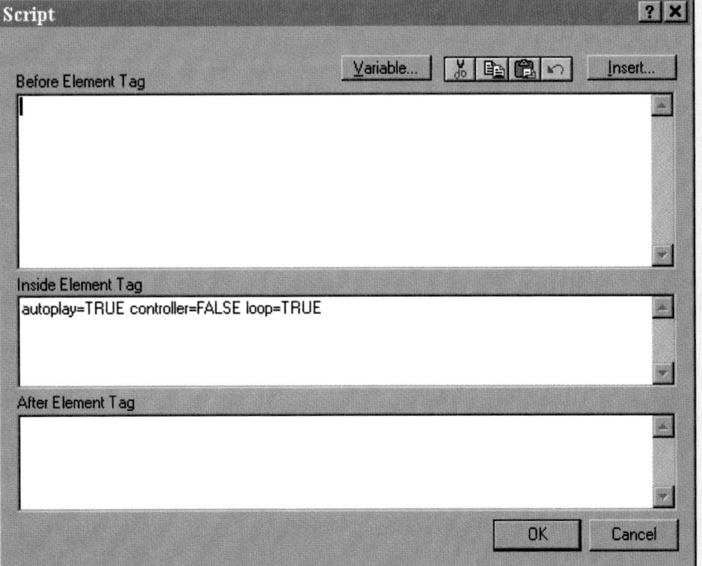

Figure 7.15

Additional parameters are inserted for a QuickTime movie. If we did not specify these parameters the default setting would obtain (no autoplay, showing the controller, and no looping).

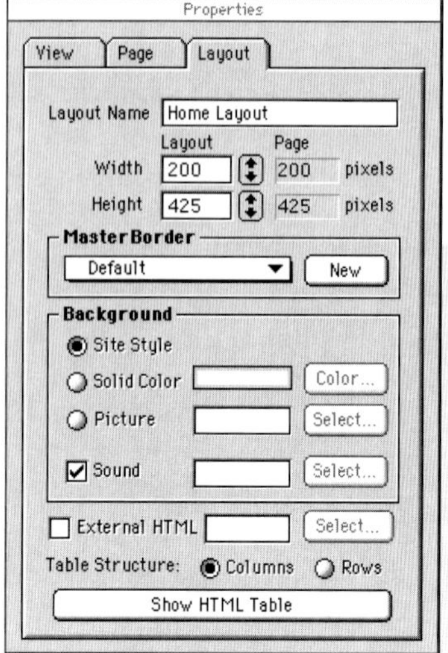

Figure 7.16
When you select a Background Sound from the Layout tab of the Properties Palette you are asked to select the file and to indicate whether you want it to loop.

insert a background sound. For this you do not use the rich media tool, the background sound is considered part of the layout (like a background image). Figure 7.17 shows the Layout palette and the option to select Continuous Loop or not. Note that unless you have chosen to optimize your HTML to work with Internet Explorer the <BGSOUND> element will not be inserted, only the <EMBED> that is preferred by Netscape.

ONE DIFFERENCE BETWEEN THE MACINTOSH AND WINDOWS PLATFORMS IS THE TOOL TO THE RIGHT OF THE JAVA TOOL. ON WINDOWS IT IS THE ACTIVEX TOOL (TO ADD ACTIVEX COMPONENTS) AND ON THE MACINTOSH PLATFORM IT IS A QUICKTIME TOOL.

Components, Java and ActiveX

The architecture of NetObjects Fusion allows for expansion to incorporate various enhancements as the technology becomes available. There are separate tools for inserting Java Applets and (on Windows) ActiveX elements. The real room for expansion is in the nfx components.

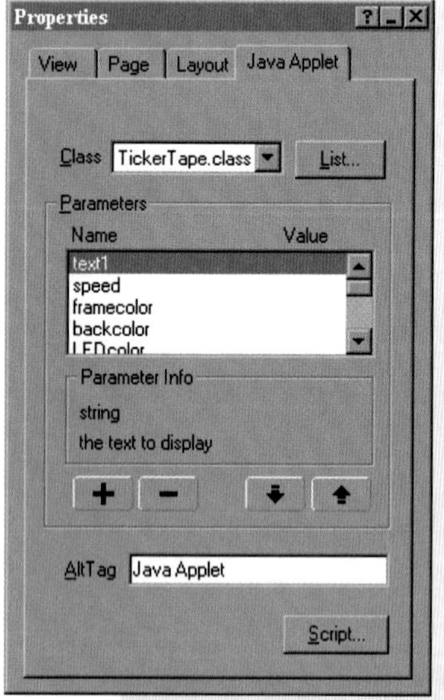

Figure 7.17
The Java Applet tab when the TickerTape.class that comes with NetObjects Fusion has been placed on a page. Here you can edit and add parameters to customize your Applet.

Java and ActiveX

These two elements work similarly in terms of the NetObjects Fusion interface. Figure 7.17 shows the Java Applet tab of the Properties palette where you can easily edit parameters without fear of accidentally corrupting the Java code.

There are substantial differences between Java and ActiveX that are beyond the scope of this book. ActiveX is not cross-platform (Windows only) and it does not have the same limitations as Java in terms of not being able to affect the user's hard disk.

nfx Components

Figure 7.19
The nfx components secondary tools.

Here the door is wide open for developers to provide packages that will enhance web sites that work directly with NetObjects Fusion. Figure 7.17 shows the secondary tools that appear under when the nfx tool is selected. Note that the first tool brings up a list of installed components (which are evidently not popular enough to rate their own buttons). We mentioned the Message Board BBS component and DynaButtons earlier in this chapter. The other components that shipped with version 2.0 (Windows) are:

- Rotating Picture
- Picture Loader
- Time Based Picture
- Ticker Tape
- SiteMapper
- AutoForm

part 3

the practice

case studies

The chapters that follow will take you through the process that was involved in designing and implementing three sites. In Part 1, you reviewed the ideal world of the design process in theory and now the theory will be brought to the real world. You will see where we deviate from the golden rules and you can judge the results for yourselves. We will highlight, however, the way in which referring back to DADI and other principles avoided certain pitfalls and helped solve thorny design problems.

Part 2 examined the strengths of NetObjects Fusion as a tool to facilitate the design process—now you will see some examples of the role the application plays in the building of a specific site. This will not be a step-by-step description of the entire design or implementation process; rather, we will describe in detail one or two areas where NetObjects Fusion was helpful in meeting a specific challenge.

The sites that follow represent a variety in terms of the client, the purpose of the site, the nature of the site content, and the unique design issues presented. The case studies include a volunteer effort for a non-profit group, a site selling fonts on the Web, and a site to promote a small business.

UPDATES

VISIT OUR WEB SITE FOR
THE LATEST ADDITIONS
DESIGNPRACTICE.COM

8

A Community Site:

AIGAphilly.org

THE MISSION OF THE AIGA IS TO ADVANCE EXCELLENCE IN GRAPHIC DESIGN AS A DISCIPLINE, PROFESSION, AND CULTURAL FORCE.

The first site we build in NetObjects Fusion, www.AIGAphilly.org, was part of a volunteer effort. This situation is unique in that busy professionals were giving their time and there was no rigid hierarchy of decision-making. This example, however, reinforces the fact that although the client may be your own company or group, the design process is the same. For each case study, we will begin by introducing the clients, especially what sets them apart from similar companies or organizations.

The AIGA, American Institute of Graphic Arts, is a national non-profit organization that promotes excellence in graphic design. Founded in 1914, the AIGA advances the graphic design profession through competitions, exhibitions, publications, professional seminars, educational activities, and projects in the public interest.

Figure 8.1
Our first online community effort, AIGAlink. This packet was sent to the membership inviting participation in a virtual environment.

When the national organization began to have local chapters in 1981, AIGA Philadelphia was the first to be recognized (there are now 37 chapters). They were also the first to attempt to connect their chapter members online (Figure 8.1). The Philadelphia chapter serves an area radiating out from Philadelphia east into most of southern New Jersey, toward Pittsburgh, and south into Delaware.

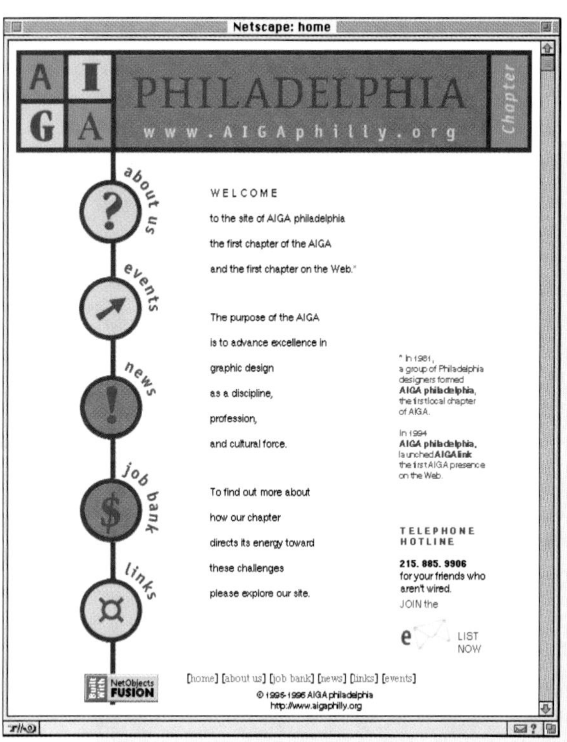

Figure 8.2
Visit www.AIGAphilly.org before reading this chapter to get the full flabor of the story.

Anyone who joins the national organization is assigned to a local chapter and part of his or her dues support that chapter. As one would imagine, the largest body of active members who can attend events generally come from within an hour radius of the city.

The chapter is active with a calendar of yearly events including its acclaimed Dialogues on Design series, an auction, a holiday sale, and membership meetings. In the past, members communicated through newsletters, special mailings to announce events or request Board nominations, and a telephone hotline. The recorded information on the hotline was formerly the only place for non-members to get information about the chapter. The chapter doesn't have physical office space or any paid staff. There is a president (one-year term), a long-suffering treasurer, and an Executive Board that emerges from a nomination and confirmation process. Standing committees, address concerns such as the environment, design education, design practice, and technology. Due to the nature of volunteer organizations, these committees tend to cycle through periods of activity and periods of dormancy, but the Board keeps them as standing committees, so there is a mechanism for interested parties to contribute whenever someone with energy and enthusiasm appears. You can see the results of our enthusiasm at www.AIGAphilly.org (Figure 8.2).

Definition: Ear, Voice, Community

In the fall of 1993, I was trying to interest my fellow AIGA members in electronic communication. This interest fit with the chapter's desire to reach out to members who are distant geographically and to involve more members in a dialog with the leadership of the chapter. Therefore, I was assigned to create a new committee to explore the use of technology as a means to build a community.

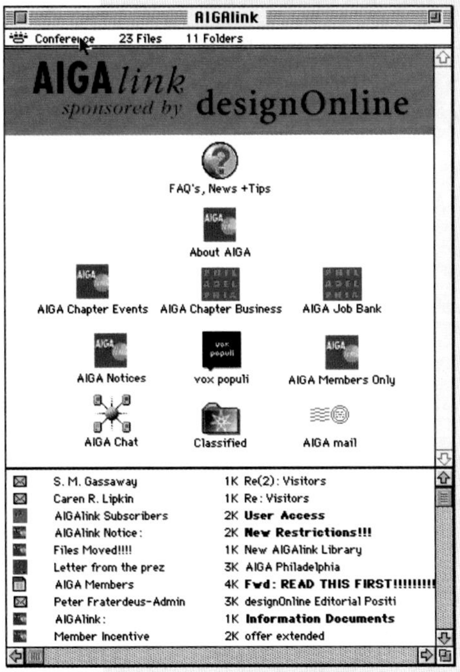

Our journey of exploration led to a Bulletin Board (BBS) conference called AIGAlink (Figure 8.3). The first web pages we put up in January 1995 were under the banner AIGAlink, because they were an outgrowth of the BBS and had a national rather than local audience. Therefore, information about the AIGA in general had greater prominence than chapter information; there was no national AIGA web presence at the time. Once again, we seemed to be getting national attention (and press) but were not able to get information from the relevant committees to post event information in advance. We were hampered by the slow adoption of this new communication technology by designers. In early 1995, the number of email addresses among chapter members was minuscule—"Can I fax it to you?"

Figure 8.3
The First Class Bulletin Board Conference set up on DesignOnline for AIGAlink.

IF YOU ARE CONSIDERING A WEB SITE FOR YOUR GROUP, FIND OUT HOW MANY MEMBERS HAVE EMAIL ADDRESSES. THIS WILL GIVE YOU AN INDICATION OF THE PROBABLE RESPONSE TO THE SITE

By the fall of 1996, however, the time was finally ripe for a site dedicated to AIGA Philadelphia. Many more members were online, and the Board and committees were enthusiastic to make the most of the medium. Monthly Board meetings were now supplemented by considerable conversation through email and we were beginning to get material for the web—"I'll email you the poster image and the text file." It was time to remove the chapter information from under AIGAlink and carve our own identity as AIGAphilly.org.

Goals

There was not much debate about goals when the committee began to tackle the new design for the web site because we had been in pursuit of these aims for two years. Basically the goals were:

- To open a new means of communication with the membership, reaching out particularly to the geographically distant
- To represent the chapter in ways that would increase both membership and sponsorship

The web is the most effective in its ability to make information instantly available to anyone that has access. The simple posting of information about the organization or events should not be taken for granted or underrated. The key, we all realized, would be getting and posting updated information in a timely manner. Therefore, a goal set by the committee was to set up regular email correspondence with other committee chairs and Board members about how the site could serve them.

The Team

For this project, we had an interesting team made up of AIGA Philadelphia technology committee members. Our group had already been managing the AIGAlink site that served the entire AIGA community; now we had to switch to serving only our chapter. In the group, the experience ranges from those who are web designers, to those who have dabbled, to those who had only done a bit of surfing. Part of the reason for our technical committee was to involve those that wanted to gain experience with new technologies and media.

In general, we attempted to involve everyone in the process, a consideration that is often disregarded in a commercial web project. The process of assigning roles and using each person's talents to the best advantage is crucial to the success of any project. In this case, we tried to challenge designers who had not handled web projects to come up with

« SITE CONTENT LIST

- **Give information about our events including:**
  - The Dialogues on Design series
  - Annual Spring Auction
  - Annual Holiday Sale
  - Annual Membership Meeting
  - New Member Quarterly Studio Parties
- **Provide information on past events of chapter**
- **Create an online Job Bank**
- **Supplement our print materials by supplying information online (discounts for members)**
- **Allow members and non-members to submit their email addresses to generate email lists**
  - Email list to inform non-members of upcoming events without costly postage
  - Membership email list for notification of special member events and notices from the National office
  - General list (member and non-member) for notifications of cancellations or rescheduled events
- **Make the Board more visible and accessible to the membership:**
  - Create bio pages for Board and committee members
  - Include links to their studio sites
  - Include email addresses
- **Give more exposure to members**
- **Offer exposure to sponsors**
- **Link to our virtual Gallery Space**

proposals for the visual look and feel of the site. The content, navigation, and structure would be hammered out by the group as a whole in several meetings and the initial implementation handled by our studio.

We had to look at how long-term maintenance would be accomplished. How could we create templates and styles that volunteers could implement? What about when the committee membership changed and the project would be taken over by others? The chapter resources were limited, so there was no question of paying a provider to maintain the site. How could we develop an ongoing team of volunteers to work on the project? This was one place where the use of NetObjects Fusion was critical to the success of the project, as discussed in the Implementation section below.

Content

At the stage of defining the content and desired features for the site, the committee came up with an ambitious list (see site content list). Obviously, information about upcoming events should be included, but we also decided to retain information about past events. This would give a potential member a sense of the caliber of our programming and could be a valuable resource for other chapters searching for program ideas.

The building of an email list was considered important for a number of reasons. Mailings about events go out to members only, but many of our speakers are of interest to a larger audience. The admission fees paid by non-members help make the events financially viable (and the larger turn-out pleases the sponsors). It does not cost the chapter any more in printing or mailing to send an event announcement out to an email list. In addition, it was considered essential to begin email correspondence with members to supplement other means of communication.

The Job Bank had been a service that was in a voice mail system. The maintenance and tracking of fees for the Job Bank had turned into a headache that no one wanted to handle. The Board decided to make it a free service and provide the listings on the Web site for one month.

We discuss more about how we implemented both the gathering of email addresses and the Job Bank in the last section of this chapter. Some ideas for the future include interactive possibilities such as online polls and live postings.

Audience

Our primary concern is serving our members in every way possible; therefore, they are our most important audience. A second audience is made up of those interested in our activities, especially the Dialogues on Design series. Thirdly, we wanted to give potential members an idea of our past and our present and how they could play a part in the organization. Also, potential sponsors might find out about the organization and the site. Lastly, AIGA chapters are always looking to each other for help and ideas—we hoped to give them some. Our community has grown and is growing closer.

What all these audiences have in common is an interest in design. Therefore, we had to meet a high standard in terms of the organization and presentation of material. The primary platform would be Macintosh, and the monitors would generally be high resolution, with good color representation. This meant that we could entertain subtle color choices without worrying about how it would look in 16 colors. Many of the smaller firms, however, do not have high bandwidth connections, so the site has to be fast-loading.

Site Architecture: Simplicity Rules!

We gave an assignment at one meeting to come into the next meeting with a sketch of the structure of the new site. It was quite striking that we all had a similar sense of the structure that was needed: simple and straightforward. Figure 8.4 shows the major sections of the site. This is a collapsed display in NetObjects Fusion's Site view; the arrows with plus signs show where additional pages are hidden. We all agreed that there were four main content areas: About Us (the chapter, Board, and committees), Events, News (material from the newsletter), and the Job Bank.

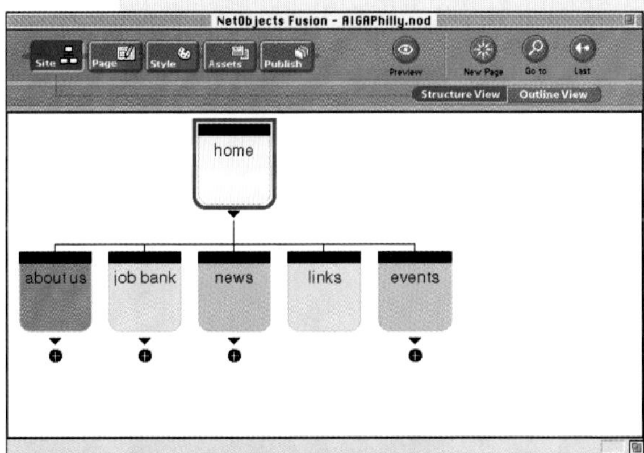

Figure 8.4
Here's a collapsed view of the site. Here we defined the major links. The site would expand from this basic structure.

No content list, no matter how thorough, is final. When we started to sketch the architecture, we realized that we should provide a page of useful links for our members. This courtesy, unique to the web, is easy to overlook when publishers are focusing on bringing their existing materials to the web.

Lopsided Growth

The foundation for AIGAphilly.org allowed for considerable growth and for lopsided expansion. The site would grow based on the interests of the current executive Board and committees. About Us would certainly be one of the first areas to grow. This section would include personal pages about the individuals involved in creating chapter activities, sponsorships, and future goals.

Figure 8.5 shows the full site structure. You can see that the Board pages stretch out and we hadn't even begun to add committee pages. As

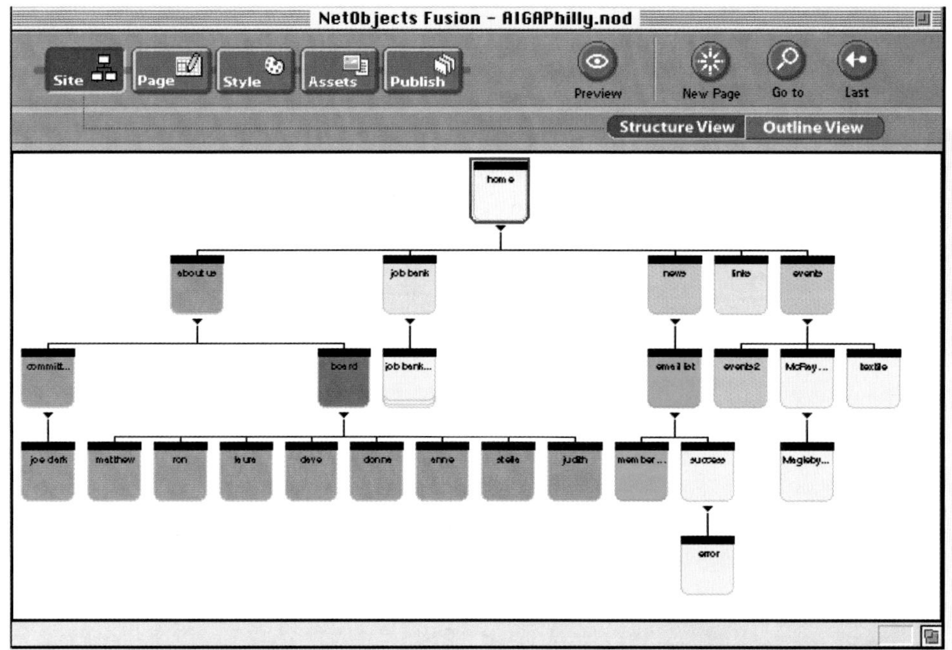

Figure 8.5
The expanded structure of AIGAphilly.org with eight Executive Board pages designated.

you can see, we made the Job Bank a set of stacked pages, so even if 100 jobs were listed it would look nice and neat on our site structure. Presumably the Events and News sections will grow as past information is kept available (subject to server space), but there is no intention of expanding the Links section beyond a single page.

The Phantom Page

If you visit AIGAphilly.org and go to the About Us section, you will have direct access to any of the Board members' bio pages directly from that page (Figure 8.6). If you look again at Figure 8.5, however, you will see a page called *board* that is the parent of all the eight bio pages for the Executive Board. This page naturally appeared in sketches of the site because it was important to keep all the Board pages together. In NetObjects Fusion terms, they are siblings. The fact that they are siblings allows for automatic next and previous links to browse in a cycle through the pages.

As we discussed in Chapter 2, "Constructing Site Frameworks," many sites make the mistake of assuming that just because a node is necessary to your diagram, an actual page should appear at the site. This leads to that anathema, a menu page without content. There is no reason why the

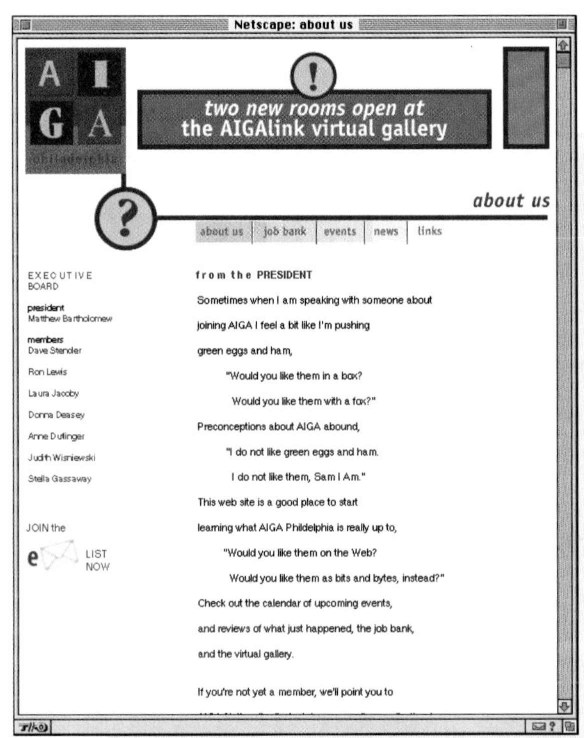

Figure 8.7

The opening page of the About Us section has links directly to the Board bio pages.

opening page of About Us should be merely a menu; we decided to put a welcoming letter from the President on the page. There is no reason why the list of Board member links should be on a separate page. When you try to draw the structure that way, however, there is no distinction between the Board pages and the others to come. In terms of NetObjects Fusion, you would lose the advantage of all the pages being siblings.

The solution that we have devised is what we call a phantom page. In other words, the page exists for structural reasons (and NetObjects Fusion reasons) but no visitor is ever directed to it. In fact, you do not have to upload the HTML page to your server (or you can remove it after NetObjects Fusion uploads it). The page serves the function of a folder or directory, grouping a set of items without having any content in and of itself.

Design and Decision by Committee

The site architecture came together relatively easily, but the visual attributes were more difficult. How could we create a site that had a distinctive Philadelphia feel? Many discussions and a few presentations of sketches ensued. In the end, an overt visual representation of Philadelphia didn't make it to the web; perhaps it will in the future.

Keeping the Look of a Printed Page

After the committee had struggled with this issue for a few meetings, we settled on the solution: give the job to the newest member. Lia Calhoun, a young designer at Kelsh Wilson Design, was charged with creating a banner and navigational elements. It was her first experience in designing for the web. After trying and discarding a map-like metaphor, Lia presented the images shown in Figure 8.7. In implementing these elements, we chose to follow through on the classic clean feel that reflects Philadelphia's historical relationship with the printed page. You remember Ben Franklin printing at Rittenhousetown, the first paper mill on the continent?

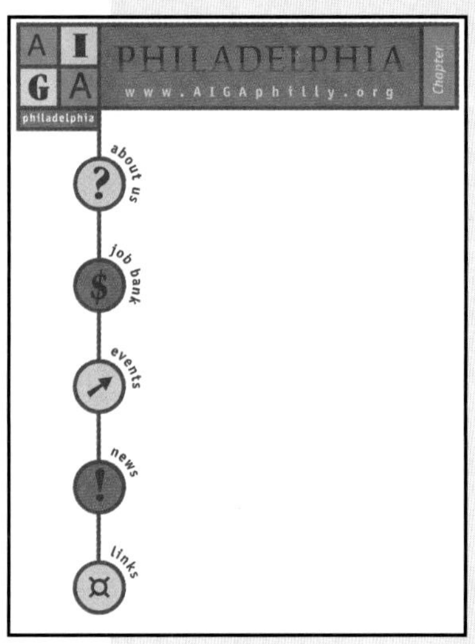

Figure 8.7
The original Illustrator file on which the site elements were based. The design was modified slightly to work onscreen, substituting fonts that would be antialiased with good results. Two of the serif fonts shown here became fuzzy and lost character.

The entire site design reflects the world of print (still the primary business of graphic design). We also decided that using the page metaphor was the most effective way to make information accessible to our members. Many visitors would probably want to print a page about an upcoming event or a Job Bank listing, so we wanted to make sure that our screen width, font sizes, and images would easily print from a laser printer onto a letter-sized sheet. At this point we weren't looking for all the latest bells and whistles, but a site that was clean, organized, and easy to implement and maintain. We had ideas for specific parts of the site becoming more interactive, but those were put on hold in favor of fulfilling the primary mission on time.

The Foundation: Page Grid and Color Palette

We had a working meeting and brought the elements together into a page design. From the modified Adobe Illustrator file we created GIF files using Adobe Illustrator's GIF plug-in and applied a color-safe palette. (For more info on these technical processes and links to resources, check out Lynda Weinman's www.lynda.com site.) It took a couple tries to get color

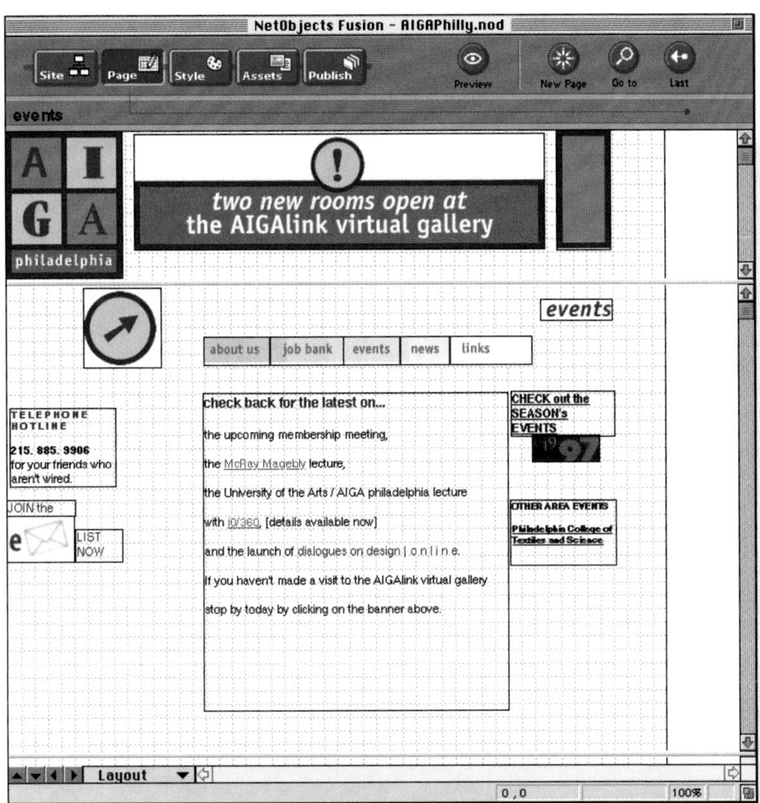

Figure 8.8

The main message of this page is in the center (wide) column, which aligns at the left with the main navigational bar. The left column contains the invitation to join the email list. The right column contains the links to the internal pages of the section.

results we were happy with. Now we could make the individual elements and create headers and footers (we were still in NetObjects Fusion 1.0 and MasterBorders weren't yet available).

We created a three-column grid that would enable us the most flexibility in adding links and sidebar elements. Using additional columns made it easy to create access to a considerable amount of information available from each content page. Figure 8.8 shows the opening page of the Events section in NetObjects Fusion and you can see how the grid works in the body of the layout.

In addition to the navigation that is specifically relevant to the page, all pages have links to the five main sections in a navigation bar at the top. Because the member who designed this bar used a fading image, we were not able to use NetObjects Fusion's auto-generated navigation bar (in which all buttons must be identical). You can also see in Figure 8.8 that the navigation bar is not contained in the header but is on the layout of the page. Because the pages were created by copying and pasting the grid elements, the navigation bar was pasted into each body. This may seem just

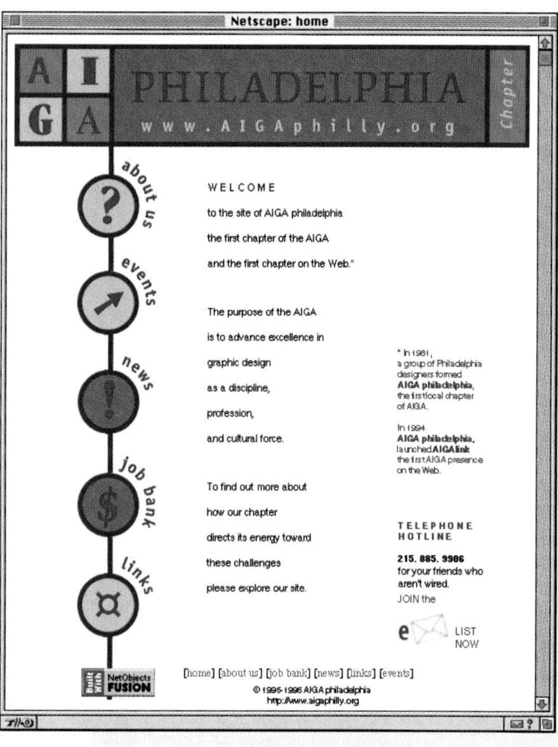

Figure 8.9
Here is the core page of AIGAphilly.org. This page has a unique header and you can see the auto-generated text navigation bar in the footer.

as easy when the site is being built, but it means any changes to the bar must be applied to each and every page. We are moving these bars to the header as we have time, in the interest of future site maintenance. The AIGA graphic in the upper left is a link to the core page and there are text links in the footer, which are described in the next section.

On the core page, the columns shift slightly to make room for the navigational icons that fill the left column. These create visual interest and clear road signs to the different areas at the site (Figure 8.9). Again, in the center column, the main thought is expressed and in the right column a side comment, our telephone hotline number, and the invitation to the email list.

THIS MULTI-COLUMN LAYOUT WOULD HAVE BEEN AN EXTREMELY DIFFICULT PAGE TO CREATE USING PREVIOUS AUTHORING TOOLS, BUT IT GAVE US THE COMBINATION WE WANTED: CONTENT AND MULTIPLE NAVIGATION MENUS. NETOBJECTS FUSION ALLOWED US TO CREATE THESE COLUMNS BY SIMPLY DRAWING AND POSITIONING TEXT BOXES, A PROCESS OUR GRAPHIC DESIGNER VOLUNTEERS WERE VERY FAMILIAR WITH.

Headers, Footers, and Backgrounds

Because MasterBorders were not yet available (they came with version 2.0), we built the site using headers and footers. Although this meant that we could not have a shared area up the left or right side of the page, it did have one advantage over the border system: all pages in the site use the same footer. This contains the copyright information, the site address, and the text navigation bar. This means that although there may be many headers used in the site, if we want to change the information at the bottom of the page it has to be done only once. The text navigation bar is a simple first-level bar, with home page checked. Note that the order of items in the bar is taken from the Site view (reading left to right). Unfortunately we

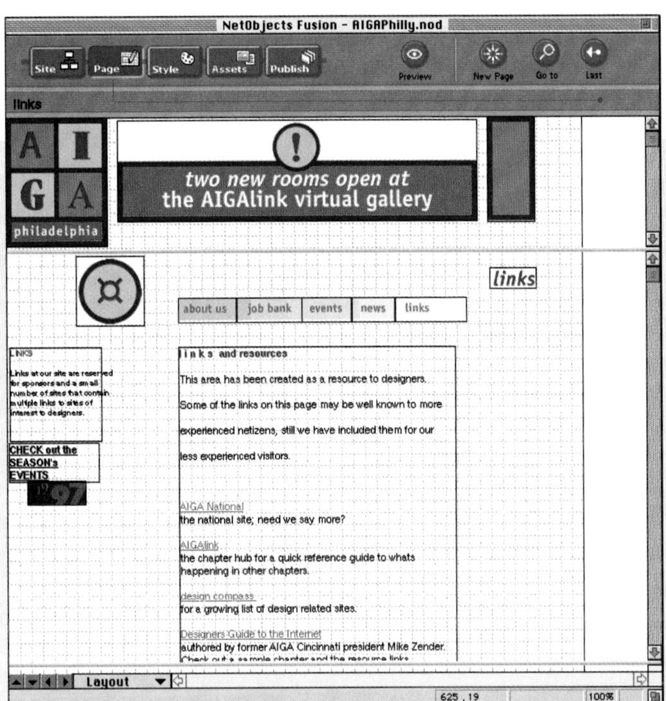

Figure 8.10

A generous area of the header is set aside for sponsors that help support the chapter. Here an in-house ad fills in until a sponsor is found.

neglected to make it consistent with the top navigation bar; another lesson learned the hard way. It's good to keep the structure consistent so that the next page in NetObjects Fusion automatic navigation is the next one in your navigation bar.

The core page uses a unique header, which you can see, and a unique background, which may be less obvious. The vertical bar is a background image, consisting of a *horizontal* GIF file 25 pixels deep × 700 pixels wide, all white except for a narrow band of dark blue. This tiles in to fill the page and form a vertical bar. You might think that a 1-pixel-deep file would be a smaller file and would load faster, but it turns out that there is a point of diminishing returns. With a 1-pixel × 700-pixel image, you watch the browser draw each line in, one row of pixels at a time. With an image 25 pixels deep, it rolls in efficiently and quite seamlessly. It might repeat on larger monitors, but that will be a clear flag to the visitor to resize their browser to a narrower width.

PLACING THE URL OF A SITE IN THE FOOTER MAY SEEM REDUNDANT BECAUSE A VISITOR CAN ALWAYS BOOKMARK THE PAGE. HOWEVER, MANY PEOPLE PRINT A PAGE TO KEEP OR TO SHOW TO SOMEONE ELSE. IN THIS SITUATION IT IS ESSENTIAL THAT YOUR URL APPEAR IN WRITING ON THE PAGE.

In our never-ending effort to gather funds with which to support chapter activities, we wanted to create space in which our generous sponsors would receive recognition (Figure 8.10). This space could be more than an acknowledgment of their contribution; it could be a link to their web sites or forms to request more information about services or products or a special offer for members. To make this

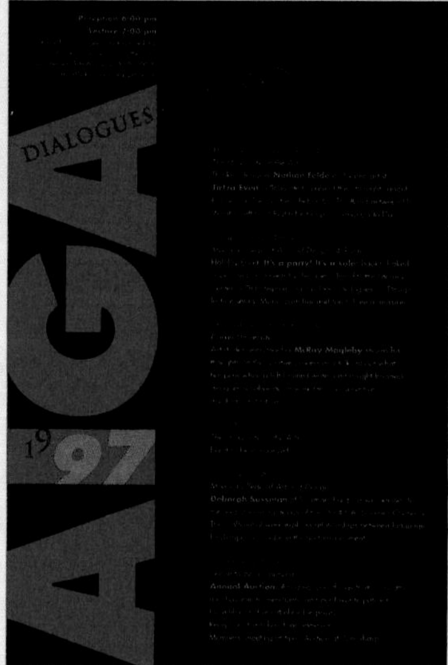

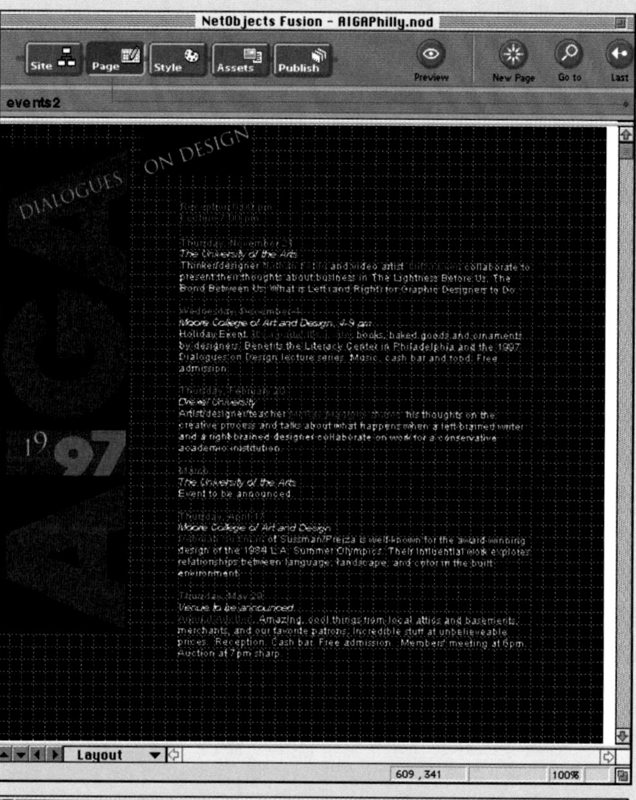

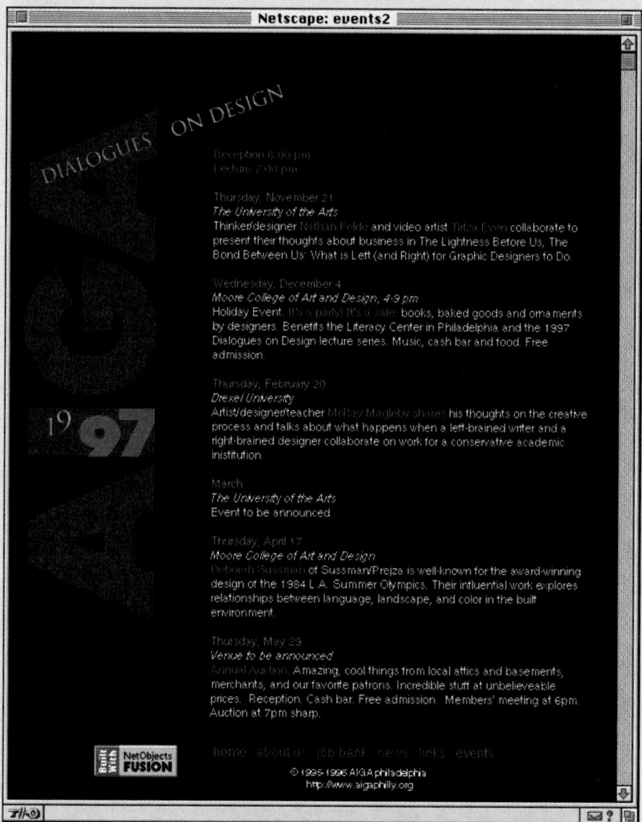

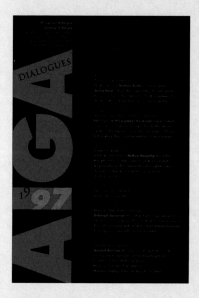

Figure 8.11

The first image is the printed card. Joe Clark, committee co-chair, created an Adobe Illustrator document to match the card and generated a GIF image. The second image is the page built in NetObjects Fusion. Choosing font, size, and color of the text was accomplished using the style palette. The third image is the result in Netscape, complete with hyperlinks. We could not have done this without NetObjects Fusion!

possible, we created headers that could be changed for different sections of the site. In Figure 8.10, the Links page is shown in NetObjects Fusion, and the area for a sponsor banner is held, for now, by an announcement of two new rooms opening at the virtual gallery. The About Us section, however, would not be sold to sponsors. The header there would emphasize various chapter-related activities, new member benefits, and online exhibitions, polls, or articles.

Reproducing a Printed Piece

An interesting deviation from our grid is the announcement of the Dialogues on Design season. Our chapter puts together what we warmly call a "refrigerator card" that lists our events for the season. This card has been a great success because everyone hangs it on his or her refrigerator or bulletin board. An event poster is mailed closer to event time and gives more details. Since this printed piece is such a trademark, we thought it would be fun and a challenge to NetObjects Fusion to try to reproduce it online (see Figure 8.11). In previous years, we either scanned the card and posted a JPEG image or created a text-only list with hyperlinks.

Implementation: A Volunteer Effort

You will have noticed that we have already been talking about building pages, and how we did it, in the design section. For jobs in our studio, the primary pages for a site are designed and approved by the client before they are brought into HTML. In this case, however, we were designing (and approving) as we were building and the two processes became quite interwoven. An advantage to this was that we were able to modify our design concepts to fit expedient page-building, rather than be held to matching a client-signed proof.

A long evening work session, however, produced only the basic pages of the site. The implementation of the deeper pages was left to the three committee members that work in our studio. Two aspects of that implementation and the role of NetObjects Fusion are worth discussing in some detail: the use of stacked pages for the Job Bank and the form for submitting email addresses.

We chose NetObjects Fusion for the AIGA Philadelphia site for many reasons. In investigating a versatile system that could accommodate years of maintenance, numerous webmasters, page builders, new design elements, expanding content, and purpose, NetObjects Fusion fit the bill. Designers on our committee, even those new to the web, were able to understand the object-based WYSIWYG page layout interface and page-building metaphor. Links within the site could be easily accomplished without any understanding of HTML and the site structure could easily be expressed and manipulated through the site and outline views.

The Job Bank: A Simple Internal Database

Chapter 6 introduced the scary concept of database publishing and defined data objects, data lists, and stacked data pages. Here is a very simple example that shows how this approach can be an excellent solution. We created an internal database, since the Macintosh version 1.0 of NetObjects Fusion does not allow linking to external data sources.

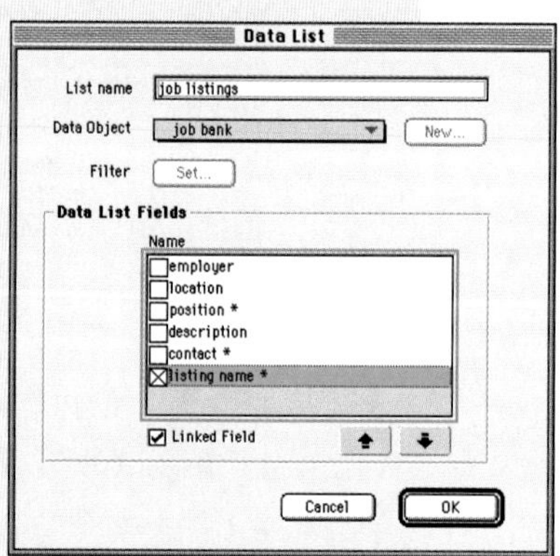

Figure 8.12

The job listings Data List of the Job Bank Data Object. The special listing name field is all that will appear on the contents page. The other asterisks indicating linked fields are left over from our efforts to use those fields as the list item, which was not workable.

While on the introductory page of the Job Bank section, we selected the Data List icon from the tool palette and created a data list (Figure 8.12). At first we had only the first five fields in the Data Object, and none of them seemed to work well for the listing of the jobs. We edited the Data Object from the Assets view to add a field that was a brief identification of the position. This was the only field we wanted listed, so that is the only field checked, and it is a linked field. In NetObjects Fusion, the data list displays as a blank box except for column titles (and one data bullet if you

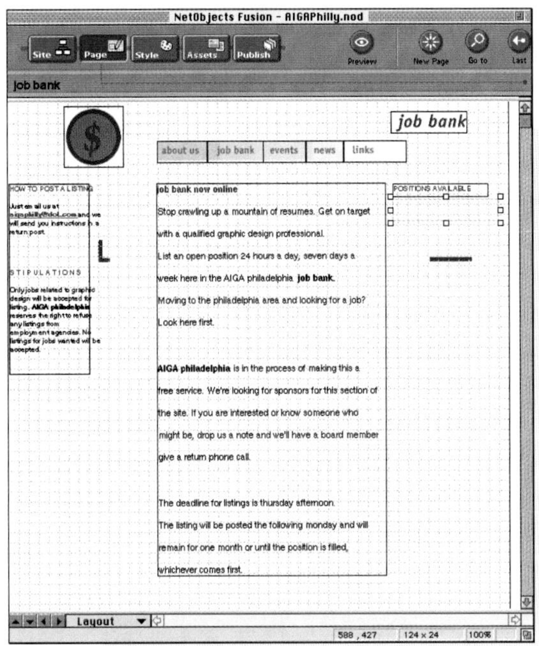

Figure 8.13

The data list is the highlighted blank box in the right column under the heading "positions available." It is impossible to tell how the list looks in terms of spacing until some records have been entered and the page previewed.

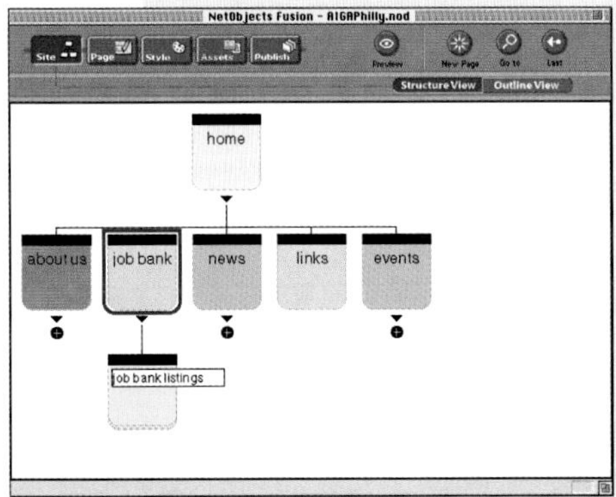

Figure 8.14

Stacked pages are added as soon as you place a data list on a page.

choose one). Here we explain how the Job Bank works in the main message column and the listing of jobs will be in the right column (see Figure 8.13).

Returning to the Site view, Figure 8.14 shows that a stack of pages has automatically been added as a child to the Job Bank page. We name this job bank listings. Double-clicking the stack takes us to the first (and, so far, only) page in the stack. Here we will add the design elements, such as the background image (the L-shaped rule), the header, and so on.

After the page had the basic format, we used the data field tool to position fields on the layout. You will remember that stacked pages are similar to the layout in a database: certain elements are on the layout, and other elements are data elements. We put the identifying field from the contents list in the upper left, for example. You can format the interior of the field as you would any other text. In Figure 8.15, you can distinguish the data fields from the text on the layout by the red outlines around the data fields. After we filled in the fields on the first page, pages were added using the small plus button at the top of the NetObjects Fusion window (below the main view choices).

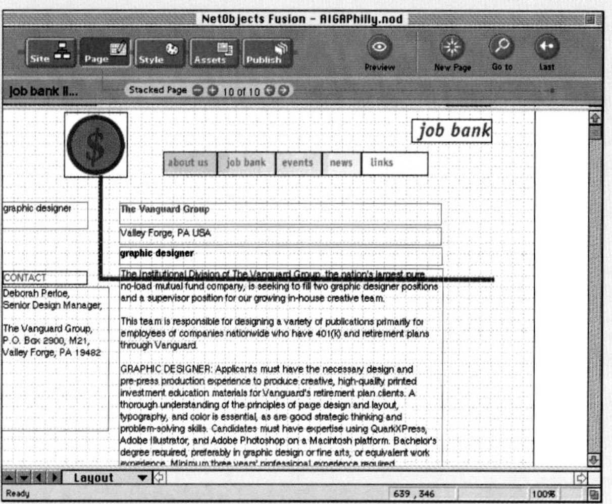

Figure 8.15

This is the tenth record in a stack of ten records, with the information entered into the data fields.

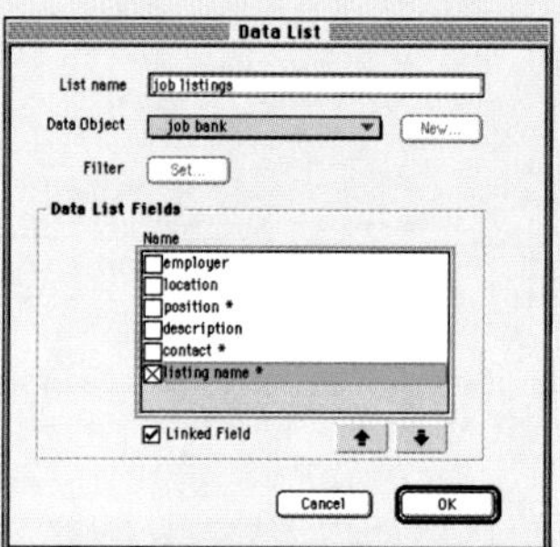

Figure 8.16

The Data List tab appears when you select a Data List in the layout. You can reach the palette shown in Figure 8.12 from the Define button.

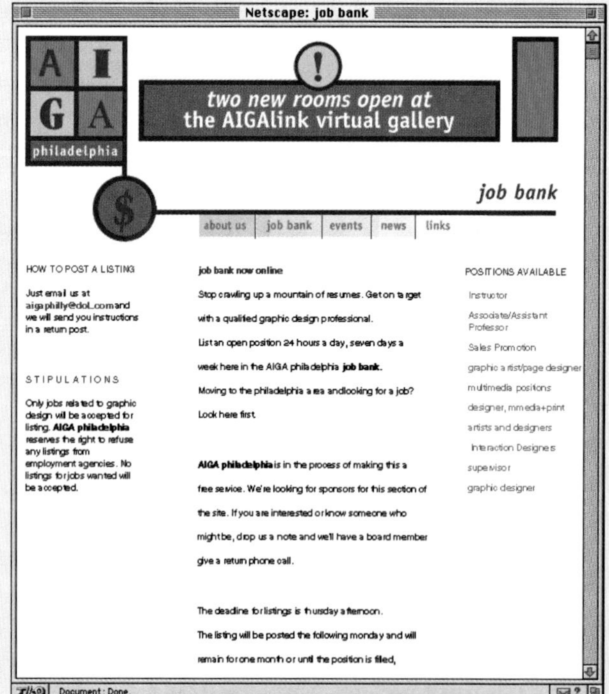

Figure 8.17

The introductory page of the Job Bank. You can see how the data list looks only by previewing in the browser.

When we had entered several records, we went to preview the pages. This was our first look at the data list that introduces the page and it didn't look at all how we wanted it to look. We went back to the properties palette in NetObjects Fusion (Figure 8.16) and changed many of the options on this palette until the list had the simple appearance we desired: no bullet, no border, no fill background. We did, however, add cell spacing so that the entries did not sit right on top of each other. We choose no column title, although you will see that there is a heading above the list. We wanted to be able to control the font color and size of the heading.

DON'T CONFUSE THE RICH TEXT FIELDS AND PLAIN TEXT. THIS CHOICE, WHICH IS MADE WHEN THE DATA OBJECT IS BUILT, DETERMINES WHETHER YOU CAN HAVE DIFFERENT FORMATTING IN A FIELD FOR EACH STACKED PAGE. IF YOU WANT TO FORMAT A FIELD ONCE AND HAVE IT APPLY TO ALL PAGES, PLAIN TEXT IS WHAT YOU WANT. YOU WILL NOT BE ABLE TO INCLUDE LINKS

In order to see the results of our choices, we had to preview the page several times. Figure 8.17 shows the final result, with a list of 10 jobs. The same formatting applies to the identifying as it appears on the stacked pages. Figure 8.18 shows two stacked pages in the browser.

This may seem like many new confusing concepts, but that is only if you are unfamiliar with the process. It may also seem like a great deal of work, but that is mostly in the initial setup. Now any new pages that are added automatically have the correct layout and the data list is automatically updated as pages are added or deleted. This is not nearly as convenient as a link to an external database, however, which is available in the Windows version only and is discussed in Chapter 6.

WE HAVE REQUESTED THAT THOSE INTERESTED IN POSTING JOBS USE JOB BANK IN THE SUBJECT OF AN EMAIL INQUIRY. THEY ARE THEN AUTOMATICALLY SENT A REPLY TELLING THEM HOW TO SET UP THEIR INFORMATION (TO CORRESPOND TO OUR FIELDS). THIS MAKES IT POSSIBLE FOR ANY WILLING VOLUNTEER TO UPDATE THE JOB BANK.

We discussed also creating Board and committee bio pages as stacked pages, except for one severe limitation in NetObjects Fusion: You cannot point an internal link to a stacked page. You can do a work-around and point to the HTML name that the stacked page will be assigned (the stack page plus a number). This link, however, must be tracked and corrected manually, losing the wonderful comfort of NetObjects Fusion's internal link management.

We decided we had to be able to rearrange member pages. Executive members have been committee members and retiring Board members often return to committees or special chapter tasks. We would want to create links to the member page from a content page where that member was involved. Instead, we created a template for

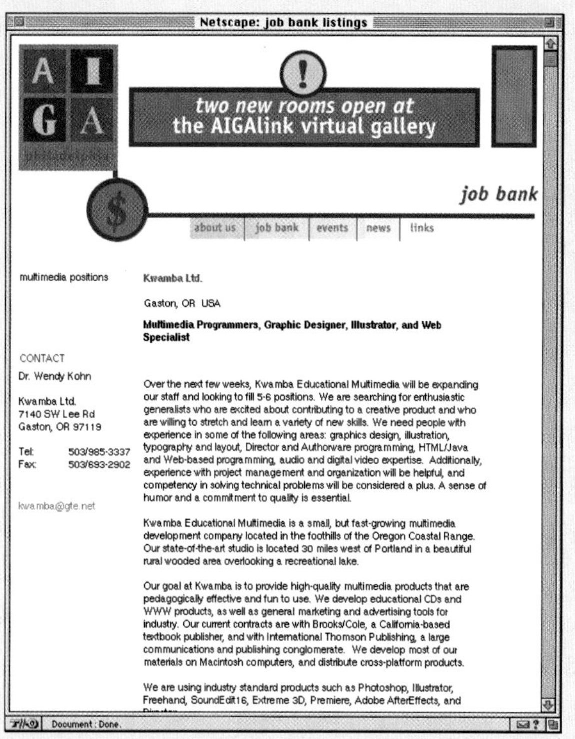

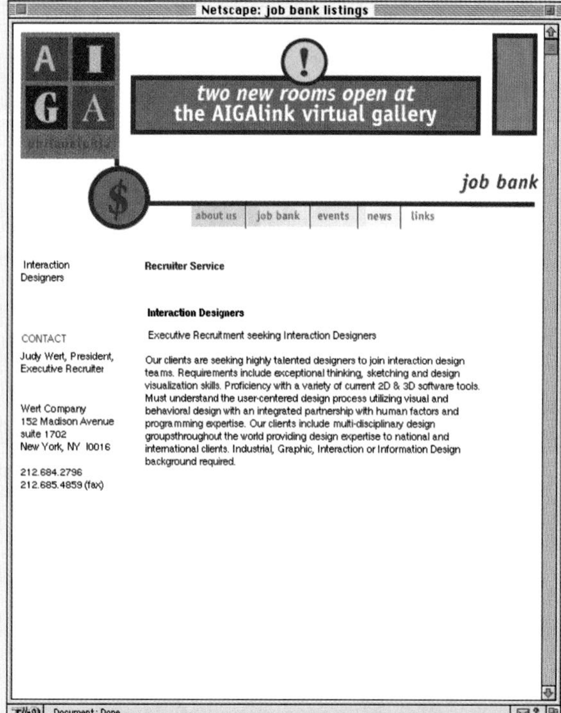

Figure 8.18

Here you can see how the data pages adjust to accommodate the longest entry. On the short page the footer is in the same position as the page with the short entry, so essential information should not be placed in the footer.

a single page, as described in Chapter 11, Fuzzy Marketing, and inserted it into the site for each bio page.

Figure 8.19

The six form tools appear when the general form tool is selected.

The Form to Submit an Email Address

The way in which you implement a form script has been improved greatly in version 2.0 of NetObjects Fusion. Here we will describe basically what we did in 1.0 for Macintosh, leaving out details that are no longer relevant, such as pasting in long scripts.

Figure 8.19 shows the six form tools that appear in the context-sensitive portion of the tools palette when you choose the general form tool (located in the lower right of upper panel). We used the lower left of the six to create normal single-line text entry fields in our form. We also used the Pop-up choice tool to make the member/non-member field and the button tool to create the submit button.

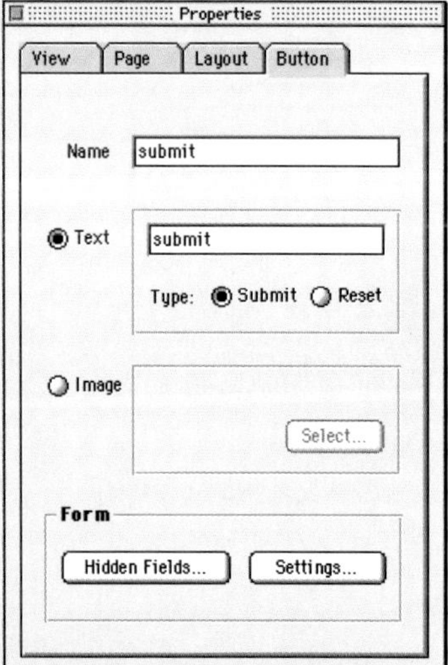

Figure 8.20

Version 1.0 (Macintosh) palette for creating a form.

Figure 8.20 shows how the submit button was set up with text that simply read submit. An image could have been used instead or other text. Figure 8.21 shows how you must specify how the form will be submitted. This has been improved in version 2.0.

Figures 8.22 and 8.23 show the final page as it appears in NetObjects Fusion and in the browser. An email address is given in case the form is not working. Nothing is more frustrating that a malfunctioning form with no other option.

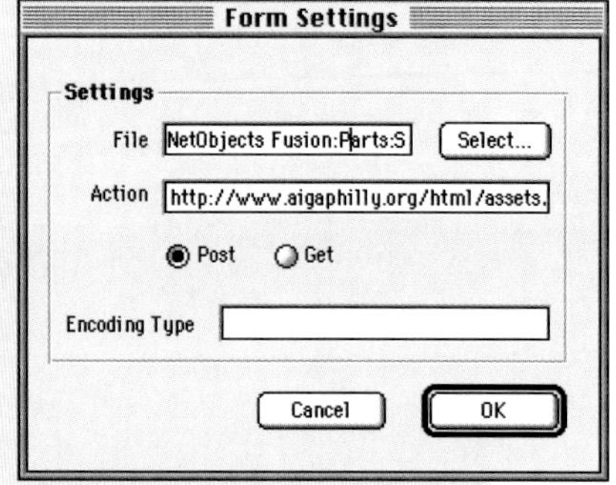

Figure 8.21

The properties of the submit button.

A Progress Report on the Site

Most of these case studies have not been on the web long (if at all) at the time of this writing. This is the first site we built in NetObjects Fusion, however, and it has been around long enough to give some feedback on how our ideas are working out.

The email list is growing with 47 members and 36 non-members on the list. The feedback has been that the notifications are greatly appreciated. The Job Bank is the busiest part of the site. We have had 28 jobs posted over the 6 months that it has been up.

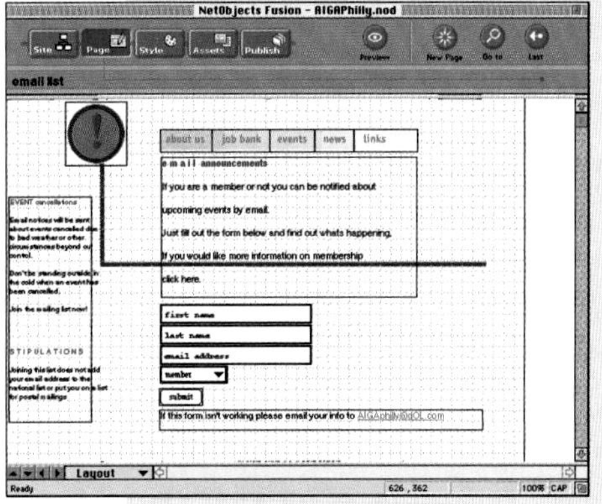

Figure 8.22

The form elements in NetObjects Fusion.

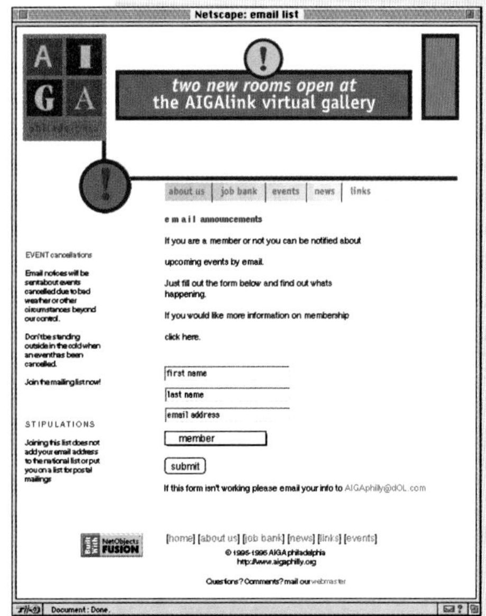

Figure 8.23

The final page in the browser.

9

Sell Those Fonts:

fontsOnline.com

Figure 9.1
*Alphabets, Inc. has been in the digital font business since 1987 and is committed to offering a technologically advanced font library and was the first third-party foundry to release a multiple master Postscript family (A*I Koch Antiqua).*

In Evanston, Illinois, just outside Chicago, is a small but highly respected firm called Alphabets, Inc. that sells typefaces (Figure 9.1). For historical reasons, such firms are called foundries, even in this digital age. Alphabets, Inc. works with a group of type designers, from the U.S. and internationally, whose fonts meet the foundry's aesthetic and technical standards. The founder, Peter Fraterdeus, is a type designer who has deep love of typography and has received two NEA grants for the study of letterforms.

OUR BACKGROUND IN CALLIGRAPHIC LETTERING AND DESIGNING FOR CARVED INSCRIPTION IN STONE AND WOOD INEVITABLY AFFECTS THE SHAPES AND SUBTLETIES OF OUR LETTERS.

PETER FRATERDEUS

Alphabets has long had a commitment to technology, enthusiastically embracing the PostScript language to create fonts, but these fonts for the digital age come from an organic background. When you take a look at the printed Alphabets font catalog, you find a library of fonts that isn't trendy or deconstructivist or postmodern stuff (Figure 9.2). These fonts are in for the long haul. Here you can find classic designs you will be able to use the year they were released and you'll surely be using them decades later (well, as long as PostScript or TrueType are around). This is an important aspect of the personality of the client.

It has become clear, with the democratization of font design and publishing, that small foundries must use all means necessary to reach an interested audience. They must struggle to make themselves known in the midst of the likes of Adobe, Agfa, and Bitstream. It is also clear that making a quality product stand out requires more and more energy and imagination. Alphabets used to send out an eight-page tabloid-size catalog to effectively display its fonts, which has become burdensome as mailing costs have increased. An online catalog would be an efficient method to display fonts, invite new designs, link to other quality foundries and places of interest to type aficionados—a place to make the fonts known and, hopefully, sell some type. The idea of fontsOnline was born.

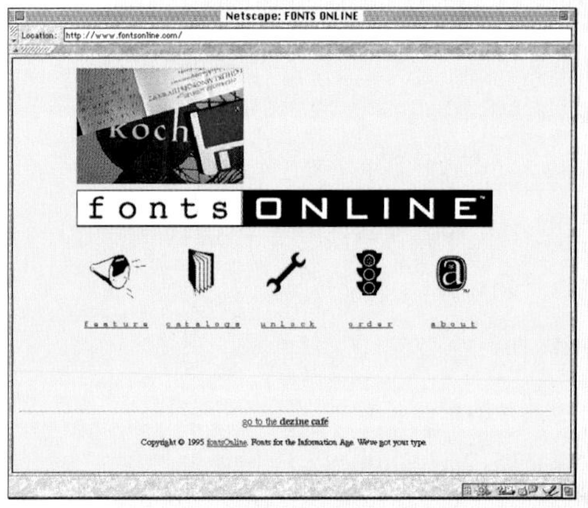

Figure 9.2
www.fontsOnline.com home page, January 1997, before our redesign. It loads fast, has simple categories, and is clean and uncluttered.

www.fontsOnline.com has been Alphabets' font marketplace on the World Wide Web since 1995 (Figure 9.2). fontsOnline is the exclusive source online for Alphabets' new releases and special offers not available anywhere else. Now with such font giants as Adobe selling directly on the web, independent foundries like Alphabets must have a strong web presence not just to compete, but to survive.

Definition: Where Are the Fonts?

As a designer with a love of typography and as an Alphabets customer, I was excited to hear the announcement of its web site. After visiting www.fontsOnline.com, however, I came away feeling unfulfilled. I had received Alphabets' printed catalog and went to the Web site to see about purchases. I investigated for a while and then asked myself, "Where are the fonts?" Why couldn't I find those glorious letterforms online? If I could see fonts on the web, I would buy them on the web. In fact, I had already done so by email—why not the web? The site was not fulfilling its purpose if it couldn't even sell *me* fonts (see Figure 9.3).

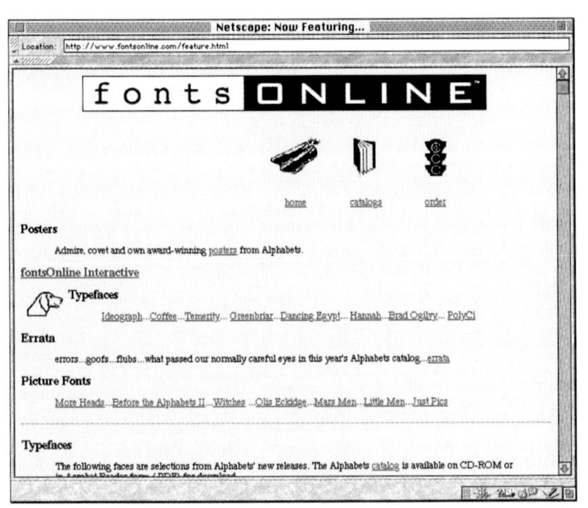

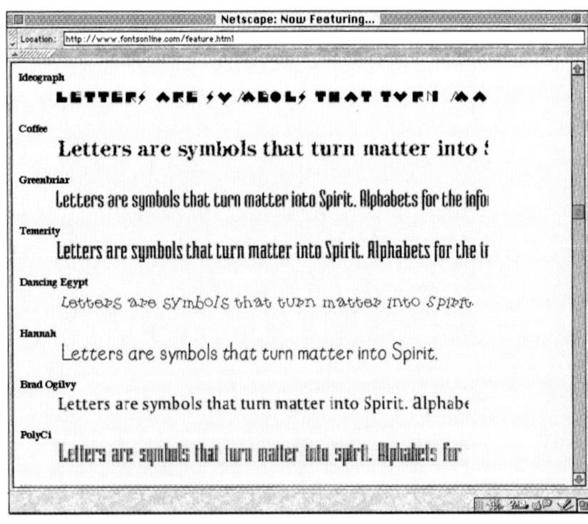

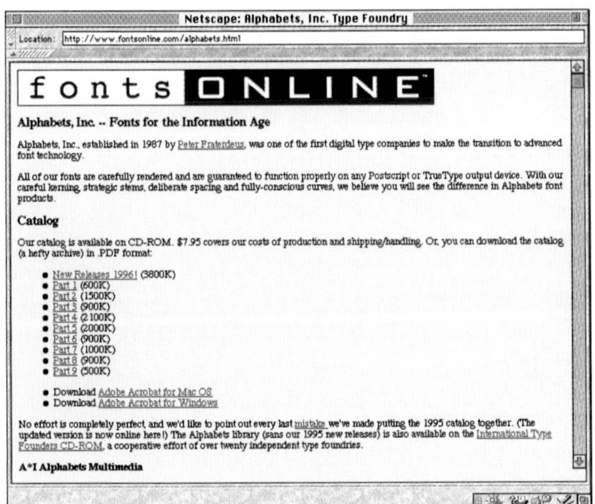

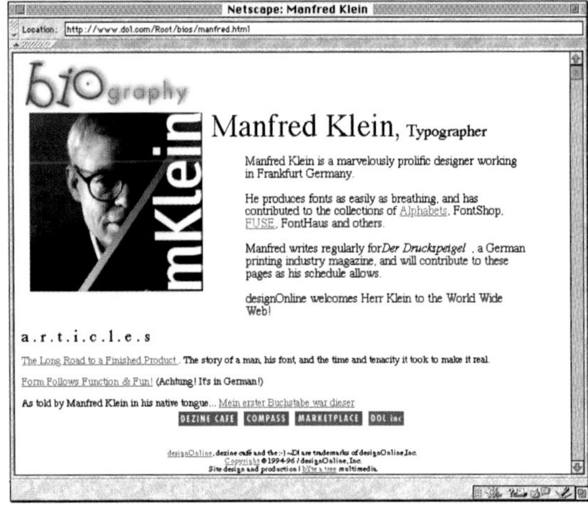

Figure 9.3

Here you can see more pages of the original fontsOnline. It had many strengths, especially for 1995, but it is clearly a first-generation web site that could use updating.

1. *The features page begins by carrying through the look of the home page.*
2. *As you scroll down (or choose an anchor), you get to small one line showings of some fonts.*
3. *The catalog link brings you to a page listing the Alphabets' catalog, which are PDF files for downloading.*
4. *Here is a bio page of a font designer that actually exists on another site, designOnline.*

I sent an email to Peter Fraterdeus, also the author of another book in this series, *Killer Web Design: Typography*, and asked him if Alphabets would be interested in a new design for fontsOnline. We discussed our mutual interest in making it a vibrant type site and a place where those interested in type could find links to the world's finest designs and type designers. These discussions brought bYte a tree the opportunity to redesign fontsOnline.

Many people are surprised that a small Philadelphia firm would be working with a small client in Evanston, Illinois. Long-distance projects are thought to be the province of large companies with teleconferencing and the budget for plane fares. For this project, almost all of our discussions about the site were carried out by email, with only one in-person meeting to discuss fontsOnline. We do have a good relationship with Peter Fraterdeus, however, from collaboration on design community projects. This relationship developed primarily through email with periodic rendezvous at conferences and the like.

Goals

The client had a firm idea of what he wanted to be contained at the site and visions for its continued growth. fontsOnline is listed in many articles and directories as an excellent resource for fonts on the web, and the home page gets over 1200 visitors every week. Despite the quality of the product offered and the reasonable prices, however, these statistics of visitors were not translating into font sales.

We made a connection to the client due to our shared interest in the soft goals in terms of providing a resource for font enthusiasts, raising the aesthetic standard of the site, and so on. Yet as close to our hearts as these issues were, the primary goal of the site had to be to sell fonts. Therefore, the goal of the redesign was to increase the sales of fonts.

After discussion with the folks in Evanston, and some of the other Alphabets, Inc. font designers around the country, the mandate was unanimous:

Make the fonts available for viewing on the web and the fonts will sell on the web.

THE ONLY POSSIBLE CONFLICT WAS PETER'S DETERMINATION TO PROVIDE LINKS TO OTHER SOURCES OF QUALITY FONTS ON THE WEB. THERE WERE ARGUMENTS ON BOTH SIDES OF THIS ISSUE: WHETHER YOU INCREASE OR DECREASE YOUR SALES BY ASSOCIATING WITH THOSE WHO SELL TO THE SAME AUDIENCE (WHEN YOUR PRODUCTS ARE, BY DEFINITION, UNIQUE). ONE ANTIQUE STORE ALONE DOES NOT DO AS WELL AS A STORE ON A STREET FULL OF ANTIQUE STORES. IN ANY CASE, THE DEBATE WAS MOOT BECAUSE PETER FRATERDEUS WAS ETHICALLY COMMITTED TO SUPPORTING OTHER INDEPENDENT FOUNDRIES.

In addition, we recommended strongly to Alphabets that a method of purchasing directly online be instituted. The immediacy of the Web leads visitors to expect immediate gratification. Peter Fraterdeus agreed to explore this and that the redesign should assume that online purchasing would be implemented.

Obviously, the other goals of glorifying letterforms and providing information were not in any way in conflict with the primary goal—the more prestigious and noteworthy a site is, the more traffic and the more potential customers it attracts.

Audience

Having an established site with visitor logs and client browser statistics helped us a great deal at this site. Usually when building a site one has to be prepared to cater to the most unsophisticated viewer. In this case, we had a working knowledge of the browser level and platform on which the browser was being used. This enabled us to approach our design within a narrower perimeter.

The visitors to fontsOnline came with the most popular browsers. Netscape Navigator was the overwhelming choice, regardless of platform, and Microsoft Explorer a distant second. It seemed safe to assume that anyone sophisticated enough to be looking for more fonts than were provided with their system would have more than the low-end 16-color monitor. Our statistics told us that most of the people visiting were using browsers with Java capability, along with QuickTime and Shockwave plug-ins. This enabled us to build for those technologies. We decided, however, that plug-in technologies would enhance the site, not drive it. We did not want to require proprietary systems just to view the site.

Type designers are an interesting group with their own subculture both on and off the web. They are involved in the making of letters, our most basic elements in passing on information. The history of making letters is, we believe, a heroic one. This heroic love of letters, of interest to all font enthusiasts, would be part of the personality expressed at fontsOnline.

The PDF Catalog

Brian Sooy, a designer who has fonts in the Alphabets library, designed and created a catalog that was distributed on CD-ROM as a PDF file and was available for download from the original Web site (Figure 9.4). This catalog never saw printed form, except when printed out by the customer. We printed ours and put it in a binder. Figure 9.5 shows a page from the catalog, displayed in Adobe Acrobat Reader (freeware from Adobe).

IF YOU WOULD LIKE A COPY OF THE CATALOG, YOU CAN ORDER THE CD-ROM FROM THE SITE OR DOWNLOAD THE CATALOG. BRIAN SOOY WILL BE CONTRIBUTING TO ANOTHER BOOK IN THIS SERIES, KILLER WEB DESIGN: TYPOGRAPHY, WRITING ABOUT THE PDF FORMAT.

There is a page for each specific face (weight or style in the font family) so there are five pages devoted to Quanta. The entire basic character set is shown on the right, and on the left is shown either paragraphs of text (for text fonts) or a display use of the font (for display and picture fonts). These are wonderful pages that really celebrate letters. This catalog was an invaluable resource and inspiration in redesigning the Web site for fontsOnline.

Making the Fonts Viewable

In our brainstorming about how to make the fonts most accessible, we came up with a long list of possibilities. Obviously, it is not possible to simply specify HTML text in the particular font, because the viewer will not have the font installed on his or her system. The fonts must be shown as images of some sort.

Here are some of the ideas we considered:

- Pages of one-line showings of fonts, as GIFs (as in the previous site)
- The entire character set for a font, as a GIF, which is helpful to those looking for that special Q, but not an effective representation for the font as it will be used
- A full paragraph of text in the font (this would need to be a large image and is only sensible for text fonts)
- Animated GIFs, showing multiple characters in succession

Figure 9.4

Another technological first, the award-winning Alphabets Inc. 1995 catalog on CD-ROM. In addition to the PDF catalog, multimedia pieces showcasing certain fonts were included.

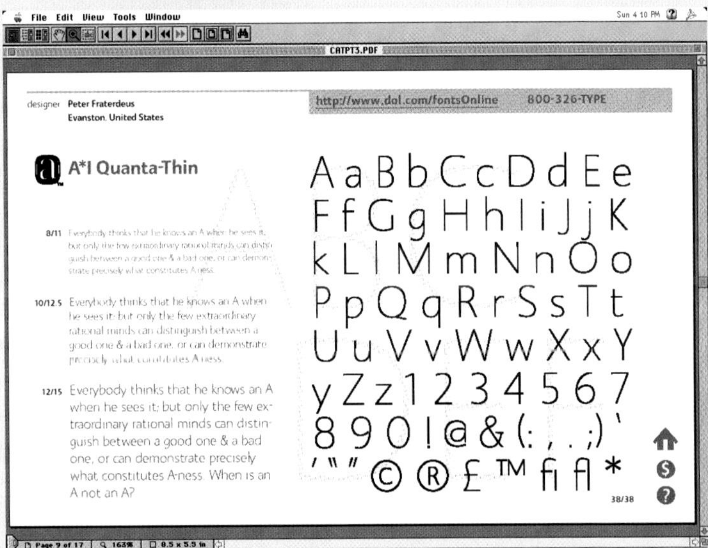

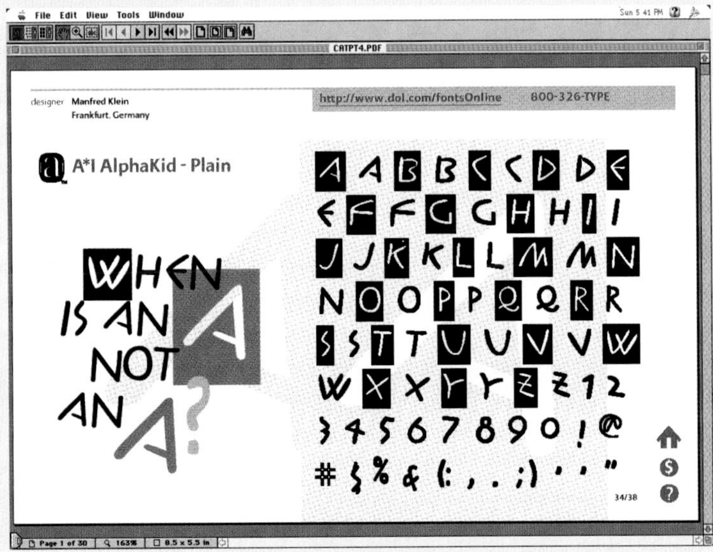

Figure 9.5

Here are a couple of pages from Brian Sooy's catalog for Alphabets. Quanta-Thin is a text font, so three paragraphs of typical font size/leading are shown. AlphaKid-Plain is a display font, so a display use of the font is shown. In both cases the complete standard character set is shown at the right.

- PDF files, using existing catalog pages, the new technology allows viewing page by page
- Director Shockwave, QuickTime Movies or Flash (formerly FutureSplash Animator) animations to really show off the personality of a font
- GIFs of posters from Alphabets, Inc. (for sale)

After discussion of all of the above, with the pros and cons of the viability and effectiveness of each, the decision was made to give options for viewing fonts in a variety of ways. It was decided to have a separate web catalog page for each font family rather than combining many font families on a page. Unlike the PDF catalog, however, we would have a single page for each font faily (not weight or style).

WE CAME OUT OF THE PLANNING MEETING FOR FONTSONLINE OVERWHELMED BY TH AMBITIOUS NATURE OF THE SITE-BUT VERY EXCITED!

Each catalog page would have a short phrase that could be shown, quite large, as a GIF. This would be in the roman (or equivalent) face of the font family. In addition, there would be an animated GIF that would show one letter at a time in various weights and styles of the family. This could be relatively small since only one letter at a time would be showing.

Then from the catalog pages, you would have the option of seeing the font in other ways, depending on your preference and the way you have configured your browser. The new plug-in technology from Adobe allows PDF documents to be read directly in the browser page by page. We would, therefore, have a link from the web page to the appropriate page (or pages) in the Acrobat catalog. The link would always be in the same location on the page and would be something obvious like the Acrobat logo. Similarly, we would have a link from each page taking you to a Macromedia Shockwave presentation (either FreeHand, Flash, or Director).

Content

The web font catalog would be the primary content of the site, what the vegetarian Fraterdeus will not allow us to call the meat. Let's call it the heart of the site. Building on that we developed the site content list. You will

« SITE CONTENT LIST

1. Web catalog of all Alphabets fonts (plus those of cooperating foundries, if any)
2. Designer biography pages (with photos)
3. Access to Acrobat PDF catalog
4. Comments from designers about fonts
5. Articles by font designers
6. Articles about the state of typography
7. Links to other foundries
8. Links to other sites of typographical interest
9. Pricing information
9. Order information
11.Online purchasing
12. Room for advertising banners
13. Special offers page or section
14. Sales of other fontsOnline products, such as posters, type books, and T-shirts.

note that there is a mention of showing pages of fonts by foundries other than Alphabets.

We felt that pages about the type designers were important because pages about people on the web are always popular. Many of the designers are authors of books or articles about typography, or have other credentials or interesting facts to list.

One of the huge issues in type design has been the battle for fonts as the intellectual property of the designer. Embedding fonts and making outlines safe from those who would choose to steal the designs is a major issue. We had to consider these facts in how we would display fonts at the site. The Acrobat files had to be locked to prevent the font outlines from being available to font thieves and any outlines had to be protected. Links to resources on this issue would be included at the site.

Architecture: Accessing the Fonts

Obviously, the heart of the site, the web font catalog, should be prominent in the structure of the site. We also needed to create a structure that would accommodate minor updates to content (usually quarterly), special offers, and additional visual-interest elements featuring quotes about typography, hints about using type, and links to articles of interest elsewhere on the web. After considering many organizational possibilities, we chose one and proceeded down one path. Then, as you will see, we changed the navigational structure of the site completely. It was the testing of the logical prototype that made us realize the problems before we had designed and implemented all the pages!

The Linear Organization

In approaching the organization for fontsOnline, we reviewed the structure that was used for the successful PDF catalog and decided to do a slightly different version of that approach.

The PDF Catalog Structure

The introductory page of the PDF catalog gives the table of contents (Figure 9.6). It shows three ways of viewing the font list: by designer, by name (alphabetical), and by category. When you choose the list by designers, you get a list of the Alphabets, Inc. designers. When you choose a designer, you go to the catalog page of the first font (alphabetically) by that designer. If you use the "next" arrow provided in Acrobat Reader, you are taken through all of the fonts by that designer (and then on into other fonts by other designers).

If you choose the type list by name, you get an alphabetical list of links to the font pages. This is a quick way to find the showing of a font that you already know the name of. If you choose to browse from there using the "next" arrow in Acrobat, however, you get the next font by that designer (not the next on the alphabetical list you just saw). If you choose the type list by category, there is a list of fonts under each category, but they are not actually links (Figure 9.7).

In analyzing this structure, it became apparent that *by designer* was the default organization of the pages. If you browsed through, page by page, the fonts were grouped by designer, and alphabetically within designer.

FONT TERMINOLOGY

TYPE 1 FONTS ARE WRITTEN IN THE POSTSCRIPT LANGUAGE. THERE ARE TWO FILES FOR EACH FONT. ONE IS AN OUTLINE FONT FOR THE PRINTER AND THE OTHER IS A BITMAP FOR THE SCREEN (UNLESS A UTILITY SUCH AS ATM IS USED TO DRAW UPON THE OUTLINE DATA FOR SCREEN DISPLAY).

TRUETYPE FONTS CONSIST OF ONE FILE THAT IS USED FOR BOTH DISPLAY AND PRINTING.

MULTIPLE MASTER FONTS ARE CUSTOMIZABLE TYPE 1 FONTS. THE CHARACTERISTICS ARE DESCRIBED IN TERMS OF LINEAR AXES. THESE INCLUDE WEIGHT, STYLE, AND OPTICAL SIZE. ALTHOUGH THESE FONTS CAN BE CUSTOMIZED ALMOST INFINITELY IN VARIETY, THE MAXIMUM NUMBER OF AXES IS FOUR.

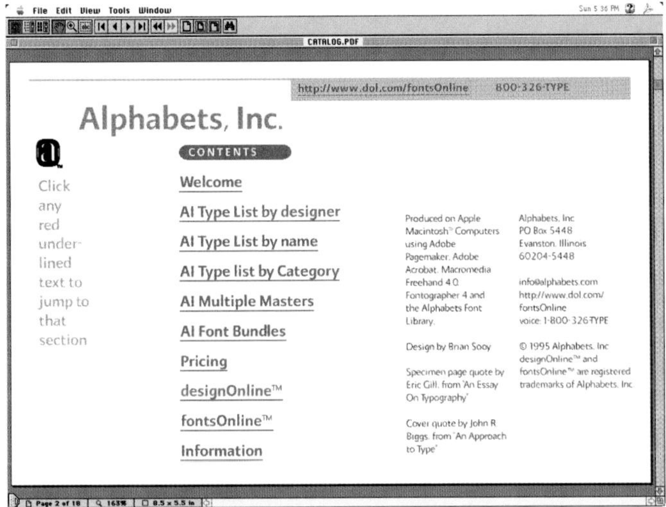

Figure 9.6

This is the Contents page of the PDF catalog. The first choice, after Welcome, is to view the type list by designer. This does not actually go to a type list but a list of designers, from which you go directly to the catalog pages.

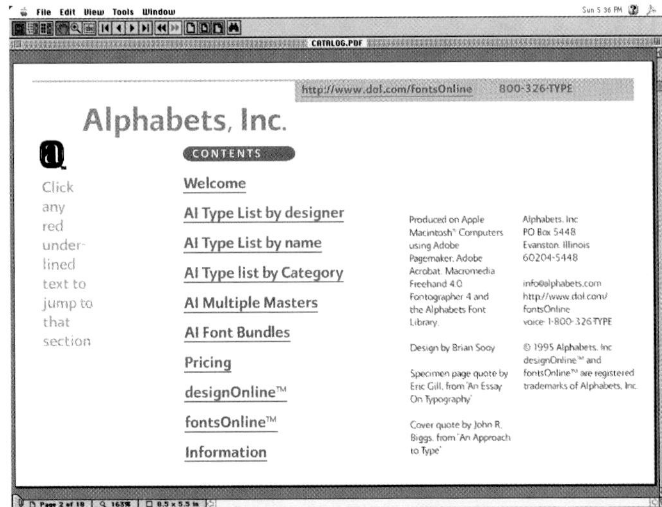

Figure 9.7

This is the second page of the type list by category, where the font families are separated by the type of font that they are. Fonts can belong to more than one category (such as, Multiple Master and Text).

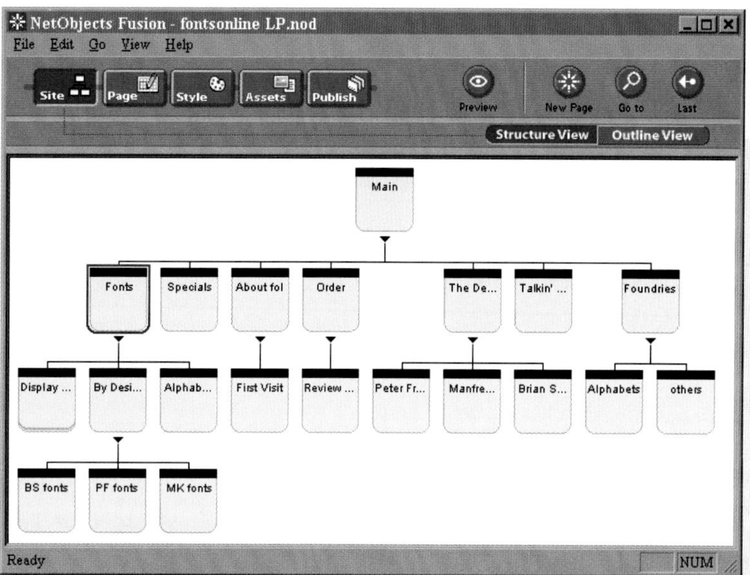

Figure 9.8

The Site view of the first logical prototype for fontsOnline. At the main level were Fonts, Specials, About fontsOnline, How to Order, The Designers, Talkin' Type, and Foundries. You will notice that there are two sections that are related to the designers, the designer bios (Peter Fraterdeus, Brian Sooy, and Manfred Klein are shown) and the fonts sorted by designer (BS fonts, PF fonts, MK fonts).

Our First Prototype

We decided to take a similar approach as Brian Sooy had taken in the PDF catalog, but with the addition of the designer bios and other pages about type. Figure 9.8 shows the Site view of the first logical prototype for fontsOnline. We chose *category* as our default organization, reasoning that if a designer was looking for a font to serve a specific purpose, she would want to page through possible candidates. We planned to build stacked pages, drawing on Alphabets' database and use NetObjects Fusion's automatic previous and next links. In addition, a search engine and alphabetical list would be offered to use if visitors already know the name of the font they are looking for.

The navigation bar throughout the site is the first level of pages. We wanted as much as possible available to the visitor without layers of navigation. The Foundries section was available if other foundries chose to join fontsOnline. The section temporarily dubbed Talkin' Type would be articles and links to type-related sites. A section for designer bios would have mutual links to the pages listing the fonts by each designer. There would also be information about special bundled fonts, and general information about fontsOnline.

We added text describing the content and function of each page, and set up the Logical Prototype for testing. The opening page to the Fonts section is shown in Figure 9.9. We decided to make separate stacks of pages

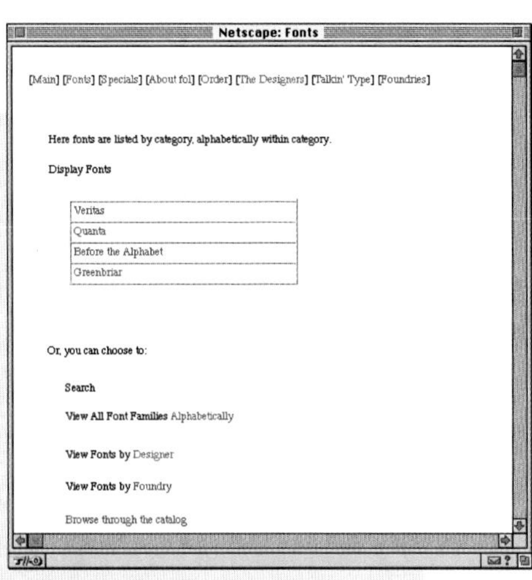

Figure 9.9

The entry to the Fonts section in the first logical prototype. Navigation to the top level of the site is shown at the top. The data list from the sample fonts database is shown below the head "Display Fonts." If this was really a complete list, it would be a long scrolling page. Also from this page the options for other organizations of the fonts had to be available. How were we really going to fit all this on one page?

for each category and show the data list under the heading (here, display fonts is shown as an example). This is because although you can sort the data by category, no dividers are inserted in the data list to separate one category from another. If you choose to display the field "category," it will repeat with every font name.

If you were to choose View Fonts by Designer from the page shown in Figure 9.9, you would get a list of designers' names (like the PDF catalog). You then had a choice of seeing a list of a designer's fonts, or a bio of that designer. Figure 9.10 shows the page "PF fonts," where the font family name links to the catalog page, and it also contains a link to Peter's biography. We were considering merging these two functions onto one page, but some designers have substantial biographies and substantial font lists.

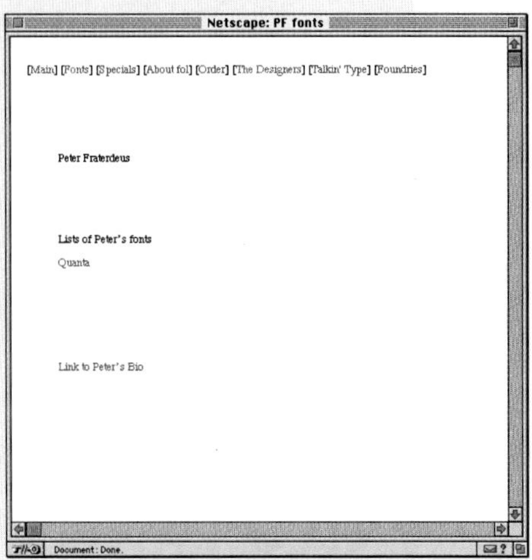

Figure 9.10

One of two pages dedicated to a font designer. This one has a list of the designer's fonts, which were to be links to the catalog pages. These links could not be generated or maintained by NetObjects Fusion because they would be links to stacked pages. The other page about the designer is a biography page, and the two are mutually linked (although in different sections of the site structure).

Testing the First Prototype

In building and testing the logical prototype in NetObjects Fusion, we began to question some of our linear ideas about the site architecture. A common response was "there is too much back and forth required." This became frustrating for testers and some lost interest in investigating any further. The repetitive clicking seemed like one step forward, two steps back. This was not what we had in mind.

It is true that from the core page (through the first visit page if appropriate) you can get to a list of fonts by category in one click, and to the showing of a font with another click. However, if you are interested in seeing fonts by Brian Sooy, you have to click back and forth between his list of fonts and the catalog pages. Also, if you want to choose fonts alphabetically, you must go from the list, to the page, back to the list, and so on. A search is a nice feature, but it requires that the spelling be correct—hit or miss at best.

It was time to rethink our navigational and interface options. Back to the drawing board.

The Nonlinear Organization

The organization and development of a structure for fontsOnline really came down to accessing the same data by several different means. So far the methods by which you could access fonts by any organizational method other than font category were seriously flawed.

Same Data, Multiple Ways to Access

Was there any way to re-sort the pages based on user demand? Sure, in a dynamic database online. Unfortunately, this was a bit beyond the resources and budget for the project. Also, dynamically built pages tend to be slower to load because of having to draw upon the data while you are waiting,as we discussed in Chapter 6, "Database Publishing."

We could set up three or four different data lists, each sorted differently and each with its own set of stacked pages. These data lists would still

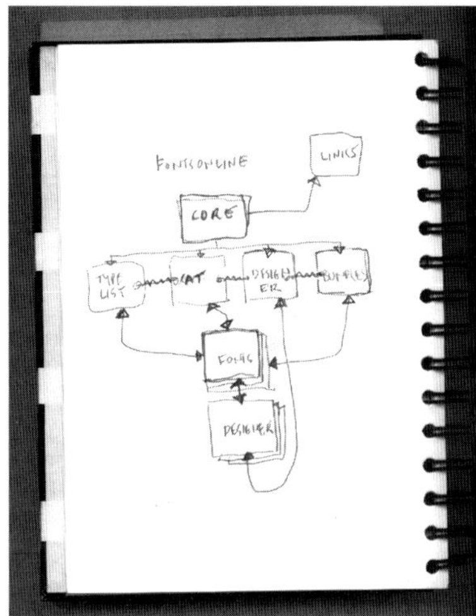

Figure 9.11
We sat down and decided to draw a map of the site again. Here's a look at the drawing in my sketchbook. It's obvious. All roads point to fonts.

draw upon the same external data source (see Chapter 6 if these terms are bewildering). This had two drawbacks: the excess server space taken by three copies of the 90-odd pages of font families and the fact that the layout of each one would have to be updated separately.

Figure 9.11 shows my sketch of the structure that we wanted to achieve. Visitors should be able to choose to view fonts by an alphabetical type list, by category, by designer, or see fonts that are bundled as specials, and all would lead to the same catalog pages. But how to avoid the jumping back and forth?

Our new map made it clear we had to make multiple avenues of access to the same information. In this case be changeable menus allowing access by category, type list, designer, and bundles would be more powerful than a search engine. This still follows the Acrobat catalog, retaining continuity, but instead of different lists, we needed context-sensitive menus. There would be additional sections (articles about type, links, and so on) available from the core page, but major levels and their context-sensitive submenus would be available on each page. How would we accomplish this?

The original approach was too much like a paper catalog and wasn't taking advantage of the navigational abilities and structures offered by the World Wide Web. How could we make it possible for the viewer to have multilevel access with ease? What were the solutions at many other very deep sites such as Netscape, Macromedia, CNET, and the like?

Frames

Using frames isn't an intuitive process. The seemingly uncontrollable need of those browsing to click for immediate gratification is one of toughest design challenges. It takes an excellent interface to guarantee that a visitor understands the relationship from frame to frame. We have found, however, that more and more people, when given a choice, choose to view

AS A DESIGNER, I HATE FRAMES. I JUST DON'T THINK THE INTERFACE IS INTUITIVE. IT IS HARD ENOUGH TO CREATE AN INTERFACE SO THAT VISITORS UNDERSTAND WHERE THEY ARE WITHIN A SITE. IF YOU ADD ANYTHING MORE THAN A SCROLLING NAVIGATIONAL BAR, THE TASK BECOMES MORE

a site with frames. The interface possibilities are better (no frame borders in 3.0 browsers) and people are beginning to understand using them.

Some site developers use frames so that navigation is always available even when scrolling up or down on a long page. This is an effective implementation of frames, however, most of our pages are not of the long, scrolling variety. Generally, frames are used to make numerous levels of a site accessible using a never-ending menu bar. Our studio has not. We had considered frames early in the structure discussions (at the request of Peter Fraterdeus) but felt that to have a long scrolling list of all the fonts down one side frame was too cumbersome. We would rather scrolling be an activity that has a reward at the end of it, not just a shopping list.

Was there a way to break down the information into manageable bits to avoid the long scrolling list, but also avoid to many levels of navigation and too much back and forth? It was time to put some interface ideas to the test again. How could we make the interface intuitive? How could we make the landmarks at the site clear and not have this be a hall of mirrors with people madly clicking and going nowhere? Figure 9.12 shows us struggling with these issues, and a solution emerging.

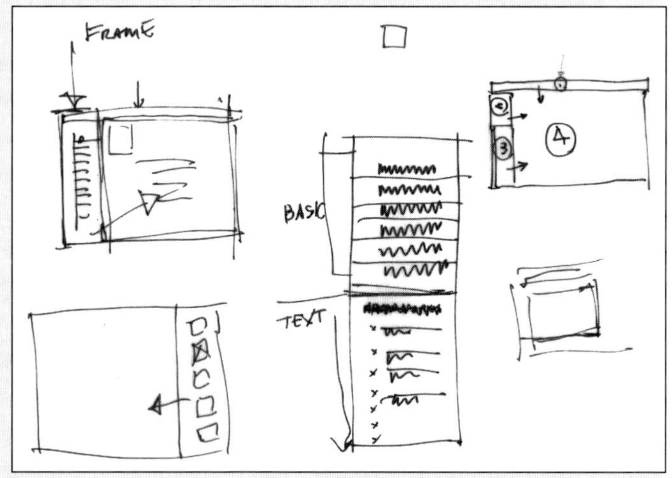

Figure 9.12
These are sketches from our interface design meetings. In the upper left you can see a two-frame solution, then the idea of splitting the left frame horizontally was raised. A relatively ambitious four-frame interface was finally developed. It would allow for growth within the site without adding additional navigational elements to every page of the site

IF YOU THINK YOU WILL GET MANY VISITORS WITH 2.0 LEVEL BROWSERS, BE ESPECIALLY CAREFUL ABOUT YOUR USE OF FRAMES. (BROWSERS OLDER THAN THAT CANNOT SEE FRAMES AT ALL.) IF A VISITOR TRIES TO USE THE BACK BUTTON WITH A 2.0 VINTAGE BROWSER (NETSCAPE OR EXPLORER) THE PREVIOUS SCREEN LOADS ONLY IN THE FIRST FRAME, RATHER THAN THE ACTIVE FRAME. THIS CAN LEAD TO SOME BIZARRE SITUATIONS. TEST YOU SITE WITH OLDER BROWSERS!

Originally we considered adding a left frame giving a list of the fonts, sorted according to the visitor's choice. We added a top banner frame to identify fontsOnline and possibly rotate headers to announce specials and places of interest within the site, or advertising banners. Where, then would the permanent navigational options appear? How do you change your mind to sort the fonts in a different way? We then decided to split the left frame and have the upper part remain constant with the same basic options. The bottom portion could then scroll without losing the primary navigation in the upper portion.

We were still left with a long alphabetical list, however, now appearing in a short frame in the lower left. Anchors from letters at the top of the frame could jump you to an appropriate letter, but how do you get back (except using those constant back to top links which make the list even longer)? We were all staring at the sketch when someone, visualizing the horizontal nature of the alphabet, suggested that the letter go across the top frame (Figure 9.13).

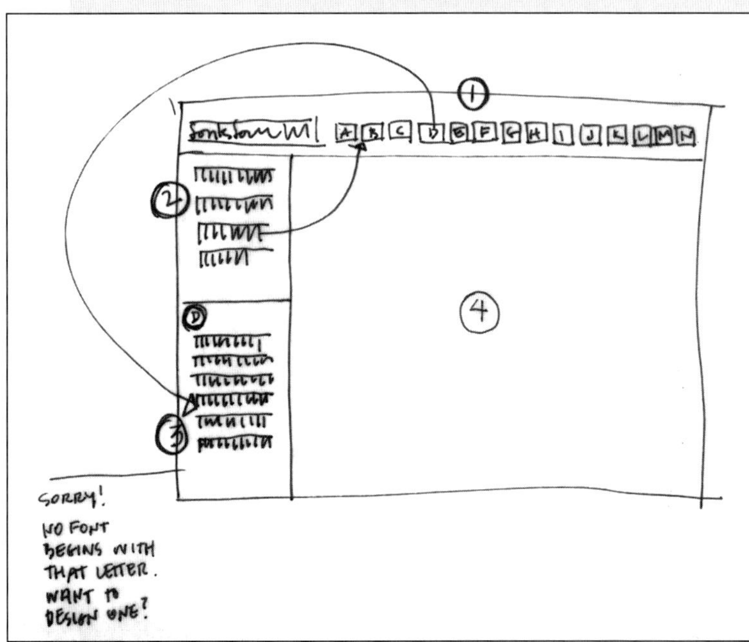

Figure 9.13
Here is a sketch of the frame set as it would appear if you chose to view fonts by the alphabetical type list. The letters of the alphabet appear across the top and the list of fonts beginning with the selected letter appear in frame 3.

The Second Logical Prototype

Our navigational solution required targeting two frames or more for simultaneous change. Now that we thought we had finally figured out how to make this interface happen, it was time to meet about what kind of scripting or engineering would need to take place to make it all happen. To do more than initiate a change in one frame based on a selected link in another frame requires applying handlers that will target frame changes. We therefore added to our team our in-house self-taught JavaScript student and involved him in the interface meetings. We had an idea it would be possible—now to look into the feasibility and test our ideas.

Figure 9.14 shows the core page of the new logical prototype. The exact number and names of links outside of the catalog has not been set, but the emphasis is on the multiple entrances to the font catalog. If the testers choose to simply enter, they are brought into the frame interface as if they had chosen the (alphabetical) type list option.

The sketches shown in the previous section became the frame layout specification set for the site, as shown in Figure 9.15. Frame 2 contains the constant navigational choices for the font catalog and a link back to the core page. The navigation in this frame would be GIFs. This frame is of fixed size and does not allow for scrolling. We decided not to have links to other sections of the site from this already crowded interface; the visitor would have to return to the core page to access the articles on type and such.

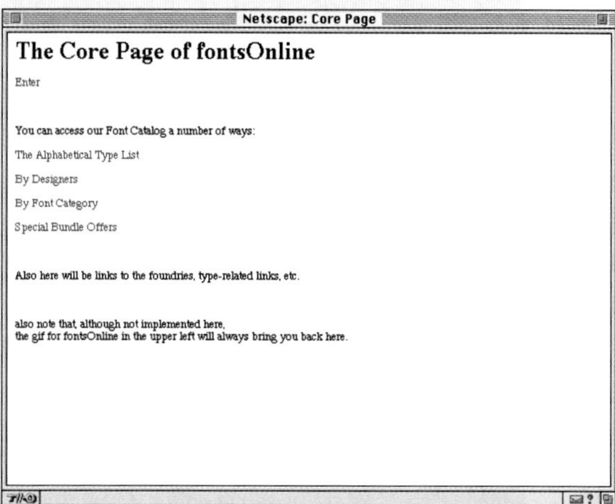

Figure 9.14
The core page in the second logical prototype. We have not abandoned the "first visit" concept, but it was not implemented in this prototype.

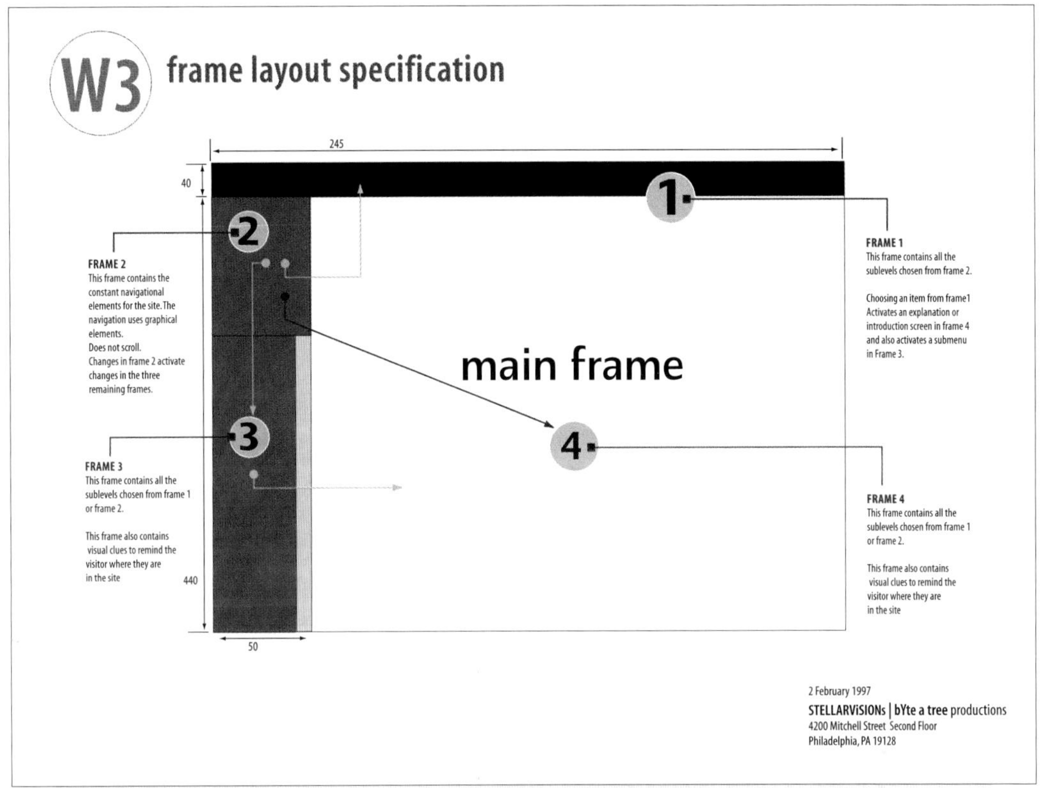

Figure 9.15
The specifications I developed for the four frames.

Figure 9.16 shows the frames' logical prototype after the visitor has entered the catalog. Frame 1 shows the choices within the alphabet, A-Z. Frame 3 tells you that a list of fonts beginning with that letter will appear there after you choose a letter above. Frame 4 is introductory copy about the catalog, how it is organized, etc., and contains no navigational links. We restrict the navigation, with few exceptions, to frame 2, followed by frames 1 and 3.

Figure 9.17 shows the reaction of the frames if you had chosen "Z" from the alphabet in frame 1. Frames 1 and 2 remain the same, so you still have access to navigation at two levels. Frame 3 becomes a list of the fonts beginning with Z (with scroll bar only if necessary). Simultaneously, to get you to actual fonts more quickly, frame 4 displays the first font that begins with the letter. You can then see subsequent fonts beginning with Z by clicking down the list.

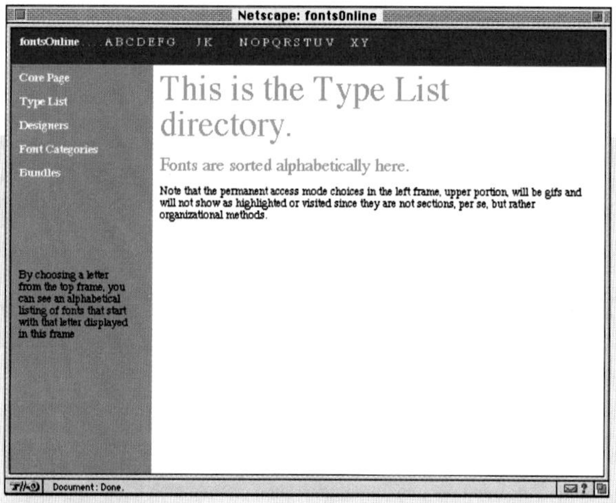

Figure 9.16

The opening of the Type List channel, or mode. The five permanent choices in Frame 2 are Core Page, Type List, Designers, Font Categories, and Bundles.

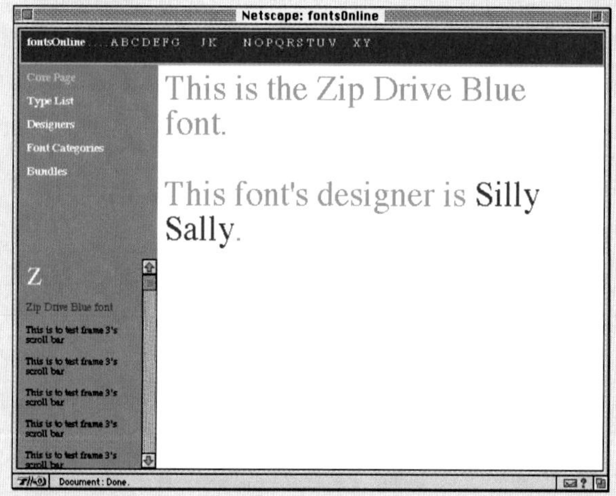

Figure 9.17

A showing of the Zip Drive Blue font. (All the fake names and humor in this prototype are to be blamed on the author of the script for the targeted frames, Arthur Knapp.)

An exactly parallel situation applies to the font categories. The categories of fonts are listed across Frame 1, as was the alphabet, and the other navigation is parallel. Instead of all the fonts beginning with Z, all the display fonts are listed in frame 3. We had to deviate from the system when it came to the designers, because they would not fit across frame 1, and the list of designers might grow at any time. Therefore, we listed the designers in frame 3. When you choose a designer you get a biography in frame 4 and simultaneously a list of his or her fonts in frame 3. In the Design section later in this chapter, there are layouts that show this clearly if you are not getting it from the description.

WHAT IF YOU CHOOSE A LETTER THAT DOESN'T HAVE ANY FONTS? RATHER THAN A DEAD LINK OR AN INCOMPLETE ALPHABET, YOU ARE SIMPLY TOLD "NO FONTS BEGIN WITH THE LETTER Z" AND INVITED TO DESIGN ONE.

The only exception, allowing navigation from frame 4, was a link to the designer's bio (from the name). This would simply bring up the biography of the designer, but not change the navigational list in frame 3 or the subcategories in frame 1. Visitors could continue browsing on the course they had chosen. It would simply be a brief side step, comparable to viewing the PDF page and coming back.

The Next/Previous Debate

NetObjects Fusion enables you to automatically place next/previous buttons on all stacked pages. This is a logical feature, because a visitor would probably want to have the option of simply browsing sequentially through the pages. In early layouts for the font catalog pages, we had forward and back arrows (actually < and >) to allow this to happen.

ALTHOUGH OUR EAGER SCRIPTER WAS INTERESTED IN THE CHALLENGE OF HAVING THE ARROWS BE CONTEXT-SENSITIVE (REFERRING TO THE BROWSER'S HISTORY LOG), WE DECIDED THAT HE HAD ENOUGH ON HIS PLATE WITH SCRIPTED FRAMES.

While we were test-driving the prototype, however, we realized that this sequential concept was incompatible with the nonlinear architecture where the same pages are organized in several ways. Is "next" the next font alphabetically, the next font by the same designer, or the next font in the same category?

We would have to choose a default organization, say alphabetically, and the next button would always take you the next font alphabetically. This is great if the visitor has chosen to browse the fonts alphabetically. We pondered, however, the reaction of a visitor who has chosen to organize the fonts according to their designer. Figure 9.19 shows a screen from the frames Logical Prototype when you are looking at a font, having chosen to view fonts in the red category (made up for the prototype). If there was a next arrow, it would take you to a font that is not red at all, and not on the list in frame 3! This is obviously confusing and there is no real value to seeing an unrelated font in the context of red fonts.

So the issue came down to weighing the positive of being able to quickly click through the alphabetical catalog with the negative of the disruption when browsing by designer or category. We reviewed the interface for the alphabetical listings once more. The visitor can easily click one font after another on the list in frame 3 (lower left) and we decided that this was just as convenient as the next arrow. Before we had embraced the frames interface, a next option was critical, but now it did not seem to be.

Figure 9.19
The Irish Red font, viewed in the context of the fictional category red fonts. If a next button were available, it would take you to the next font alphabetically, not the expected Lady Sings the Rouge.

The Reaction

We uploaded our prototype in a secret folder called "slinky" and asked our client what he thought. Soon we had an email from Peter Fraterdeus that said:

Slinky sends Silly Sally Soaring!

Rigorous testing raised a few items for improvement. Overall, however, the test was a huge success and all the testers felt that they were able to get to the fonts quickly and easily any way they chose.

Design: Giving the Fonts Expression

The visual personality of fontsOnline wouldn't be trendy. It would be driven by clear organization and a visual emphasis on the letters themselves. An atmosphere had to be created that would show off the letters. Make the characters themselves of interest. After all, the letters do sell themselves.

The fascinating thing about typography is the personality and history that is bound in each letter. The love of the form of letters combined with the interest in technology would be the driving forces from which the personality of the fontsOnline site would emerge (Figure 9.20).

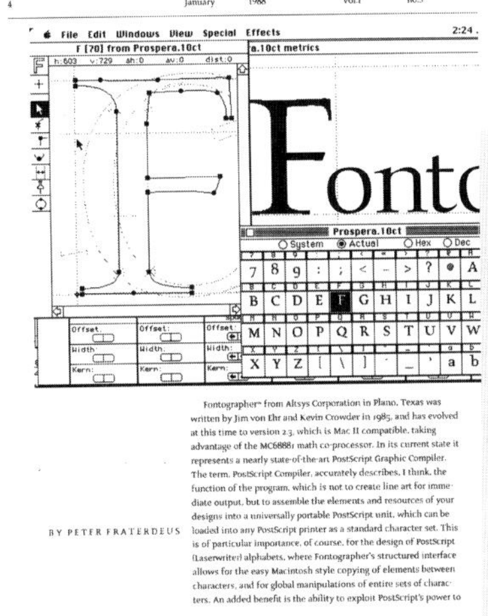
4 January 1988 vol.1 no.3

BY PETER FRATERDEUS

Fontographer™ from Altsys Corporation in Plano, Texas was written by Jim von Ehr and Kevin Crowder in 1985, and has evolved at this time to version 2.3, which is Mac II compatible, taking advantage of the MC68881 math co-processor. In its current state it represents a nearly state-of-the-art PostScript Graphic Compiler. The term, PostScript Compiler, accurately describes, I think, the function of the program, which is not to create line art for immediate output, but to assemble the elements and resources of your designs into a universally portable PostScript unit, which can be loaded into any PostScript printer as a standard character set. This is of particular importance, of course, for the design of PostScript (Laserwriter) alphabets, where Fontographer's structured interface allows for the easy Macintosh style copying of elements between characters, and for global manipulations of entire sets of characters. An added benefit is the ability to exploit PostScript's power to

Figure 9.20

Here's a screen capture of a letter in Fontographer. This kind of view, showing vectors and the creation of letters, would be used in the designing fonts section. We would show a behind-the-scenes look at fonts, letters, and designers to enhance the site.

Alphabets has been interested in technology since its beginnings, seeking to make fonts for LaserWriter desktop publishing and Postscript with PageMaker 1.0 (Figure 9.21). We would use new technologies to enhance the visibility of its family of characters.

One of the things we really like about the design of www.word.com and www.hotwired.com are the intro pages. Just a little hint of what's new inside, nothing big or elaborate, just a changing visual that lets someone know there is at least a small reason to return often. We decided to include an intro page to set the tone for the site. Each animation, image, or quote has to do with the glorification of type. They are all less than 20K and use a meta tag for refresh. The page also has a manual link in case a fast connection leaves someone waiting (Figure 9.22).

The color palette for the site can be seen in Figure 9.23. We always determine a palette and build all assets using this palette.

The design for the pages can be seen in Figures 9.24 through 9.27. These are specification sheets created in Adobe Illustrator for client approval, and to be followed by the production staff building pages in NetObjects Fusion. We chose the phrase "(?#&*!) flagrante delicto" to show as a GIF for each font because it is a highbrow version of "jeepers! I'm caught red-handed!" It shows the often distinctive letters, f, g, and r, and gives an excuse to show some punctuation. The animated GIF and the links to the Acrobat PDF and the Shockwave Flash animation are on the right. In the background is a randomly chosen image of a large letter (the five vowels). Figure 9.26 shows the font categories across frame 1, and the labeling of each font with the categories to which it belongs.

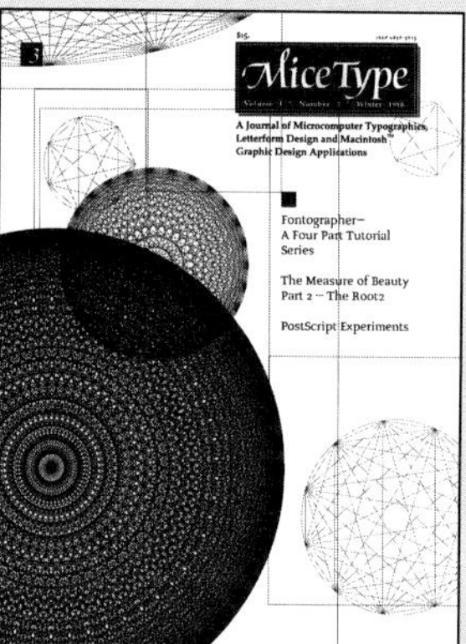

Figure 9.21
MiceType Journal's paper publishing by Alphabets, Inc. We would repurpose this art and text for access at the fontsOnline site. These early publications discuss the new Postscript language and the designing of type for the new imagesetters and the designing of type for the new imagesetters and desktop publishing industry.

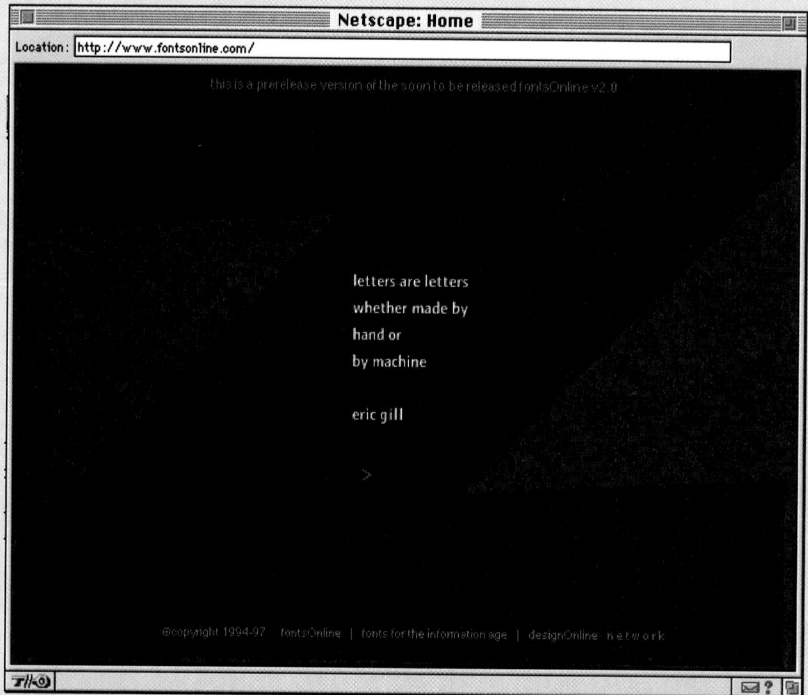

Figure 9.22
Here's the entrance page. Our first animated GIF is a quote from Eric Gill.

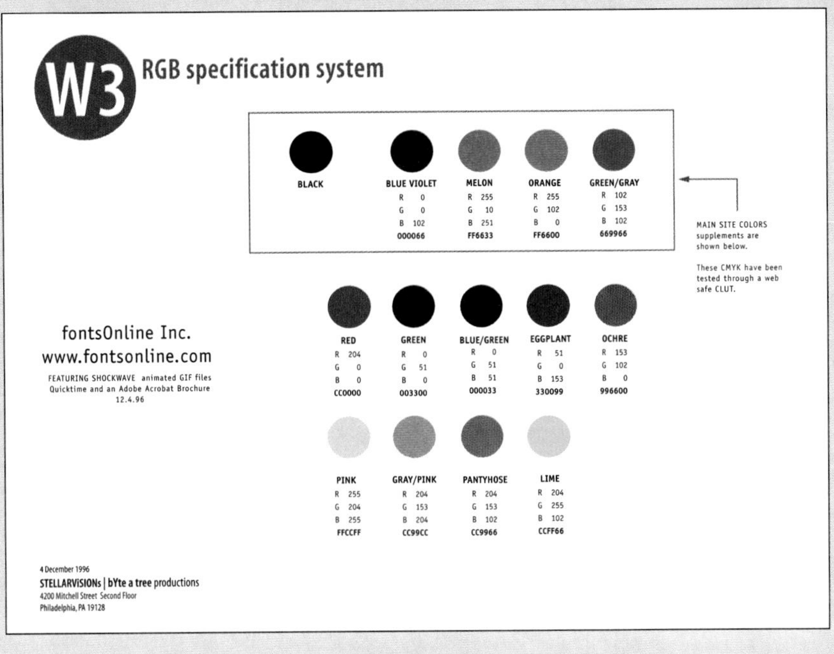

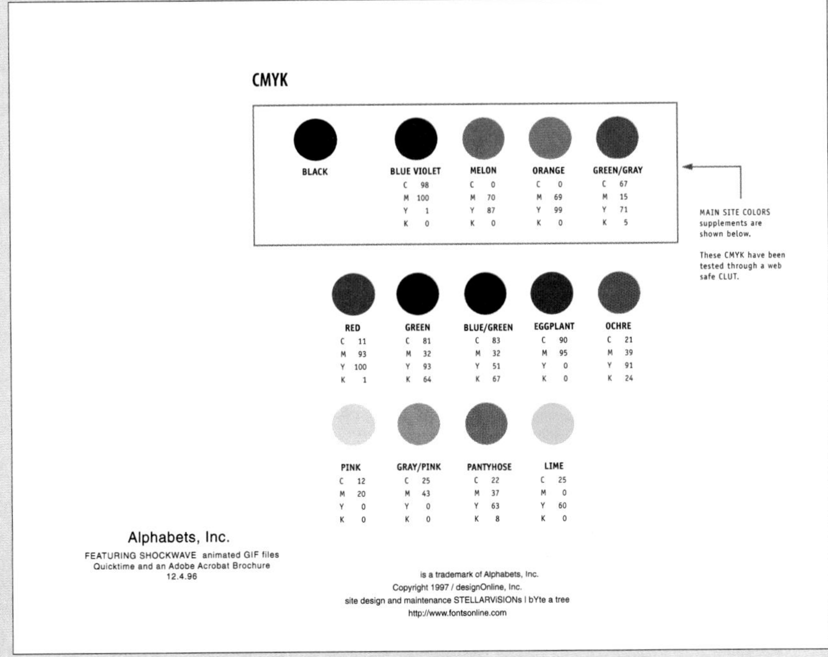

Figure 9.23

We decided on a sophisticated, subdued color palette. It contains deep blue for intro and navigational pages. To keep the weight of GIFs and GIF animations down on catalog pages, we decided to use white as the background behind the letters. This would also help if we wanted to create transparent objects and any shadows.

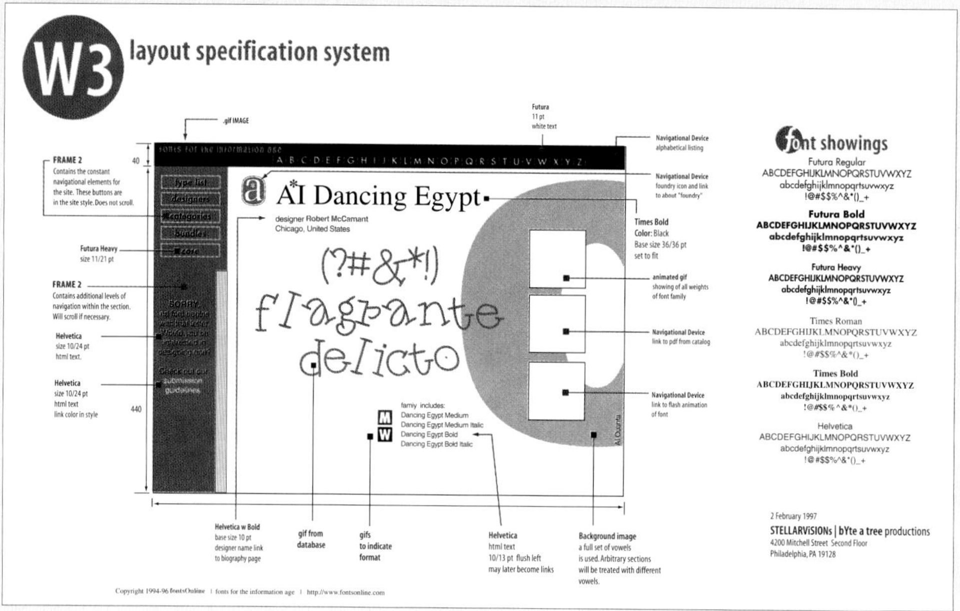

Figure 9.24

Here are the specs for the catalog pages at the site. Note the foundry mark in the upper left corner of frame 4. This would be a link to foundry information. It would also be a place to mark other fonts included at the site in the future if other small foundries joined fontsOnline. Always allow room for growth in the pages you design.

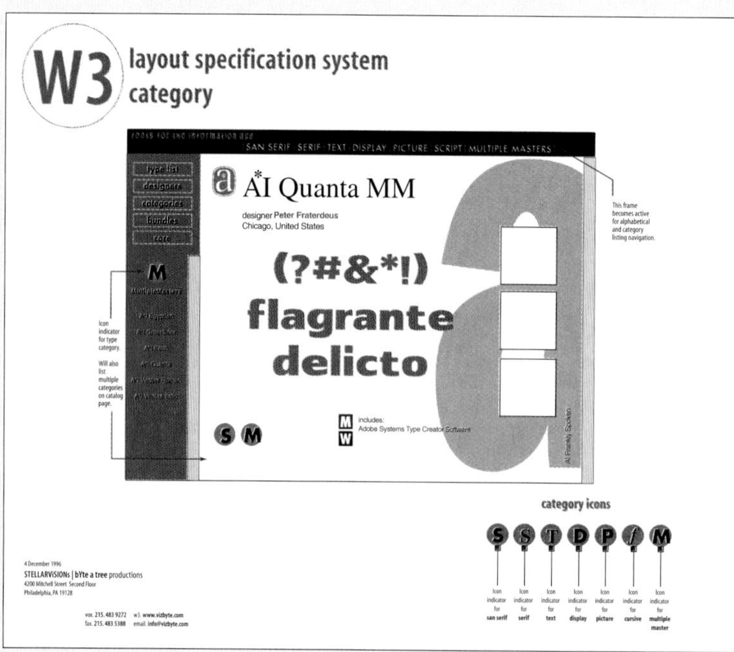

Figure 9.25

The seven categories of fonts are identified by seven characters in circles (GIFs). These category icons for san serif, serif, text, display, picture, cursive, and multiple master appear in the lower left of the catalog page. They also appear at the top of frame 3 when that category is being listed.

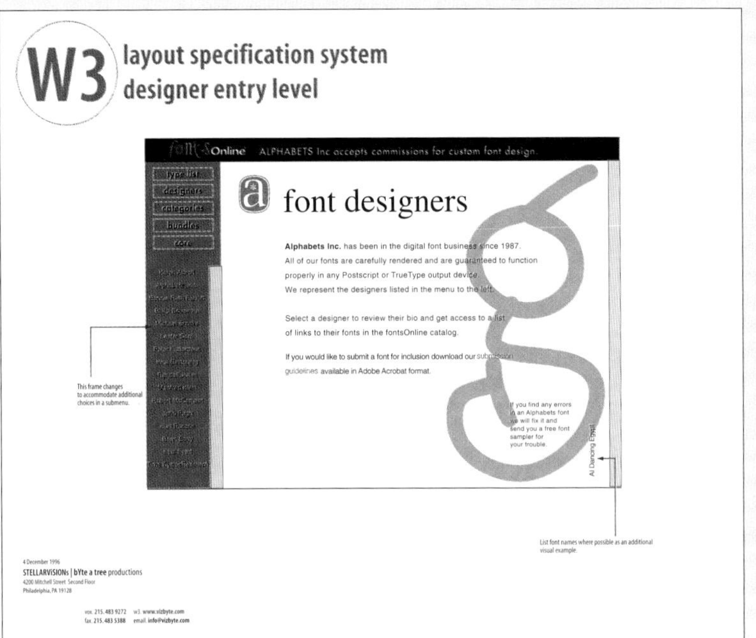

Figure 9.26

This is an example in which frame 4 had introductory copy while "waiting" for the viewer to choose a designer from the list in frame 3. In this case the subcategories appear in frame 3, not frame 1 (because they won't fit in frame 1).

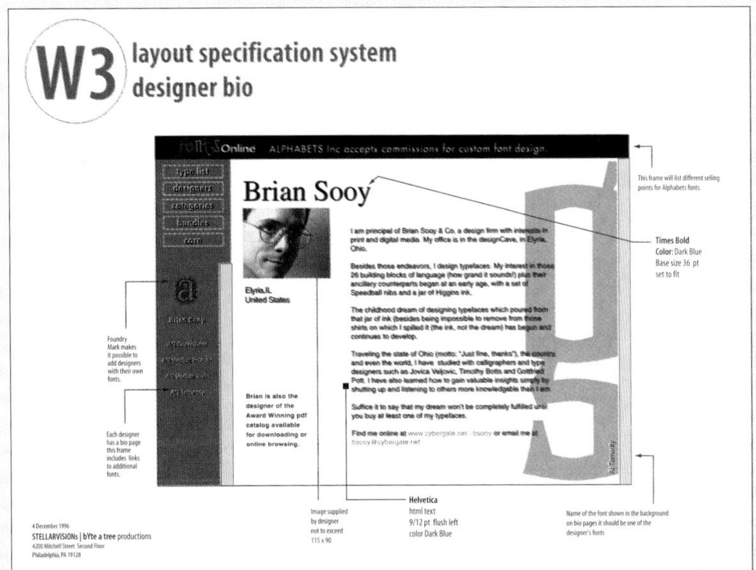

Figure 9.27

Here is the bio for Brian Sooy. You will note that in frame 1 (which is not needed for navigation) a message has appeared. This could be a random rotation. You can browse Brian's fonts by clicking in frame 3, and always get back to his bio by clicking his name.

Implementation: Making the Dream a Reality

This project is a combination of the strengths of NetObjects Fusion and bringing in JavaScript to go even further. The catalog pages are built from a database provided by Alphabets. NetObjects Fusion, however, does not enable you to link to a specific stacked page internally. Also, NetObjects Fusion does not allow a frame to split horizontally, the way we split the left frame into frames 2 and 3. Therefore, this project is an interweaving of NetObjects Fusion and conventional production.

Database Pages for the Font Catalog

Figure 9.28 shows a record from the client's database in FileMaker Pro (on the Macintosh). The fields include designers, number of weights for each family, comments about the font by the designer, and type category. In Chapter 6, we reviewed publishing databases using NetObjects Fusion, and how it is a static (update when publish) rather than a dynamic

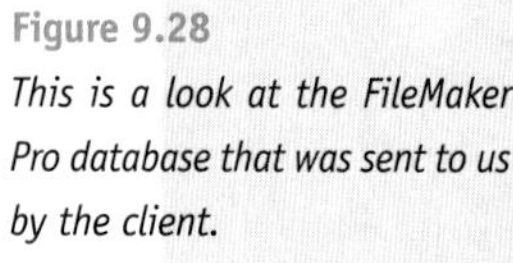

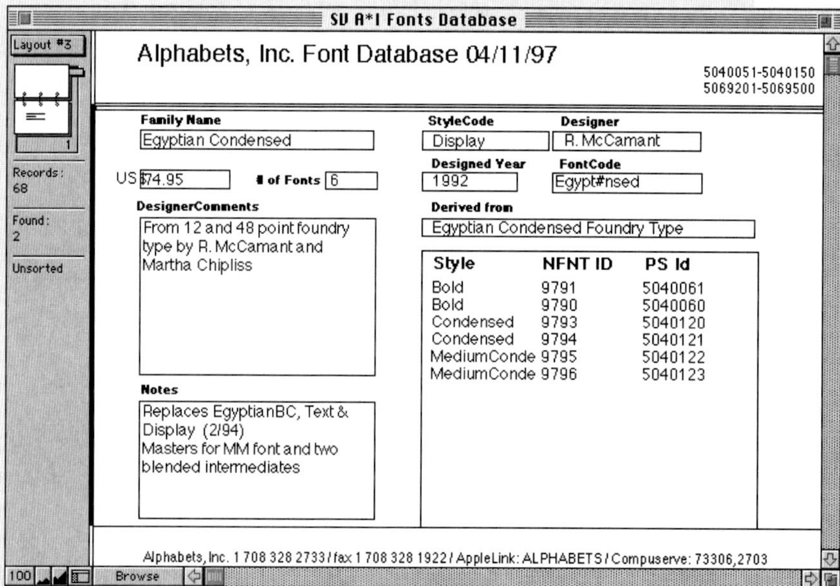

Figure 9.28

This is a look at the FileMaker Pro database that was sent to us by the client.

(update instantly) publishing system. There was no need in this case for instant updates; the fact that we can periodically update the data automatically is a wonderful advantage. Any time a new font is added, we must make the components for the catalog page (GIF, animated GIF, and so on) so there will be nothing instant about the process.

Linking to the Images

Because we did not have a database system that could cope with images, instead we entered the *name* of the image into a new field. This was scripted from the list of the images (in order) in the folder or directory. We then added scripts to the element on the layout using the Script dialog box:

Before element: <IMG SRC = "/images/

[the element has the image name]

After element: ">

In the Page view you will not see the images, but upon preview, they appear like magic. The same technique was used for the animated GIFs. The Acrobat and Shockwave images can be placed on the layout since they are constant; however, the links associated with the element change with each page. Therefore, the file names for these elements were added to the database as separate fields. We then treated these as a variable (see Chapter 6) and were able to point to the element. Since all the images were in the same location the path name was not in the database but in the script.

Creating the Lists of Links for Frame 3

We would need lists of fonts (actually font family names) to appear in frame 3 in the lower left that are links to the correct HTML *generated by* the stacked pages. This presented several logistical challenges:

- How to track the HTML names and pair them with the font names
- How to create separate lists grouped by designer, category, and bundled fonts

- How to create the links (other than by hand)

At first, it seemed overwhelming to keep track of the arbitrary names assigned by NetObjects Fusion to the stacked pages and individually code links which, of course, would not be managed by NetObjects Fusion. We considered abandoning the idea of stacked pages for this reason, but then we were faced with manually entering the text for 90 pages. We could use a template as a starting point, but if there needed to be any modifications to the design, it would have to be changed on all 90 or so pages.

Through a combination of AppleScript, spreadsheets or databases, we were able to generate text files to paste into traditional HTML documents (external HTML pages in NetObjects Fusion). If you are interested in the exact series of steps, visit our site at www.designpractice.com. It involves using AppleScript to capture file names from the Finder, a spreadsheet to add columns of HTML and then sort the rows by the different parameters. We call this kind of procedure "database assisted" publishing. Whenever you find yourself doing a great deal of cut and paste, consider a way of automating the process, getting software to do some of the work.

In general, when you are starting with a database, most manipulations will be easier to do in the database or some other application geared to sorting and massaging data. This means that when the material comes into NetObjects Fusion or into HTML, it is in the exact form you need it. It is essential that these steps be as simple and automated as possible, because they will have to be repeated every time the database is updated. In this case, it is only when new fonts are added, which is only a few times a year. Indeed, all of these spreadsheet manipulations could be easily scripted.

"THE GRAPHIC SIGNS CALLED LETTERS ARE SO COMPLETELY BLENDED WITH THE STREAM OF WRITTEN THOUGHT THAT THEIR PRESENCE THEREIN IS AS UNPERCEIVED AS THE TICKING OF A CLOCK IN THE MEASUREMENT OF TIME. ONLY BY AN EFFORT OF ATTENTION DOES THE LAYMAN DISCOVER THAT THEY EXIST AT ALL. IT COMES AS A SURPRISE TO HIM THAT THESE SIGNS SHOULD BE A MATTER OF CONCERN TO ANY ONE OF THE CRAFTS OF MEN. BUT TO BE CONCERNED WITH THE SHAPES OF LETTERS IS TO WORK IN AN ANCIENT AND FUNDAMENTAL MATERIAL. THE QUALITIES OF CLASSIC TIME: ORDER, SIMPLICITY, GRACE. TO TRY TO LEARN AND REPEAT THEIR EXCELLENCE IS TO PUT ONESELF UNDER TRAINING IN A SIMPLE AND SEVERE SCHOOL OF DESIGN."

WILLIAM ADDISON DWIGGINS

10

Warm Fuzzy Marketing:

TimeCycle.com

Figure 10.1
Designing the logo in 1989 was the beginning of our business relationship with TimeCycle. This mark and the color of their fluorescent yellow jerseys have become synonymous with speedy delivery and their cool image.

TimeCycle Couriers is the premier bicycle courier service in the Philadelphia metropolitan area (Figure 10.1). Having virtually annihilated most of the competition and developed an extremely loyal client base, it is now expanding its range of services. There are several factors in this success, one of which is early integration of technology.

WHEN YOU CALL TIMECYCLE, THE MINUTE YOU SAY YOUR BUSINESS NAME (OR, MORE LIKELY, THE MINUTE THEY RECOGNIZE YOUR VOICE), THE DISPATCHERS HAVE YOUR INFORMATION ON A DATABASE SCREEN. YOU DO NOT HAVE TO GIVE AN ACCOUNT NUMBER—THEY WILL QUICKLY CONFIRM YOUR LOCATION, AND PROBABLY ALSO HAVE THE ADDRESS OF YOUR DESTINATION IN THE DATABASE. THIS HAS LED MANY CLIENTS TO BELIEVE THAT THE DISPATCHERS ARE PSYCHIC.

TimeCycle has been receptive to the use of technology both to serve its clients and to maintain an ecological office. It uses much less paper in the course of doing business than other courier services—dispatching without paper and billing in monthly cycles. It uses bicycles wherever possible, calling upon gas power only outside of the Center City area (and not always then). It is not surprising that a partnership with an interest in efficient technology, from bicycles to Macintosh computers, and a commitment to ecological goals would be interested in making use of the World Wide Web.

Figure 10.2

Here is the logo on the front of the jersey; on the back it is much larger. Clients have actually inquired about purchasing TimeCycle jerseys and other gear. This exemplifies the power of the TimeCycle image.

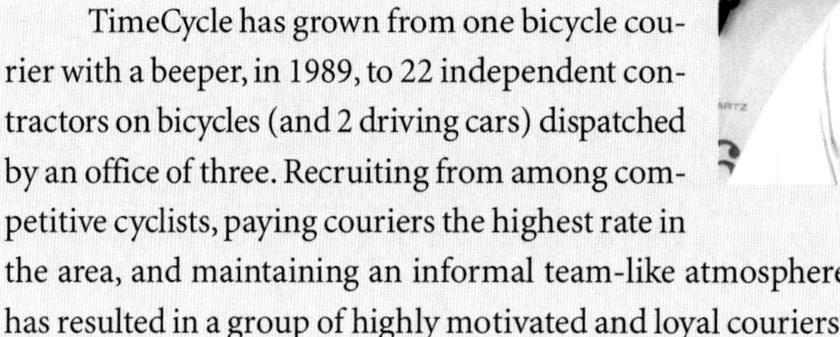

TimeCycle has grown from one bicycle courier with a beeper, in 1989, to 22 independent contractors on bicycles (and 2 driving cars) dispatched by an office of three. Recruiting from among competitive cyclists, paying couriers the highest rate in the area, and maintaining an informal team-like atmosphere has resulted in a group of highly motivated and loyal couriers.

"YOU RODE FROM THERE ON A BICYCLE? NO WAY!" TIMECYCLE WAS FOUNDED BY A COMPETITIVE CYCLIST AS A WAY TO TRAIN AND ALSO MAKE A LIVING. MOST OF THE COURIERS ARE INVOLVED IN RACING AND THEIR SPEED AND ENDURANCE IS TRULY AMAZING. MANY OF THEIR YUPPIE DESK-JOCKEY CLIENTS LOOK UPON THESE ATHLETES WITH ADMIRATION AND SOME ENVY.

A unique characteristic of TimeCycle is the personality of the founder, Jeff Appeltans, which affects every aspect of the business. Jeff will strike up a conversation, find a common interest within minutes, remember it, and call you the next time that band is in town. He weaves connections among people out of genuine interest and good will. His business partner and longtime friend, Eric Nordberg, supervises the dispatching operations, often talking on the telephone, the radio and to someone in the office simultaneously while screens fly past on the monitor. We have found that the character of a small business is inextricably linked to the personality of the owners, and in this case it is especially true. Figure 10.2 shows partner Eric Nordberg with TimeCycle clock.

In categorizing the type of Web site, this case study falls into what we characterize as warm fuzzy marketing because while the information is there for marketing purposes, a key marketing tool is interpersonal. As a glimse ahead to the published site see Figure 10.3

Fuzzy Definition: Coming into Focus

Jeff Appeltans, founder and partner, approached us at the end of 1996 to design a Web presence for TimeCycle Couriers. He wanted this to be a site that wouwd enhance his service to existing clients, explain new services, and give a broader sense of the people that make up TimeCycle.

We carried on our correspondence and even transferred text files by email. Paper documents or disks were carried—you guessed it—by courier.

Goals

In talking with Jeff, it emerged that the primary goal was to reinforce and extend the feeling of connection that he tries to develop with his customers, which is becoming a challenge to maintain as the business has grown. In addition, the web site could provide convenient access to information about services, which might lead clients to expand their use of the couriers. Although a potential client *might* find TimeCycle on the web, Jeff realistically imagined the site would act more powerfully as a supplemental resource for him when pursuing a new account.

Figure 10.3

Visit the site at www.TimeCycle.com *before reading this chapter to get a full appreciation of the we process describe.*

Therefore we articulated two goals for the site:

- To represent TimeCycle, its personality and its services
- To increase customer interest and involvement

The design challenge was to create a visually hip site that reinforced the personality of TimeCycle while maintaining instant accessibility to key features. The site had to be damn speedy, too!

Research or Yard Sale?

Before this project we already knew quite a bit about this company. They have been our client—and, conversely, we have been a customer—as long as TimeCycle Couriers has been in existence. We began gathering information (and objects) with the aim of getting all the material freshly in front of us to review possible content for the site.

We pulled all of the printed samples from the archives and, where practical, located the corresponding digital files. We asked TimeCycle to bring in any source material we could use, including press clippings and television video. We had a member of the team log all this into our client library database. This enabled us to view the material in different ways and make annotations about it. It is helpful in determining where we need photography, scans, or image enhancement.

A CLIENT LIBRARY FILE CAN BE SORTED AND SEARCHED AND SHOULD BE KEPT AFTER THE PROJECT HAS BEEN COMPLETED. WE ADD TO THIS DATABASE ANY TIME WE ACCEPT ANOTHER JOB FOR A PARTICULAR CLIENT. IN THIS WAY WE HAVE EASY ACCESS TO A WHOLE CLIENT LIBRARY THAT USED TO BE PAPER ARCHIVES (READ FILING CABINETS). WE HAVE BEEN GRADUALLY DEVISING DIGITAL METHODS TO REPLACE MANY ANALOG SYSTEMS. THIS IS INTEGRAL TO THE DESIGN AND BUSINESS PRACTICE IN A DIGITALLY BASED STUDIO.

In addition to printed material and information, we gathered the tools of the couriers' trade. Tires, radios, beepers, bags, clipboard, water bottles, helmets, jackets—anything that could be recognized as being TimeCycle. We felt that these were important to have a physical sense of the business, a complete picture (remember Figure 1.6?).

This pile of paraphernalia also helped to start thinking about visual symbols that could be used at the site. Although the stage of setting the personality and visual look of the site comes later in the design process, most of us can't help beginning to visualize things. Don't fight it; let those images stew quietly on the back burner and they will probably have taken shape by the time you need them. Also, talking to a client about some visual ideas can help get the client excited about the project.

Content: Features and Functions

We sat for the afternoon brainstorming about what we thought could be included at the site. Most obviously we would need to include the information about services that appeared in the printed brochure. This included expanded services, numerous delivery options, and maps showing zones. Also included were instructions about how to request a delivery, how to prepare your package, and so on. We recognized that there was a complex matrix of information—geographic, temporal, and financial—that we struggled to present clearly in print and would need to be reanalyzed. Also, although space considerations were at a premium

Hill racing cyclist energetically delivers the goods

in the printed material, at the site we could actually expand the information. For example, we could include more specific geographical locations.

There was a stack of news coverage of TimeCycle, mostly pure human interest gems from weather-related articles (how do they deliver in all that ice and snow?) to coverage of their participation in the Cycle Messenger World Championships (Figure 10.4). The sheer amount of coverage speaks to the appeal of TimeCycle and the wealth of stories, not to say legends, about these couriers. How could we exploit this best?

This internal brainstorming helped us formulate questions for our next brainstorming meeting which, this time, included our client. We got their reactions to many of our ideas, and asked them to think of what they would like to see at the site (temporarily ignoring any obstacles). What did they want to promote at the site? What kind of features did they want, such as email and online requests for deliveries? Did they want to feature the couriers? Had they thought of featuring clients too? How often did they want visitors to return to the site? Who are the customers? Who are the companies that are their competition? How is TimeCycle different?

Hell on Two Wheels: How to Bike Center City

By Joseph Stinson

Wearing a lime-colored jersey, sunglasses, gloves, bicycle shoes and a helmet, Jeff Appeltans pumps the pedals on his Schwinn one-speed and shoots right down the dotted white line separating two lanes of cars on Walnut Street. This is a perfect time to pay attention to every rearview mirror, every pedestrian, every back-end of a bus. It's also the perfect time not to think too hard. I'm following a good block behind Appeltans, trying not to clip every rearview mirror on either side of me.

Appeltans, a veteran bicycle messenger and co-owner of Time Cycle Courier service, is an expert on staying alive while riding breakneck through the busiest traffic in Philadelphia. And riding around town behind Appeltans, I begin to learn his secrets: Pay attention to everything, wear the right gear, know when to juice it and when to put on the brakes and don't freak out. I came away with a lesson every urban biker should memorize: Dress brightly to be seen, but ride as though you're invisible.

But to Noel Weyrich, president of the Bicycle Coalition of the Delaware Valley, Appeltans' riding style is not only

BIKING

dangerous, it gives all bikers a bad name. I spoke to Weyrich by phone after riding with Appeltans. Though Weyrich tends to take the air out of Appeltans' pumped up riding style, they both agree that brightly colored clothing, helmets and reflectors are mandatory. And despite their differing viewpoints on style, both offer tips useful to anyone navigating Philadelphia's city streets on two-wheels.

"Bicycle couriers are to bicyclists what New York cabbies are to other motorists," says Weyrich, who advocates a law-abiding and safety-first approach to biking. "You don't have to bike like a total animal out there."

According to Weyrich, bikers should obey traffic laws, use hand signals, put a flashing red light on the rear of the bike and use a front headlight while riding after dark. Weyrich recommends a riding style far different from the gutsy courier method ("I stop when I come to a red light," says Appeltans when asked. "And if no one's coming, I proceed.")

Weyrich hopes bikers will win automobile drivers' respect by setting a good

that bikers try to make contact with drivers to get their respect and attention.

"Make sure you're not completely oblivious to the drivers around you. People in cars respond if you acknowledge them," says Weyrich. "If you feel pressure riding, you have to set up a relationship with the motorist, no matter how brief, just make sure you show them you know where they are."

But Appeltans and his colleagues don't interact much with those behind windshields. Though far from poster boys for bicycle safety, the courier's basic philosophy is based on what works and what doesn't at warp speed on the city streets. Though the messengers' style seems aggressive, they see themselves as riding defensively.

"You always have to be aware of what's going on behind you," says Appeltans. "You don't want to take your eyes away from the road, but a quick glance under your arm is important."

Appeltans' job takes him through the busiest intersections in the city. He has to contend with sinking, rut-filled streets, Buicks and oblivious jay-walking Philadelphians.

"We're fending for ourselves with cars, taxis and pedestrians and it gets discouraging dealing with people's ignorance," says Appeltans. "People driving in cars seem totally oblivious to what's happening around them except for what's straight-ahead. And even then, you can't be sure they see you."

Says Appeltans: "I go out of my way to stay out of their way."

And for Appeltans, at least, his methods have worked: A bicycle messenger since 1988, he's never had a mishap while riding that involved more than minor scrapes and scratches.

In the end, every urban biker in Philadelphia needs to develop his or her own style of riding, based on what works

From this productive session we concluded that TimeCycle wanted a way to have an ongoing conversation with its clients. On the one hand it wanted to inform clients about new options and give them an expanded view of the services that were available. On a more human level it wanted to let clients know more about the people who make up the company. It also wanted to reach the recreational and competitive cycling community.

Figure 10.4

A couple of the clippings that would be incorporated into the about TimeCycle section of the site.

One feature that was not considered due to technological barriers was the idea of ordering deliveries online. This requires a continuous open connection that is not feasible for TimeCycle, now or in the near future.

At this point we had expanded the two objectives to a list of 11 functions we thought the site should fulfill:

1. Provide expanded service information.

2. Announce new services.
3. Allow potential clients to request a brochure.
4. Allow clients to request email invoices.
5. Allow clients to request proof of delivery online.
6. Tell about the people that make up the company.
7. Open up a conversation with clients.
8. Sell TimeCycle merchandise.
9. Give additional exposure to sponsors.
10. Promote TimeCycle's racing team (extension to the site).
11. Link to sites of interest to the cycling community.

These are not in priority order (yet) but the result of freewheeling brainstorming. We are not going to discuss all of these points here, but a few are worth considering in more detail.

Conversation?

The most amorphous of these 11 ideas was number 7, Open up a conversation. Many ideas were considered and rejected: chat rooms, threaded discussion, contests, and so forth. Several ideas emerged unscathed, one of which was to have a page for TimeCycle Tales. We would invite customers to submit stories about how TimeCycle had saved their butt, which would be amusing and also give the client exposure. There would be an online form where customers could submit their story for inclusion at the site (to be reviewed before publication!). The idea is that the changing feature story would bring visitors back for repeat visits. An archive of previous features could be available as long as server space permitted.

Another aspect of conversation is that the site would open up a connection that could be followed up in person, as in: "Hey, Sarah, congrats on winning that race last weekend! I didn't know you raced mountain bikes." This, of course, relates to number 6, as discussed in the next section.

Special Interests on a Commercial Web Site: Distraction or Asset?

Our original objectives for the site were strictly aimed at customers of TimeCycle. Even if we weren't directly pushing services, we were pursuing the softer goal of building a closer connection with the customer. What's this cycling community stuff? It's not in the company's brochure, after all. Should we try to talk our client out of this, or what?

On the web, many sites have areas devoted to topics that are close to the hearts of the site publisher. This is very true of personal sites, often true of sites where an individual is primarily promoting his or her business, and occasionally true of larger business sites. It is a unique characteristic of the web, and is appreciated by web surfers—these guys have something they care about. As long as it is not a topic that will alienate large numbers of customers, why not include it?

The World Wide Web is a network of interests and related topics. Newbie surfers quickly reach boredom unless have a hobby or interest about which they can explore a vast interlinked world of information. Cycling is an interest that is shared by many, and the demographics (relatively young, relatively affluent, mostly male) ensure that it is well represented within the online community. The cycling information and links are most likely to earn free reciprocal links from other cycling-related sites (organizations, manufacturers) and generally increase traffic at the site. Unlike distributing printed materials, greater traffic at the site (up to a point) does not cost more. The chances of a news story or other coverage of the site are also increased.

There have been situations, however, in which the time and energy needed to keep up with the hobby side of a site drains resources. In this case it was decided that we would incorporate the pages devoted to the racing team as an extension of the site, but plan that the pages would be maintained by the team members.

1. **Provide expanded service information**
   - Matrices and tables listing areas served and the rates for delivery
   - Maps of zones and special service areas
   - Step by step instructions on how to request a delivery
   - Tips on how to prepare a package to prevent damage
   - Expanded explanation of billing codes
   - Account services (billing, signature confirmation)

2. **Announce new services**
   - Now have driver services
   - Maps of zones and with rates for drivers
   - Expanded service area: tri-state
   - New timewarp 15-minute delivery

3. **Open up a conversation with clients**
   - Email forms for suggestions
   - Email address for everyday mail
   - Client stories about how TimeCycle saved their butts
   - Email notices about special services or holiday closings

4. **Enable potential clients to request a brochure**
   - Email form

5. **Allow clients to request proof of delivery electronically**
   - Email, PDF, specific Web address

6. **Tell about the people that make up the company**
   - Courier bios and photos
   - News features from local press print and broadcast
   - History of TimeCycle couriers
   - Adjacent racing team site
   - Participation in the World Cycling Championships.

7. **Promote TimeCycle merchandise or gear**
   - Create an online catalog
   - Special seasonal offers
   - Gear of interest to cyclists

8. **Give additional exposure to sponsors**
   - Create a link page for sponsors
   - Link to clients' sites from within client testimonial pages

9. **Build racing team extension site**
   - Feature TimeCycle members and results
   - Add links to other racing sites of interest
   - Lists and links to additional competition result sites

10. **Provide additional cyclist interest site links**
    - Link to recreational sites
    - Link to equipment sponsor sites
    - Link to rails to trails, Pennsylvania wheelmen, and bicycle coalition

« SITE CONTENT LIST

The Couriers

About our staff pages can be pretty dull, but at most web sites they are quite well visited. It seems to be human nature to be curious about other people. In addition, clients and potential clients are interested in the abilities of the couriers, their training habits and race results. The competitive cyclists that make up TimeCycle have individual achievements as well as their association with the TimeCycle-sponsored racing team. Again we have moved from a discussion of one function (number 6) to the concept of providing information of interest to the cycling community (number 11).

In addition, featuring information about the couriers at the site involves each and every person at TimeCycle in the making of the web site. This serves the internal agenda of morale and the courier's investment in the company. For example, one courier has designed a piece of equipment that the owners will allow him to promote at the site.

A List Is Not a Structure

Some elements on our list turned out not to be easy to fully implement, or as important as we had originally thought. Figure 10.5 shows how this functions as a working list of desired functions or features of the site.

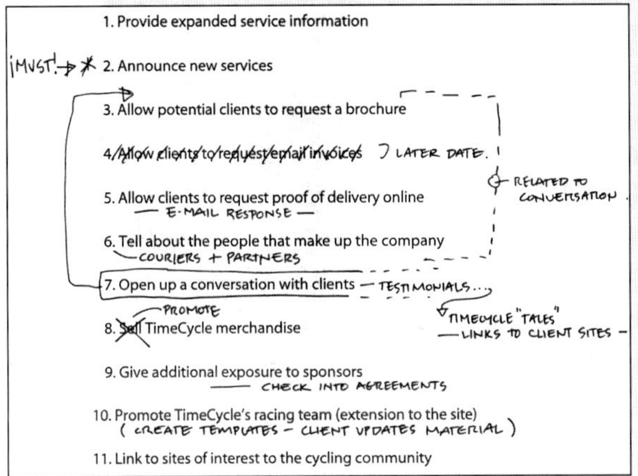
1. Provide expanded service information
¡MUST! → * 2. Announce new services
3. Allow potential clients to request a brochure
4. ~~Allow clients to request email invoices~~ ? LATER DATE.
5. Allow clients to request proof of delivery online — E-MAIL RESPONSE — RELATED TO CONVERSATION
6. Tell about the people that make up the company — COURIERS + PARTNERS
7. Open up a conversation with clients — TESTIMONIALS... TIMECYCLE "TALES" — LINKS TO CLIENT SITES
8. ~~Sell~~ PROMOTE TimeCycle merchandise
9. Give additional exposure to sponsors — CHECK INTO AGREEMENTS
10. Promote TimeCycle's racing team (extension to the site) (CREATE TEMPLATES – CLIENT UPDATES MATERIAL)
11. Link to sites of interest to the cycling community

Figure 10.5

The fate of that nice neat list of 11 agreed-upon functions. It turned out that the logistics of sending an invoice by email are a bit of a challenge, so that was put on hold.

Over time, we developed a more detailed list or outline of the site content, as you can see in the accompanying box. This still is just a list; to call it an outline implies that it is more structured than it really is. It has no direct relationship to site structure.

The Audience and Their Technology

Who is the audience? First we looked at who TimeCycle's existing customers were—this would probably make up a good portion of the visitors to the site. The base consists of designers and other members of the creative community including photographers, service bureaus, and printers. In addition, TimeCycle serves lawyers, travel agents, newspapers, anyone who has to move physical items quickly (you can't email airline tickets yet). They range from small to medium-sized businesses with a few larger operations.

An additional base of visitors would include cyclists, couriers (looking for a new job?), and bicycle enthusiasts. As we discussed above, being a cyclist makes you part of a community that has many interests—including legislative needs.

Most of these individuals would have connection to the Internet (or email at the very least) from their offices. A large number of the customers would be coming from the creative professions—on larger monitors and faster computers (and more Macintosh computers) than the business community as a whole. However, although they have good computers, many of these smaller businesses do not have the fast connection speeds that exist in corporate offices.

Therefore we are left with the familiar challenge: make the site available comfortably at 28.8 dial-up and exciting at 36, ISDN, and T1.

Creating the Architecture

Now it was time to create the blueprint for the site. How would we reach the goals defined? What devices would we use to achieve the desired functions? The goals helped to determine and define the key messages. Now we needed to implement a design that would accomplish the goals and serve the functions.

Defining Structural Relationships

At first attempt, the material for the TimeCycle site seemed to fall into two major categories and a bunch of miscellaneous, hard-to-categorize material.

1. Information related to deliveries
2. Information about TimeCycle and its couriers
3. Everything else: cycling-related stuff, links to sponsors and clients, TimeCycle gear for sale

We discussed in Chapter 2, "Constructing Site Frameworks", the pitfall of giving an arbitrary name to an unrelated group of material and expecting the visitor to have any idea what is contained in that section. To come up with a catch-all name for number three wouild be misleading and impede access to the material. Many of the items will be impulse visits so they need to be readily accessible directly.

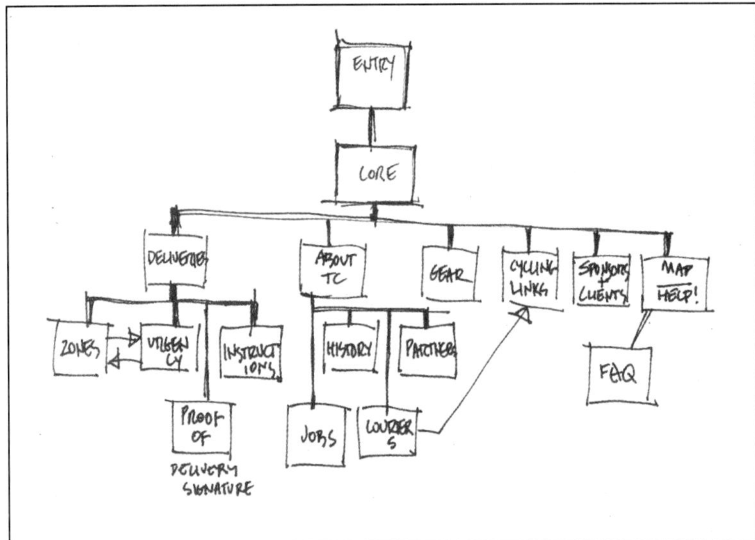

Figure 10.6

A structural sketch from our team meeting. This is our draft of the architecture of the site.

Figure 10.6 shows an early version of the architectural sketch. We refined this drawing and created a version to our client before we created the Logical Prototype. Recently we have begun thinking about structure using the prototype built in NetObjects Fusion from the beginning and rarely submit a drawing before we have worked with some .nod files internally.

Here you see an entry page to lead into the core page, which is the navigational touchstone. Also included are a site map/help section and an FAQ page. We hadn't mentioned an FAQ page in our brainstorming, but it was a component of the NetObjects Fusion template for a company Internet site and seemed like a good idea. FAQ is another uniquely web feature that can be forgotten if you are only focused on existing material about the company.

Developing and Testing the Logical Prototype

You are familiar from Part 1 and the other case studies how we develop a Logical Prototype to assess the navigational features and content. This is a text-only series of screens that summarizes the content of each page and shows the links available from that page (Figure 10.7). NetObjects Fusion is the ideal tool for creating and revising these prototypes quickly.

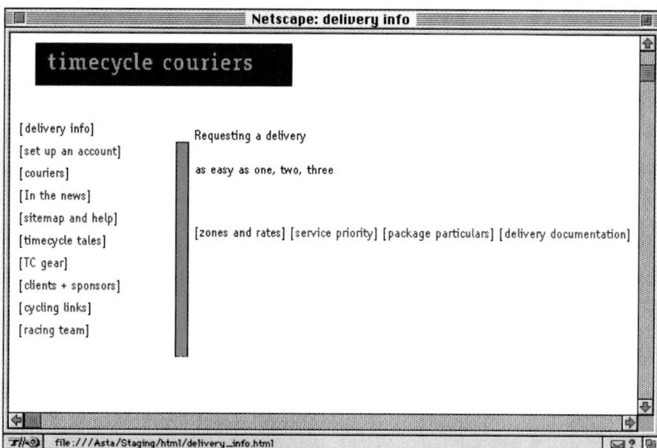

Figure 10.7
This is a screen from one stage of the Logical Prototype for the TimeCycle site. The navigation on the left is a vertical navigation bar showing all links at the first level of the site.

We had many (friendly) fights over how many avenues of navigation should be available on each screen at the site. One of the main concerns here is that any part of the site can be arrived at quickly without having to navigate through levels of menu screens. We tried to compress the number of navigational items to the top level of our site map. That would make for about six links. With access only to these the viewer could get frustrated trying to get to certain places quickly. We tested this and found the navigation insufficient. What to do? Could we get away with 14 or 16 links on almost every level? This has clear implications for the choice between icon- or text-driven menus!

A test drive by each member of the studio helped us discover unmet expectations. For example, the Center City area, which accounts for a large percentage of deliveries, needs to be treated separately. All information relevant to Center City—prices, delivery speeds, zones—is visible at once. We then tested the revised prototype with a small group of testers, including the client. We asked testers to imagine themselves to be the following:

1. You are unhappy with your courier service. You are looking at the site to evaluate if TimeCycle can fill your requirements. What do you want to look for and were you able to find it?
2. A friend recommended TimeCycle and you are in a bind. You want to contact TimeCycle now to make a pick-up. If you go to the site (you've been given the address), can you find the information you need to request a pick-up?
3. Your courier gave you a flyer about a new timewarp delivery. 15 minutes from your call it will be delivered. It has limited areas. Can you easily find out where it is available?
4. You're a competitive cyclist and you've heard TimeCycle is looking for new couriers. Can you find out what it takes to be a TimeCycle courier?

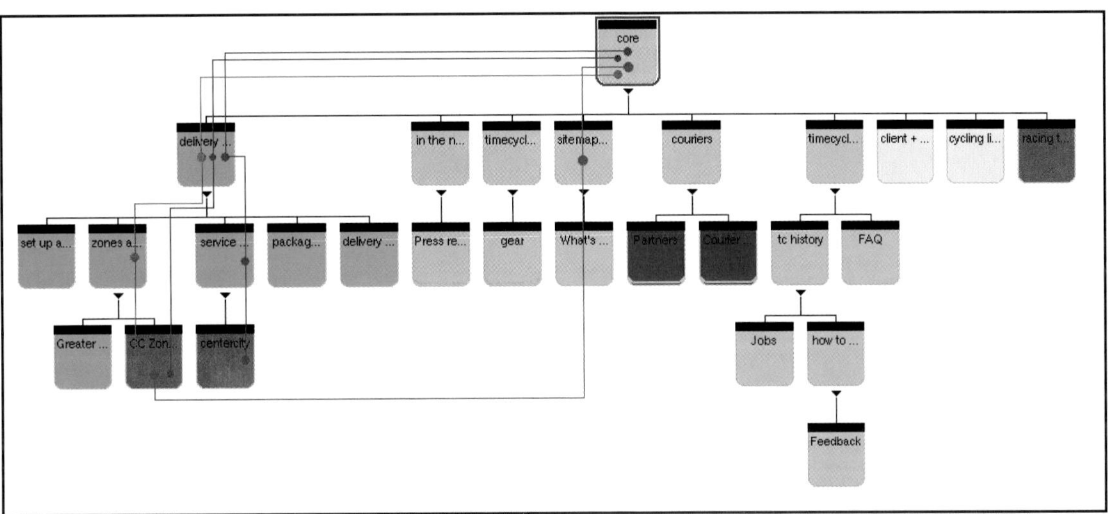

Figure 10.8

This illustration shows the paths that the testers traveled in the third scenario—searching for TimeWarp Zone. Most found it easily either through the main delivery screen or from the site map. Some missed our direct Center City link and went through the general Zones page, which tells us the Center City link must be prominent.

We have discussed how testing is an important part of structure design in Chapter 2, "Constructing Site Frameworks." Remember to be sure that most of the testers have not been involved in the design process in any way and that at least some of them are not familiar with TimeCycle. The results are summarized in Figure 10.8, using lines drawn on top of the Site view from NetObjects Fusion.

Notice that we have not tested some of the softer issues of human interest. These are much more difficult to test in a logic-only situation, and it is not as critical that a direct path be available for these aspects of the site.

The revised site is shown in Figure 10.9. Stacked pages have been introduced for the merchandise pages promoting TimeCycle Gear (jerseys, hats) and the pages about the couriers, which will be based on databases if possible.

The Challenge of Different Information Types

As we worked with the pages for the zones, rates, and levels of urgency, we became involved in seemingly endless debates about which comes first: the chicken or the map. There are maps of zones and lists of zones (alphabetical or geographical?). There are rates to and from Center City for each zone—but what about when it is from suburb to suburb?

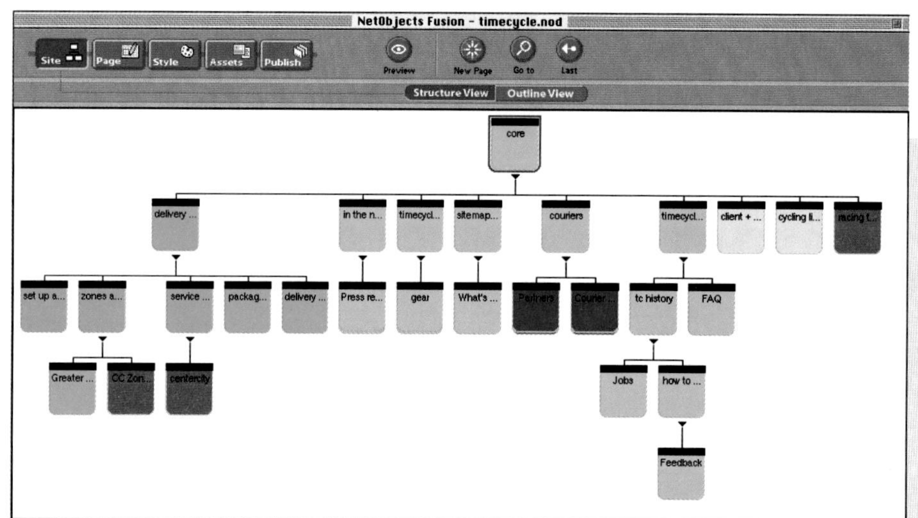

Figure 10.9
This is the Site view for TimeCycle. The color coding shows general groupings across sections or highlights within a section (that is, red = Center City).

There are four levels of service within the heart of Center City, and three everywhere else. How much it costs depends on where you start, where you finish, and how soon you need it there! So we began to work with different ways of linking key pieces of information, looking always from the visitor's viewpoint.

A previous version of TimeCycle's printed brochure is an example of an unfortunate presentation of information. We produced the list of zones as it was given to us by the client without challenging this on behalf of the poor customer:

Suburban Zones:

Zone 9 Bryn Mawr, Conshohocken, Fort Washington, Glenside, Haverford, Jenkintown, Plymouth Meeting, Springfield, Havertown, Broomall, Glenolden, Folcroft, Folsom; (NJ) Cherry Hill, Haddonfield, Maple Shade

$25.00

Zone10 Ambler, Blue Bell, Norristown, Willow Grove, Media, Berwyn, Bridgeport, Wayne (Montgomery County), Radnor: (NJ) Marlton

$30.00

The zones are in expanding circles around Center City Philadelphia, so they include towns on opposite sides of the map. Readers have to look under each zone for the locality they are seeking. Suburban Zones is an in-house TimeCycle construct that is meaningless to a customer. Therefore, one thing we agreed upon from the beginning was that we would divide the suburban zones first by major area (New Jersey + Penna Counties), and then list all localities alphabetically in one column and give the price after each. Because we cited TimeCycle for the original poor organization, we should credit the folks there for suggesting this improved method of reorganization.

"YOU'VE GOT THE COOLEST BUSINESS IN PHILADELPHIA."

"I JUST LOVE THOSE GUYS AT TIMECYCLE."

"THEY HANDLE COMPLICATED MULTI-PART PICK-UPS THAT I WOULDN'T TRUST TO ANYONE ELSE."

Design: It's Got to Have Personality

Creating this site presented numerous design challenges. TimeCycle has a well established identity. It is extremely visible when on the job. It has an excellent reputation for speed of delivery. The couriers are known for their courtesy and intelligence. How would we transfer this identity to the web? Above all, it's got to be cool.

The Cool Look and Feel

The obvious visual elements are the logo and the trademark yellow. If you see a cyclist and she is wearing that fluorescent yellow, you automatically think TimeCycle (Figure 10.10). These are the visual keys we used in developing the personality of the site.

Figure 10.10
This is Jeff Appeltans, founder and partner of TimeCycle Couriers, Inc.. This is how he looked when photographed for the image map on the core page.

We came to the conclusion that the look and feel of www.timecycle.com should be just like the experience with the company:

courteous, reliable, and fast

The graphic file sizes should be small; we would use text links to drive most of the site. Headlines would be GIFs in a reduced color palette.

Almost everyone locally recognizes Jeff Appeltans, the founder of TimeCycle. When we were having photos developed

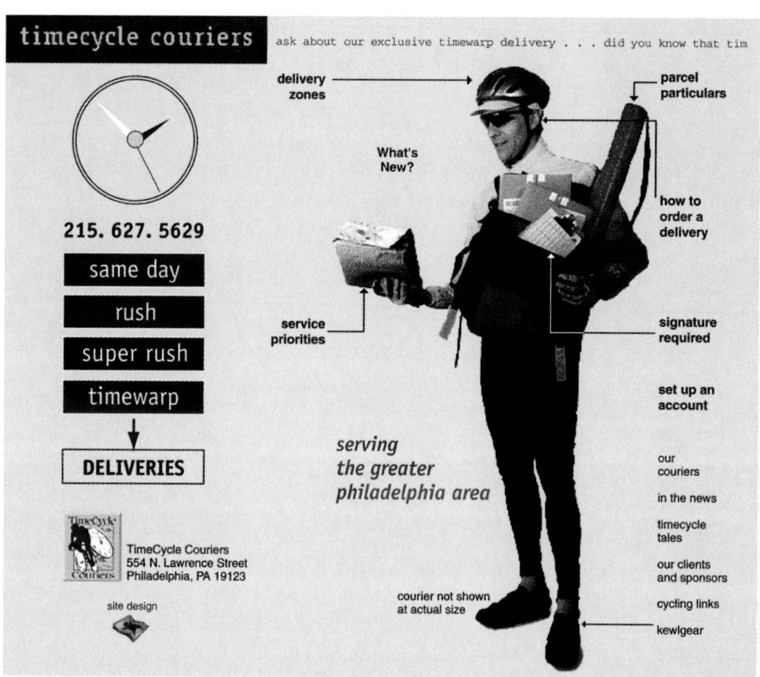

Figure 10.11
Jeff Appeltans, transformed into an image map. "Anatomy of a courier." Key messages are conveyed on this page and it has links to almost everywhere on the site.

for the site, the lab technician asked, "Is that Jeff Appeltans?" Jeff is an icon for the company. As we said at the beginning of this chapter, he is a personable guy, he has the ability to start a conversation, remember your name, remember things you are interested in, and generally make you feel comfortable doing business with him. We make use of his persona to reinforce the TimeCycle identity at the site (Figure 10.11).

Now it was time to determine the new assets that would have to be created. Our first priority was to arrange for photography. TimeCycle has a cycling enthusiast (who happens to be a professional photographer) take photos of the staff for yearly posters. We added to last year's shots using the same photographer and style.

Several iconic illustrations are used on pages, such as tires, radios, beepers, bags, waterbottles, helmets, and so on. We scanned as much of the material as possible and added simple sounds and animation where appropriate. These sound files and animations are enhancements and are not required to get the essential messages from the site (see Chapter 7, "Multimedia Enhancements."

Because of the desirability of many navigational choices, text is being used for navigation instead of icons. Text links work well on the core

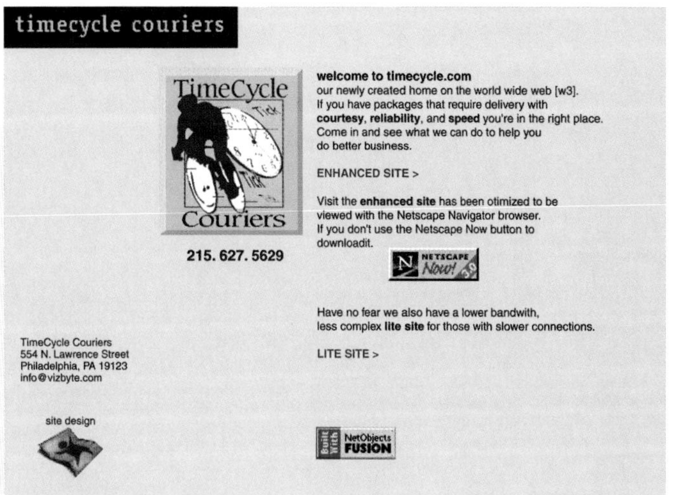

Figure 10.12
This is the entry screen to the TimeCycle site. Viewers with all kinds of bandwidth will probably be visiting the site. We want to give them options before they enter, not surprise them once they are in the site.

page, which is dominated by the image of the courier and the text GIF emphasizing the delivery services; other imagery would dilute the effect.

For the entry page, shown in Figure 10.12, the key concept was to convey that there are two different paths through the site, one for higher bandwidth and another lite site. At this point we want to make sure that visitors know where they are and whose site it is. The page is the TimeCycle yellow with its logo and fast-loading text. You can find out the phone number and the mailing address immediately from this page—you don't have to enter the site if you don't want to.

NETOBJECTS FUSION ALLOWS YOU TO PUBLISH A TEXT-ONLY SITE VERY EASILY. ALTHOUGH WE HAVE ALWAYS ENDORSED THE THEORY THAT A TEXT-ONLY VERSION OF A SITE IS A GOOD THING, WE NEVER GOT AROUND TO MAKING THEM UNTIL WE HAD THIS APPLICATION!

Page Design

Finally! It was time to create the page grid and structure. As we said, due to their cutomer base, the largest number of visitors to the TimeCycle site are from the creative community. This means that they will be on Macintosh computers and probably have 17-inch monitors or greater. We will design for a smaller monitor (15-inch), but we'll take into consideration that a visitor might actually be able to view the site on a 19 or 20-inch monitor.

We'll make sure that the most important information and navigation will be within reach of a smaller monitor, but primarily consider the larger monitor experience. That means the links cannot sit at the bottom of the page.

WE EXPERIMENTED WITH OTHER METHODS, INCLUDING A SMALL HIGHLIGHT ICON SUCH AS AN ARROW NEXT TO THE LOCATION. THESE ICON EFFORTS MADE FOR A MORE CONFUSING INTERFACE. TOO MUCH ATTENTION WAS DRAWN TO A LINK WHERE THE VISITOR ALREADY WAS; EVERYONE WANTED TO CLICK THAT LITTLE ARROW AND IT DIDN'T TAKE YOU ANYWHERE.

Position and Design of Navigational Elements

For the visitor's experience to evoke speed and efficiency, we designed TimeCycle.com with single screens. Only in areas with nonessential material (defined as not important to making a request for delivery) is scrolling used. Each screen would carry enough information to create easy steps that could be followed by a first-time visitor. Each screen is small enough to be printed onto a letter-sized page

We couldn't cut back on the accessibility to the areas of the site. Essential and/or interesting information must be accessed from any page (with some exceptions). The price for this is a long list of text as navigation. To remind visitors where they are, we made the current location in the list bold (see Figure 10.13).

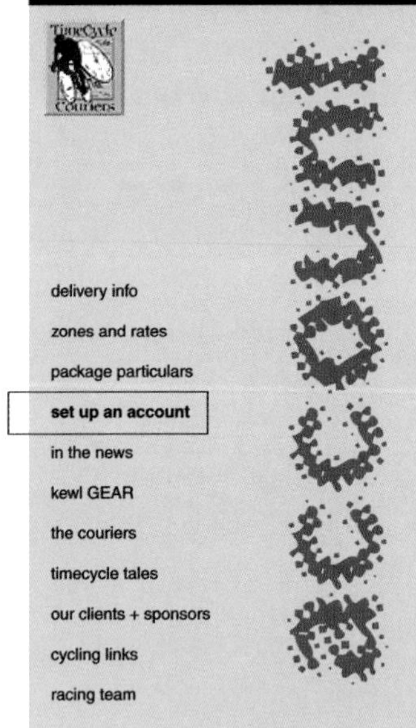

Figure 10.13

The navigation list appears on every page, on the left. This shows the left panel of the standard screen. The area where you now are (delivery info) is bold. The large word request refers to the instructions on how to request a delivery.

The type in the upper left corner, TimeCycle Couriers, is present throughout the site and always takes you back to the core page.

Page Grid and Color Palette

As described in Chapter 3, "Web Page Design," we created color palette templates for the site in Adobe Illustrator (see Figure 10.14). One of the templates shows the CMYK equivalents (for use in applications like Adobe Illustrator) and the second shows the RGB values and the hexadecimal values for the colors. Numerous team members will be making art and we want the color formulas to be readily available. This template uses color names and formulas so that anyone creating art can be sure to meet the color matching standards for the site.

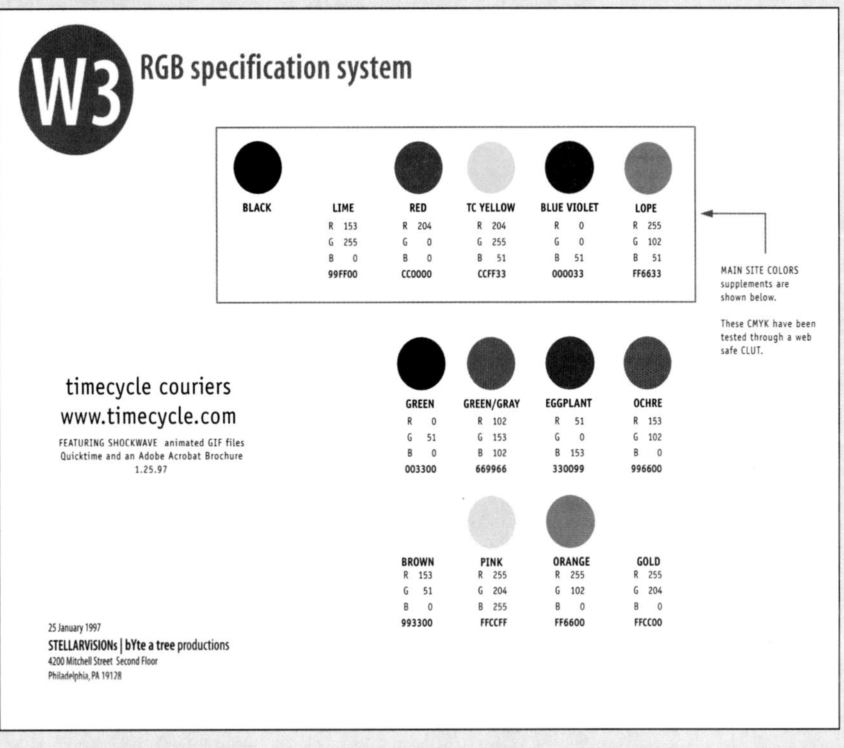

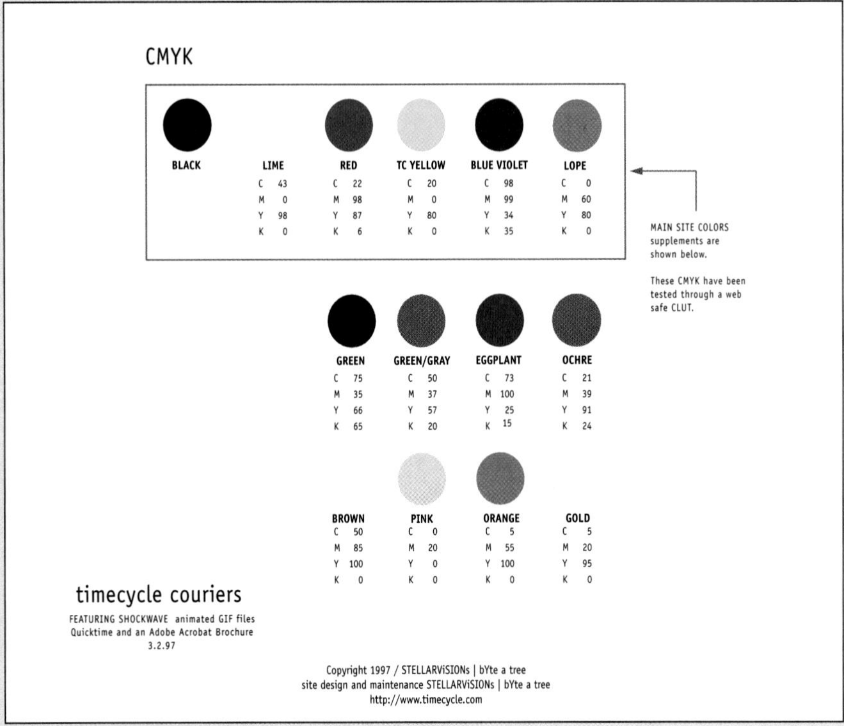

Figure 10.14

Here is our color palette template for the TimeCycle site. On the top you can see CMYK equivalents and below the RGB.

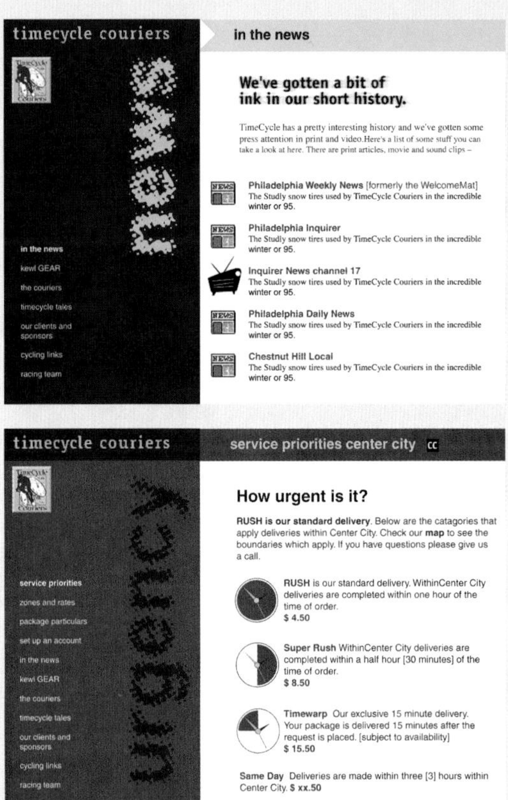

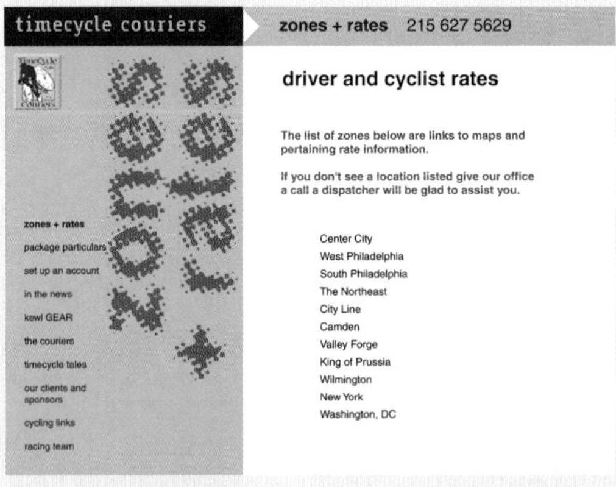

timecycle couriers

need account info call 215 627 5629

account

It's fast and easy.

Fill out the form below and we'll get the process going. Fill out all of the fields in the form below. That will get the process started. A representative will contact you to discuss your needs and how TimeCycle can help you do business better.

company

first name last name

title

street address 1

street address 2

city state

telephone fax

email address

delivery info

zones and rates

package particulars

set up an account

in the news

kewl GEAR

the couriers

timecycle tales

our clients + sponsors

cycling links

racing team

Figure 10.15

Here you can see the color coding scheme for the different sections of the site. The news page uses the dark blue, the Center City page uses the urgent red, and the zones and rates page uses the green of the delivery section. Even though Center City is within the delivery section, it is highlighted with red because it is such a key source of critical information. The news section opener is an exception to the white body because it is simply a menu to other pages that contain news items.

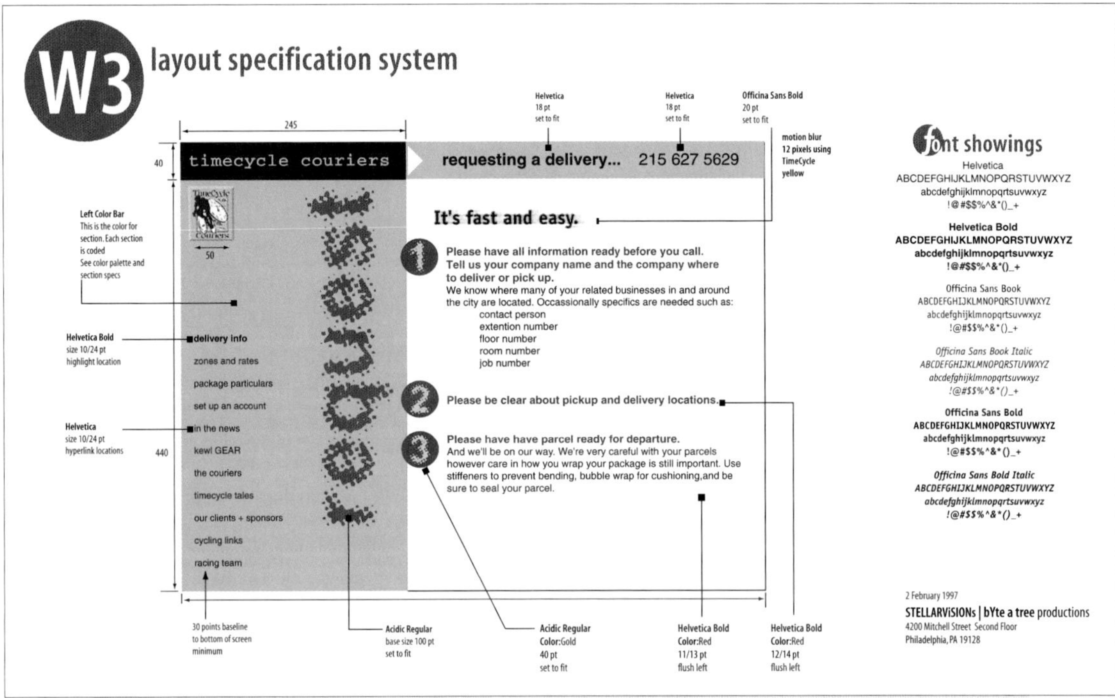

Figure 10.16

Here is the base grid for most pages in the site. Also shown are the fonts that will be specified. Helvetica, with Arial as an alternate, is displayed in the browser except in the banner at the upper right, which is a GIF. Acidic and Officina are used only in GIFs.

Each of the key sections would be color-coded to help viewers understand where they were. This is much like the color coding of multiple-level garages. You know you are in the garage, but what floor did you park on? The red level of course. Remember the color coding we did in the Site view of NetObjects Fusion? Well, that translates right over to the color coding on the pages themselves (Figure 10.15). Don't keep your structure secret if it will be helpful to the visitor.

Although the TimeCycle yellow is our trademark, it does not make a good background for reading text, even in printed material. With the addition of illumination on a screen reading body text against this background becomes painful. Therefore the body of the pages is white or, at times, dark blue. TimeCycle yellow is used in the opening pages and in the headers and behind the navigation bar in the yellow section of the site (the default color).

We decided against the same font from in the logo in the headers. The results of creating image files of serif type at small sizes were unacceptable. We would instead brand each page with a logo button. This lets viewers know that they are still within the TimeCycle site and the button would be another hyperlink back to the core page.

We finally settled on the ITC Officina family as the typeface for the site, even though it looks best as *timecycle couriers* instead of the *TimeCycle Couriers* in the logo. This face would now be incorporated into new printed materials as well. It has clean square serifs that make readability excellent. For display, the eaten away face acidic is used.

ICONS CAN BE VERY EFFECTIVE, BUT 16 OF THEM IS CRAZY NO MATTER HOW WELL DESIGNED. YOUR NAVIGATIONAL SPACE WILL BEGIN TO LOOK LIKE A SALAD WITH ALL KINDS OF STUFF STICKING OUT EVERYWHERE. THIS SHOWS THE ADVANTAGE OF TESTING THE NAVIGATION BEFORE CREATING GRAPHICS. IF WE HAD BEEN IN LOVE WITH FOUR PERFECT ICONS, WE WOULD HAVE FORCED THE SITE STRUCTURE TO FOLLOW THE GRAPHICS RATHER THAN VICE-VERSA.

The screens are divided into three rectangles (Figure 10.16):

- A narrow header strip across the top included TimeCycle type, an arrow, and a headline that would pertain to a section (similar to a banner). In the section about deliveries, the header would include the telephone number.
- The left side rectangle would be the navigation bar, again color-coded for each section. The section location would be reinforced with text GIF traveling vertically up the color bar, in this case request.
- The body rectangle would be white and would carry the essential information for each screen. We would limit links in the section except for screens that are primarily a list of links, such as the entrance to the in the news section.

The Core Page

We have already met Jeff on the core page, but as the core it deserves a bit more design discussion. The core page for TimeCycle makes use of the most recognizable aspects of TimeCycle. The background color is TimeCycle yellow, and a courier is the imagemap and icon to navigate the site (although the links around the edge are in text). Telephone number and essential services are listed at this level. A clock Applet shows what time it is based on the visitor's own computer clock, echoing the clock in the logo—the other TimeCycle image.

Figure 10.17
Here is one of the bio images in grayscale—and the same image after we had color-enhanced it.

On the core page the hyperlinks would be more descriptive than the standard navigational menu. For example, How to order a delivery takes you to the delivery info page. At the core page we wanted to help first-time visitors find the information they needed and get used to what is available. Links to the delivery section of the site were all placed near the top of the courier's body map. Links near the bottom, such as the gear that is for sale, are less critical.

Courier Pages

The images on the courier biographical pages used a technique we had used previously for printed material for TimeCycle. The image was made into a color monotone, all dark blue. Then the bright TimeCycle yellow jersey image would be put on an overlay (a Photoshop layer) so that yellow is the only color in an otherwise grayscale image (Figure 10.17). Note that when you combine the layers in Photoshop, use multiply as the interaction between the layers or the yellow will lighten the dark areas on the jersey (such as the logo) and make it look washed out. The page is shown in FIgure 10.18.

Figure 10.18
The courier bio page design.

Implementation: How Did We *Really* Build this Site?

When we went into our page-building stage, where we try to figure out where NetObjects Fusion can save us the most work, we were met with many challenges with this design. Certainly, the client-side image map for the courier on the core page was a snap. And of course we were able to position all of the elements exactly how we wanted them, but overall we were unable to use some of the most powerful NetObjects Fusion attributes such as banners, navigation bars, and MasterBorders as you will see below.

Color Coding Disrupts Universal Styles

The biggest culprit was the color coding of sections. It is easy to combine color coding of sections using different backgrounds colors (or colored background images) and NetObjects Fusion's navigation bars and banners. If the color coding is held in the background, that is associated with the layout of the page, not the SiteStyle (or MasterBorder). So a black banner with white type can appear on a green, red, or blue background. But the banner itself cannot change color without creating a custom GIF for each banner.

If there was no color coding, a NetObjects Fusion banner element could be used for the headline banner in the upper right of the pages. A custom style with shorter-than-usual banners would have to be created. Set the specifications for the headline type so that the longest headline fits nicely. You would use the Custom Names feature to list the exact headline you wanted in the banner.

Oh, for Those Handy Navigation Bars!

When we first chose to have a simple vertical text menu for navigation, we assumed we would use the text version of the vertical navigation bar in NetObjects Fusion. You can control the font (one in the visitor's system), color, and size of the text in this bar if you don't mind changing the default text for the entire style. However, you are stuck with the brackets: [home] [next]. These work fine for horizontal navigation at the bottom of a page, but look really silly in a vertical navigation bar. Also, there was no way to highlight (bold) the current page. Probably the good folks at NetObjects will give us a choice about those brackets and more control the text attributes in the navigation bar for the next release of the program.

So, this meant we had to link each of the items in the navigational menu by hand (a matter of two clicks for an internal link). Fortunately you can copy and paste the text from page to page and the internal links remain intact. It's really not that hard to do once, but now every time we change our mind about a page name we have to change it manually on every page. NetObjects Fusion would have done it magically had it been a navigation bar. Again, it is the maintenance or revision process where the application saves you the most hours.

We created a single page site that had the basic grid and the navigational menu on the left. It contained a background image 25 pixels deep and 700 pixels wide that is part green and part white. This image repeats, filling in vertically, until the background is green on the left and white on the right. This file was saved as a template (.nft file). We then began the .nod file, built the unique core page, and then inserted this template several times using the Import Section command. Each time we imported the template (.nft file) we only got one file because there was only one page in the original template. So we just imported as many times as we needed pages. We added additional elements as needed, added text, and changed the background image (red + white, yellow + white depending on the section).

The Good News: Database Integration for TimeCycle Gear

The TimeCycle Gear pages are set up as stacked pages, and will link to the external database provided periodically by TimeCycle. They can maintain this database in FileMaker (which they used until recently for all dispatching, tracking, and invoicing). When we want to update, they will simply export the records as tab-separated text and save the file with the extension .tab. In the .nod file in Windows 95, we have set up an external database linking to the tab-separated text file. Each time we stage or publish, it will pull the most recent information from the database. See Chapter 6, "Database Publishing," for more information about how to do this. This is very good news for maintenance!

Index

A

B

C

D

E

F

G - H

I

J - K

L

M

N

O

P

R

S

T

Index

U - V

W